LEARNING NEW LANGUAGES A GUIDE TO SECOND LANGUAGE ACQUISITION

Tom Scovel

San Francisco State University

A TeacherSource Book

Donald Freeman
Series Editor

HEINLE & HEINLE
TM
THOMSON LEARNING

Australia • Canada • Mexico • Singapore • Spain • United Kingdom • United States

HEINLE & HEINLE
THOMSON LEARNING

Learning New Languages: A Guide to Second Language Acquisition
Tom Scovel

Vice President, Editorial Director ESL: Nancy Leonhardt
Acquisitions Editor: Sherrise Roehr
Marketing Manager: Charlotte Sturdy
Production Editor: Jeffrey M. Freeland

Sr. Manufacturing Coordinator: Mary Beth Hennebury
Compositor: Ethos Marketing and Design
Cover Designer: Ha Nguyen
Printer: Webcom

Printed in Canada
1 2 3 4 5 6 7 8   05 04 03 02 01

For more information contact Heinle & Heinle, 20 Park Plaza, Boston, Massachusetts 02116 USA, or you can visit our Internet site at http://www.heinle.com

For permission to use material from this text or product contact us:
Tel   1-800-730-2214
Fax   1-800-730-2215
Web   www.thomsonrights.com

Library of Congress Cataloging-in-Publication Data

Scovel, Thomas, 1939–
    Learning new languages: a guide to second language acquisition/Tom Scovel.
        p. cm—(A TeacherSource book)
    Includes bibliographical references.
    ISBN: 0-8384-6677-X (alk. paper)
    1. Language and languages—Study and teaching.
    2. Second language acquisition.
    I. Title. II. TeacherSource.

    P53 .S36 2001
    418'.007—dc21
                                                00-053987

ASIA (excluding India)
Thomson Learning
60 Albert Street #15-01
Albert Complex
Singapore 189969

AUSTRALIA/NEW ZEALAND
Nelson/Thomson Learning
102 Dodds Street
South Melbourne
Victoria 3205 Australia

CANADA
Nelson/Thomson Learning
1120 Birchmount Road
Scarborough, Ontario
Canada M1K 5G4

LATIN AMERICA
Thomson Learning
Seneca, 53
Colonia Polanco
11560 México D.F. México

SPAIN
Thomson Learning
Calle Magallanes, 25
28015-Madrid
España

UK/EUROPE/MIDDLE EAST
Thomson Learning
Berkshire House
168–173 High Holborn
London, WC1V 7AA, United Kingdom

For Asia

Thank You

The series editor, authors, and publisher would like to thank the following individuals who offered many helpful insights throughout the development of the **TeacherSource** series.

Linda Lonon Blanton	University of New Orleans
Tommie Brasel	New Mexico School for the Deaf
Jill Burton	University of South Australia
Margaret B. Cassidy	Brattleboro Union High School, Vermont
Florence Decker	University of Texas at El Paso
Silvia G. Diaz	Dade County Public Schools, Florida
Margo Downey	Boston University
Alvino Fantini	School for International Training
Sandra Fradd	University of Miami
Jerry Gebhard	Indiana University of Pennsylvania
Fred Genesee	McGill University
Stacy Gildenston	Colorado State University
Jeannette Gordon	Illinois Resource Center
Else Hamayan	Illinois Resource Center
Sarah Hudelson	Arizona State University
Joan Jamieson	Northern Arizona University
Elliot L. Judd	University of Illinois at Chicago
Donald N. Larson	Bethel College, Minnesota (Emeritus)
Numa Markee	University of Illinois at Urbana Champaign
Denise E. Murray	NCELTR Macquarie University
Meredith Pike-Baky	University of California at Berkeley
Sara L. Sanders	Coastal Carolina University
Lilia Savova	Indiana University of Pennsylvania
Donna Sievers	Garden Grove Unified School District, California
Ruth Spack	Tufts University
Leo van Lier	Monterey Institute of International Studies

TABLE OF CONTENTS

ACKNOWLEDGMENTS

When you have devoted almost an entire lifetime to learning new languages and studying how they are acquired, there are indeed many people to thank for all that you have learned. I would never have gotten into linguistics or second language acquisition without the choice my parents made many decades ago to become medical missionaries, first to China and later to India. They gave me a multicultural heritage, and they also fostered within me a love of language and languages, a gift I have already acknowledged in print (Mendelsohn, 1999). I also owe a debt of gratitude to my wife, Janene, who bravely accompanied me by freighter across the Pacific in 1964 when I returned to Asia to teach English in Thailand. There we learned a new language together, there we raised two children, and there we nurtured many enriching memories. And later, when we were invited to teach in China in 1979, she joined me for yet another Asian adventure and, with our two children, learned yet another new language. I have always been grateful for her love, support, and friendship. Even now, when I press the wrong key and the screen suddenly freezes over, she has more than once helped save me and this manuscript.

I gratefully acknowledge the many teachers, students, faculty colleagues, and academic friends who have taught me much about languages and how they are learned. I have had opportunities to teach courses in second language acquisition in several institutions around the globe, and these experiences have contributed enormously to my understanding of this complex field. At San Francisco State University, I am most fortunate to be surrounded by a group of intelligent, experienced, and committed colleagues, and they have taught me much about what it means to be a good teacher. Among them, Doug Brown has stood out as a longtime friend and mentor, and to him I am especially grateful for insights into second language learning. And among my many academic friends, I must single out two who have shared much wisdom with me over the years. Mark Clarke and Earl Stevick have taught me a great deal about how to think rigorously, speak clearly, and live wisely.

The production of any book is a team effort, and so it is appropriate to recognize the many people who helped me put this work together. I very much appreciate Donald Freeman's initial invitation to contribute to this fine TeacherSource series and his patient guidance throughout the composition process. I also want to acknowledge the assistance given to me by the staff at Heinle & Heinle, and a special vote of gratitude goes to Tab Hamlin who did a superb job copyediting this manuscript. I also wish to thank the teachers who are named in the text and who contributed the Teacher's Voices. Several of my former students generously shared their Learner's Accounts for this book, and since they are not named in the text, I wish to acknowledge them here: Deneene Bell, Karin Cintron, Marisa Da Prato, Stefan Frazier, Kim Mahr, Marta Meuller, Kazuhiro Nunome, Karyn Panitch, Maureen Persico, Jeana Vaccaro, and Laura Vaudreuil.

Finally, a brief note about the dedication, in case you're wondering. Yes, in a way it is to acknowledge my debt to Asia and to the thousands of Asian students I have enjoyed teaching and the hundreds of Asian teachers I have had the pleasure to work with. But really, this book is dedicated to our first grandchild, Asia Siree Sherwood. Some day, I hope that by learning new languages, her world will be enriched, just as her grandfather's has been!

SERIES EDITOR'S PREFACE

As I was driving just south of White River Junction, the snow had started falling in earnest. The light was flat, although it was mid-morning, making it almost impossible to distinguish the highway in the gray-white swirling snow. I turned on the radio, partly as a distraction and partly to help me concentrate on the road ahead; the announcer was talking about the snow. "The state highway department advises motorists to use extreme caution and to drive with their headlights on to ensure maximum visibility." He went on, his tone shifting slightly, "Ray Burke, the state highway supervisor, just called to say that one of the plows almost hit a car just south of Exit 6 because the person driving hadn't turned on his lights. He really wants people to put their headlights on because it is very tough to see in this stuff." I checked, almost reflexively, to be sure that my headlights were on, as I drove into the churning snow.

How can information serve those who hear or read it in making sense of their own worlds? How can it enable them to reason about what they do and to take appropriate actions based on that reasoning? My experience with the radio in the snowstorm illustrates two different ways of providing the same message: the need to use your headlights when you drive in heavy snow. The first offers dispassionate information; the second tells the same content in a personal, compelling story. The first disguises its point of view; the second explicitly grounds the general information in a particular time and place. Each means of giving information has its role, but I believe the second is ultimately more useful in helping people make sense of what they are doing. When I heard Ray Burke's story about the plow, I made sure my headlights were on.

In what is written about teaching, it is rare to find accounts in which the author's experience and point of view are central. A point of view is not simply an opinion; neither is it a whimsical or impressionistic claim. Rather, a point of view lays out what the author thinks and why; to borrow the phrase from writing teacher Natalie Goldberg, "it sets down the bones." The problem is that much of what is available in professional development in language-teacher education concentrates on telling rather than on point of view. The telling is prescriptive, like the radio announcer's first statement. It emphasizes what is important to know and do, what is current in theory and research, and therefore what you—as a practicing teacher—should do. But this telling disguises the teller; it hides the point of view that can enable you to make sense of what is told.

The **TeacherSource** series offers you a point of view on second/foreign language teaching. Each author in this series has had to lay out what she or he believes is central to the topic, and how she or he has come to this understanding. So as a reader, you will find this book has a personality; it is not anonymous. It comes as a story, not as a directive, and it is meant to create a relationship with you rather than assume your attention. As a practitioner, its point of view can help you in your own work by providing a sounding board for your ideas and a metric for your own thinking. It can suggest courses of action and explain why these make sense to the author. You in turn can take from it what you will, and do with it what you can. This book will not tell you what to think; it is meant to help you make sense of what you do.

The point of view in **TeacherSource** is built out of three strands: **Teachers' Voices**, **Frameworks**, and **Investigations**. Each author draws together these strands uniquely, as suits his or her topic and—more crucially—his or her point of view. All materials in **TeacherSource** have these three strands. The **Teachers' Voices** are practicing language teachers from various settings who tell about their experience of the topic. The **Frameworks** lay out what the author believes is important to know about his or her topic and its key concepts and issues. These fundamentals define the area of language teaching and learning about which she or he is writing. The **Investigations** are meant to engage you, the reader, in relating the topic to your own teaching, students, and classroom. They are activities that you can do alone or with colleagues, to reflect on teaching and learning and/or try out ideas in practice.

Each strand offers a point of view on the book's topic. The **Teachers' Voices** relate the points of view of various practitioners; the **Frameworks** establish the point of view of the professional community; and the **Investigations** invite you to develop your own point of view, through experience with reference to your setting. Together these strands should serve in making sense of the topic.

In *Learning New Languages: A Guide to Second Language Acquisition,* Tom Scovel brings together experiences as a learner and a teacher drawing on, in his words "a lifetime of learning new languages and studying how they are acquired." This book is about the core of language teaching and learning: how students gain access to and come to master new languages. Scovel writes from the diverse and complementary perspectives of someone who has learned to speak several languages, who teaches English on a regular basis, who prepares second language teachers, and who researches how people learn languages. Using the framework of People, Language, Attention, Cognition, and Emotion which he has developed from these experiences, Scovel organizes and synthesizes the complex and diverse research literature on second language acquisition to help readers understand and think more closely about how people learn new languages in their classrooms. The multiplicity and depth of the author's perspectives lead to a book that is unique in its ability to blend questions and insights into language learning with the ongoing demands of teaching.

—*Donald Freeman, Series Editor*

1

INTRODUCTION

"What's the best way to lose weight?" This question pervades many a conversation in the United States and has spawned a huge industry of talk shows, videotapes, books, self-help courses, and magazine articles. Its pervasiveness reveals a perversity of the American psyche: Appearances matter a lot, and it matters most to appear slim—especially if you are a woman

But when we try to avoid the media blitz on weight loss and dieting and turn to the real experts, we find that the question is not easy to answer. People who have spent a lifetime studying nutrition often counter with the query, "Why would you want to lose weight, anyway?" Rather than quickly and confidently prescribing a neatly packaged diet program, genuine experts end up with a discussion of all the factors that go into maintaining a healthy lifestyle. What appeared to be a simple and legitimate question with a supposedly straightforward solution turns out instead to be a "weighty" problem whose ultimate resolution depends on the complex interplay of a large number of disparate variables.

Language learning and teaching, like dieting, is another popular social activity, and many have asked the related question, "What's the best way to learn (or to teach) a foreign language?" Again, there is a virtual cottage industry of neatly packaged programs that can be readily purchased at a not-so-modest price that purport to help anyone learn almost any language quickly, effectively, and with almost no work. But alas, when we turn again to the experts—applied linguists who have devoted lifetimes of research to the vagaries of language acquisition—there are no quick and easy answers.

I have written this book to demonstrate that because learning a new language is as complex and multifaceted as nutrition, the process is equally fascinating and miraculous. The goals of this modest introduction to the field are not unlike the goals of a book on personal health. I hope to challenge you to look beyond the pat answers and popular myths that pervade the field of second language acquisition, to help you to understand the complex network of variables that influence your success, or the success of your students, in learning new languages, and, above all, to encourage you to appreciate the miracle of speaking a new tongue.

Like the ability to maintain a healthy weight, the ability to become bilingual requires time, attention, and experience, but even more than good health, the successful acquisition of one or more languages can open up a whole world of new opportunities and relationships that can enrich not only your life and the lives of your students, but the lives of those you and they encounter. As a language learner yourself, I hope you have already experienced this singular sense of accomplishment. As a language teacher, I hope you will be able to sense the manifold joy that comes with sharing this accomplishment with your students.

With such an abundance of factors influencing our ability to pick up a new language, how can we be confident that we will account for all of them, or how can we ensure that a modest introduction such as this will adequately and fairly cover them all? Applied linguists, like scientists in any discipline, always begin their research by delimiting the domain of their inquiry. Just as a nutritionist might talk about diet and health in terms of food intake and then in terms of various types of food and subcategories of each type, an expert in second language acquisition attempts to categorize the various factors that impinge upon language learning and then discusses each of these categories separately.

Two words of circumspection are pertinent here. Although it is the nature of science, and of texts like this, to divide human experience into categories and subcategories, we must never forget that these classifications are not a natural part of nature. If you look at what a person eats at a meal, for example, you cannot see "carbohydrates" or "proteins" in real life. They are extrapolated from the real world by scientists as necessary constructs for the proper understanding of human nutrition. By the same token, if you observe a student in a foreign language class, you cannot see "grammar" or "motivation," and yet these notions are equally obligatory for the ultimate understanding of how people learn to speak a new tongue. These constructs may be difficult to quantify because they are not a visible part of our daily behavior, but they are needed if we wish to understand the principles and processes of acquiring another language.

The second note of caution is related to the first. We should remember that, although scientists divide in order to conquer (categorization must precede explanation), the world of nature is holistic, systematic, and indivisible. Just as your nutrition is ultimately affected not just by the amount of carbohydrates you ingest each day, but by many other interrelated and disparate factors such as exercise, climate, and amount of sleep, your ability to successfully acquire a language is affected not only by the amount of grammar you learn, but also by such variables as motivation, linguistic input, and opportunity to interact socially with speakers of the target language.

Given the two caveats above, but still accepting the dictum of science that understanding cannot be achieved without explanation, and that explanation cannot be accomplished without classification, what then are the main categories that make up the holistic process of learning another language? One author has actually come up with 74 "conditions" that affect language acquisition (Spolsky, 1989), but even a nutritionist might balk at attempting to cope with so many variables, at least within the confines of a brief, introductory text. Rather than deal with a large number of conditions or principles, I have chosen to introduce the field with only a handful of categories. These do not represent general principles; instead, I think it is more useful to divide the field into a few general domains that circumscribe the major influences on what and how much we pick up in any second language learning situation.

I like to think there are five major contexts in which languages are acquired, and although they can be labeled with more academically impressive appellations, it is probably more helpful to use simple and straightforward terminology. So, whenever we learn a new tongue, I believe we should consider the following five domains: **People**, **Language**, **Attention**, **Cognition**, and **Emotion**. Although it may not be immediately apparent, these particular categories have also been chosen because of the acronym the labels spell out—**PLACE**. This abbreviation refers to the five contexts where all language learning takes "place."

PLACE

In a moment, we'll take a quick glance at these domains, by viewing each through the eyes of a person in the throes of learning a new language. A unique aspect of this book is the presentation of various (and sometimes conflicting) perspectives that have been excerpted from the journals of students who have taken a course on Second Language Acquisition (SLA) and, as a requirement for that course, have concurrently studied a second (or foreign) language. Each chapter you are going to read contains several of these **Learner's Accounts**—short excerpts from the language learning journals that these students wrote for their SLA course. Because the great majority of these students took the SLA class as part of their graduate training in teaching of English as a second language (TESOL), their language learning accounts do not represent the voices of learners only; they also express the point of view of current or future teachers.

Each chapter also has longer excerpts labeled **Teacher's Voices**, which represent different viewpoints teachers bring to the TESOL or foreign language classroom. These teachers' perspectives not only provide variety, they also introduce some contradictory opinions about the nature of SLA. Do not be overly concerned about the way some of these views contrast; rather, imagine yourself engaged in conversation about language learning and teaching—for example, with a couple of participants at a teachers' conference after a lively presentation. The speaker is trying to amplify ideas made during the talk, but another participant is trying to clarify these points from a teacher's perspective. You too are engaged in this conversation, adding your opinions from time to time, but basically, you are trying to sift through all the information under discussion in order to decide what is really relevant for your classroom and for your students. It is not a matter of who's right and who's wrong, but what we can learn from each other *because* our viewpoints differ.

Treat this book the same way by listening carefully to the different voices presented in these pages. Certainly you should pay attention to the large amount of information about SLA introduced and described in the **Frameworks** sections, but also listen for the ways the Teachers' Voices and the Learners' Accounts offer fresh and different angles about the material under discussion. Become an active participant in this dialogue as you read along; consider the way all this information and all these various voices can help you become a more effective language teacher. In order to ensure that you participate in the ensuing conversation about language acquisition, each chapter contains **Investigations** sections where you are asked to do an activity or conduct a simple exercise.

By the time you have finished reading this text, you will have "overheard" a variety of voices and viewpoints being expressed. I hope this means that you come away with a clearer appreciation of why language acquisition is such an impressive human achievement. I hope that you will have picked up some ideas on how to be a better language teacher, as well.

Going back then to the five components of the "place" model that serve as chapters for this book, listen to the following Learner's Accounts from five different language students as they describe their attempts to acquire a strange new tongue.

What role do **People** play in SLA? A large and diverse one, of course, as the research points out, but the following excerpt from a student trying to learn American Sign Language (ASL) demonstrates this up close and personal.

Learner's Account #1

We finally did a very short group activity today. I've been craving the social interaction of using the language. I really find it more interesting and useful if I'm in the social situation. Just watching the teacher and signing back to her gets really old. The beginning of the group activity was a little awkward. I felt like I tried to instigate ASL communication, but I didn't want the others to think I was dominating. I feel like most of the others are a little slower than me and, more frustrating, they are afraid to take risks. I wanted to be accepted by the group, so I didn't really show all that I knew.

A Student of ASL

Of course, the most defining characteristic of an SLA class is that what is being taught, and presumably learned, is **Language**, not chemistry or social studies or any other subject. Then, naturally, another major domain of SLA is the language being learned, as well as the language(s) that the students employ as their mother tongue or as additional languages they have acquired. Very often, as this student of Tibetan attests, the structures of the new language can tower like a veritable linguistic Everest.

Learner's Account #2

Tibetan study is, how should I put it, a formidable mountain. The first week was fine. We learned the thirty Tibetan consonants, and all was peachy. Then came the four vowel sounds, followed by the ten suffixes, five prefixes, two post suffixes, three superfixes and four subfixes. Are you still with me? Any of these can be added to the original thirty consonants changing the sound and meaning in a myriad of ways. (It was about this time that I started finding clumps of hair in my balled-up fist....) How thankful I am that I'm not in this alone. I'm also thankful that my seven classmates are full of good humor, and we can laugh about our struggles. Hey, who knows, I may actually be able to communicate in the language at some point in the future!

A Student of Tibetan

Attention is the portal between the universe of external experiences that surrounds us and the world of internal perceptions that comprises our very being. It is central to all that we perceive and all that we learn, and that is why "attention" is placed in the middle of the PLACE model; it is the narrow gateway through which the People and Languages outside affect our internal Cognition and Emotions. Much of teaching and most of learning involves attention, as this entry suggests.

Learner's Account #3

My mind is a sieve. Tonight my instructor has taught a whole litany of new grammatical concepts including *to, from, after, in order to,* to go on foot/by bus/by plane, to change (transportation), and how to form tag questions. We've also gotten about 40 new vocabulary words. We're supposed to conjugate in the past, present, and future while paying attention to varying levels of politeness, and meanwhile, everything, I mean *everything*, is written only in Korean.

The board is a myriad of symbols, and I have no ability to sort through it or organize it in any way. All my strategies have suffered a complete meltdown. My instructor knows that I'm flailing; she always calls on me last now, so that I have plenty of time to note down everyone else's response and answer with some syllables that are moderately appropriate.

A Student of Korean

Because we are Homo sapiens, the "thinking" hominid, **Cognition** is a vital part of our everyday behavior. We think a lot about everything. We even think a lot about thinking; in fact, that's what psychologists get paid to do! And we think a lot about learning, too, as shown by this passage written by a Japanese student of English.

Learner's Account #4

When I dealt with the writing assignment, I needed to read one or two articles before I fought with the rough draft. During my reading, when I faced unfamiliar words, after I stopped reading and guessed what they meant, I consulted my dictionary. If I did so, I felt I could memorize the meaning of the word much more clearly and accurately than if I had simply looked up the word in my dictionary. To enrich my vocabulary, I wrote down the words and meanings on the small pieces of paper and put them on the wall. This habit made me feel that I was getting more and more vocabulary.

A Student of English

But we are not only cognitive animals; we also possess **Emotions**. In fact, it could be argued that we are more emotional than any other species, because our great cognitive capacity allows us to generate deep feelings and to think deeply about them. Anyone who has taken a foreign language class realizes that SLA is not only social, linguistic, attentive, and cognitive, it is also an emotional experience. Here is one concluding and convincing example.

Learner's Account #5

Had my Japanese midterm today. Don't think I did very well. I was the last student, and I still hadn't finished it all. While I was taking the test, I got more and more stressed out, and this resulted in two simultaneous reactions. I felt like I was going to be sick to my stomach, but at the same time, I was reading and understanding hiragana at a speed never before attained. Thank God I decided to take this class on a credit/no credit basis or I might have puked.

A Student of Japanese

Now that you have been introduced to the five main components of SLA, thanks to the honest testimonies of these five learners, we are ready to examine each of these domains in greater detail. Whether it is our mother tongue or some completely foreign speech, we learn language in order to communicate with others. It is only natural, therefore, to begin by examining the role that People play in the acquisition of a new language. But before we turn to the next chapter, which introduces the first letter and first component of the PLACE model, pause for a moment to read and reflect on the following Teacher's Voice.

TEACHER VERSUS RESEARCHER

It may seem a bit strange for you to have me, as the author of this book on second language acquisition, suddenly switch roles and become the voice of a teacher in this section, but I have been a language teacher for almost four decades—actually, several years longer than I've been a language researcher. When I reflect on all the experiences I've accumulated over all these many years, my views on language learning differ considerably depending on whether I'm a "teacher" in an ESL classroom or a "researcher" reading journals and conducting experiments.

Granted, there is a great deal of overlap between these two roles, but, in many ways, this professional contrast is no different from the personal contrasts you and I share as part of our everyday life. We are parents at home, but usually not in the workplace; we are husbands and wives to our spouses, but during a typical busy day at the office, we tend to forget our loved ones and become preoccupied with the job at hand.

A researcher and teacher can be the same person, but in two different places and at two separate times. Here, I want to briefly share my perspective as a teacher, not as an SLA researcher. For this and each of the Teachers' Voices excerpts that you will encounter in this book, I hope that you will feel free to join in the "conversation" as a reader. I also hope that the dialogue that ensues, however silent and distant, will widen your views of teaching and increase your wonder over the daily miracles of learning that we as teachers are privileged to witness.

Tom Scovel

I teach a low intermediate "Grammar for Writing" class in our ESL program at San Francisco State University, and though I've taught this course for several semesters and have been a TESOL teacher for well over three dozen years, there are still many things that I'm unsure of in my own teaching. Like most teachers, when I look at my students, I tend to get preoccupied with the two extremes—the quick and the bright who don't actually need me, and the slow and the weak whom I often can't really help. Ironically, I suppose I'm most helpful for the "silent majority," the students in the middle, whom I tend to forget once the term is over. Take a recent semester for example. I can instantly remember Carlos and Minami (not their real names).

Carlos is especially hard to forget because I taught him two semesters in a row. He took the course over again with me after I gave him an incomplete the first time around. We have a policy of not giving D's and F's in our ESL classes but using incompletes instead, largely because we want our students to get credit for all their required ESL courses, but we don't want to drag their grade point averages down with low grades in these required language courses. On the other hand, by giving incompletes, we can be sure that students like Carlos, who do poorly in one class, don't get automatically promoted to the next ESL class until they're ready.

We also have a general practice of not allowing a student who got an incomplete with one teacher to repeat that course with the same instructor, but Carlos talked to me at the beginning of the term and pleaded to be allowed to enroll in my section. I don't think it was so much because he liked me as a teacher, but it seemed that his academic and work schedule was such that the only way he could fit in his ESL class was to take it during my time slot. I was reluctant to let him in at first, partly because I thought he'd be bored to death, repeating the same course with the same book and the same instructor, but deep down, I think I was also worried that maybe *I'd* be bored to death facing Carlos again! It's not that I disliked him. He was quiet and hardworking, and except for his propensity to unexpectedly cut class about once a fortnight, he was a fairly conscientious student. He simply had very weak English skills, and because his homework and performance on quizzes and exams were so poor, coupled with the occasional missed class and assignment, he continually ended up at the bottom of my grade book.

From his compositions, I knew he'd had a tough life, living in the United States with his sister after the death of both parents in Mexico, and I also knew that most of his absences were legitimate. After all, I had seen him late in the afternoon emptying trash bins around the Student Union at his part-time job, and I admired him for the pride and energy he must have had to support himself and still keep up with his studies. But I knew that the academic dice seemed loaded against him, and I doubt that experts in second language acquisition have any idea why a kid like Carlos barely scrapes by in my English class. Why is English so hard for him when he himself is trying so hard? The experts don't seem to know or care much about individual students, but as a teacher, I still think of Carlos, even though it's been more than a year since he took that class the second time around. Oh, by the way, he did manage to pass with a C−.

Now Minami is another story, and I remember her as clearly as Carlos, even though she ended up near the top of my grade book. She wasn't the brightest student out of the 27 who took my class that semester—that honor goes to Catherine, one of about a half dozen Chinese girls who all sat together to my left in the horseshoe arrangement of tables and chairs that formed the classroom. It took me several weeks to get all the students' names straight, and because of that and also because they all tended to be pretty timid in class (except for the voluble woman from Turkey who sat smack in the middle and whose name I picked up the very first day!), I didn't quite realize that quiet Catherine was the brightest student of the bunch until I had passed back the second dictation.

At the same time, however, I was aware that Minami was a whiz at English. From her compositions, and sometimes from a few of her comments in class, I learned quite a lot about her personal background. Although she was Japanese and was a foreign student, unlike most of my class who were U.S. residents or immigrants, Minami had spent a considerable chunk of her childhood in the States—in Alaska, of all places! Her father was in some kind of business there, so her early schooling was all in English. Because of this, unlike the other two Japanese students in the class, Minami was confident, fluent, and comfortable when responding to my questions or when busy in pair or group work with her ESL classmates.

She was a dance major, so she seemed to be quite creative and outgoing, and I sensed that she commanded some degree of admiration from the other students, who tended to major in mundane fields such as accounting and engineering. I also wondered if her experience as a dancer had anything to do with the confidence and competence she displayed in her spoken English. This might be stretching it a bit, but it seems that compared to the other students in my class, Minami was able to "dance" her way through ESL—sort of like a choreographer of grammar! If my class had been devoted to strictly oral communication, she would have easily aced the course. But just like some native speakers who aren't strong in their writing skills, Minami had trouble with some of the grammatical structures we covered, especially on dictations, where she tended to make errors. This was in stark contrast to Catherine, who seemed to have a great ear for every syllable I pronounced and a great eye to catch every little grammatical nuance I tried to introduce into the dictation exercises.

I guess the so-called experts in SLA might be able to answer some of my questions about Minami, but certainly not all of them. Though they might be able to explain the mismatch between her great oral fluency and her relative lack of success in written accuracy, I don't think they could give me any valuable advice about how I could have helped Minami improve. As I said at the beginning—because she was already so good in English when she entered my class (or at least in the communicative use of the language), there wasn't much that I could do to help her.

Going back to my initial concern, as a teacher I tend to remember the weak students like Carlos and the good ones like Minami (or even Catherine), and maybe I remember them because these were the students I was unable to help. It seems to me that from most of what I've read about second language learning, almost all the research is devoted to anonymous groups of students. The researchers look at faceless blocks of "control" and "experimental" groups just the way politicians look at blocks of voters ("the women's vote," "the Hispanic vote," etc.).

And yet when I look back at all the "Grammar for Writing" classes that I have taught at my university, most of the students quickly fade from memory, but the "exceptional" students stand out. I can see their faces right now, and there are times I still wonder how I could have helped them. As an ESL teacher, I'm not at all interested in them as generic statistics or as representing certain linguistic or psychological profiles. I'm interested in them as individuals. That's the way I treat them, and that's the way I remember them.

Looking back now, I feel somewhat frustrated that I wasn't able to help Carlos very much because I could never overcome his individual weakness in my class. At least he passed the second time, but did I really help him succeed or was I simply moving him up and out? I'm also annoyed that I couldn't help Minami very much either. She finished my ESL class with good skills in the language (at least in spoken English) because that's the way she entered.

I guess what I'm trying to say is that I don't teach blocks or groups of subjects, I teach individuals. I wish the SLA experts could somehow look at ESL students the same way we do as teachers—as persons and not as groups. I wish they could explain the Carloses and the Minamis of the world to me.

1.1 *What's the Best Way to Learn a Foreign Language?*

Investigations

When you ask friends, family members, or neighbors—people who are not in the business of language teaching—what's the most important ingredient for successful language learning, you naturally get a variety of answers:

(a) "The main thing is to live in the country where the language is spoken."

(b) "Some people just have a good ear for languages, and some people don't."

(c) "Some languages are easy to learn—like Spanish, and others are really tough—like Hungarian."

First, think about the five major factors introduced in this chapter and rank them in an order from most important to least important. I know this may be hard to do, and, if you're like me, you'll want to have several ties, but for the purposes of this exercise, force yourself to come up with a clear ranking from first to fifth.

Next, conduct a little survey to discover which of these five factors people feel is the most important in determining the successful acquisition of a new tongue. If you're currently teaching, you could ask your students to rank the five categories from 1 (most important) to 5 (least important) and thus collect somewhat formal data. If you don't have immediate or easy access to a class of language learners, ask some people you know what they think is most important in determining successful second language acquisition, and then try to catalogue each answer into one of the five factors introduced in this chapter. Going back to the three responses above, (a) seems to imply that People are most important, (b) suggests that individual ability, probably Cognition, is primary, and (c) gives the impression that the structure of the Language to be learned is crucial.

After you've completed your survey, reflect on the rankings that you've compiled. How close did the survey come to your own personal ranking of these factors? What do you think influences people to weigh some factors as very important and others as relatively insignificant? When you've finished reading this book, you might want to return to your personal ranking list and see if you would change it, based on what you've read.

1.2 *Looking at the Individual, Not the Group*

As teachers, we think about our students both as individuals and as members of a group. If you listen to teachers discuss their classes, they invariably talk about individual students—we might even call it "gossip"! You hear things such as, "So you've got X this semester—good luck!" or "I wish Y were in my class; she does everything well." But teachers also look at their students collectively. Again, you often overhear teachers making comments like "I could never teach first graders; their attention span is so short," or "It's like pulling teeth to get my Japanese students to speak up in class." Comments like these are natural and pervasive, but they raise at least one intriguing question: How do we come up with these generalizations about either individual students or entire groups of them?

Find a colleague or two with whom to discuss this issue. It may seem trivial at first, but this is a complex topic that many cognitive psychologists have debated long and hard. After all, first graders can be riveted to a video game for a long time, so why do we ignore this fact when we come up with the notion that young kids have short attention spans? And anyone who has ever been to Japan and watched some of the corny evening TV talk shows knows that Japanese people can be irrepressibly loquacious, so where does the stereotype of shyness come from?

This book is full of generalizations about learners, but there are two distinct ways in which these claims differ from the everyday stereotyping teachers make. For one thing, because second language acquisition research comes to us from the traditions of social science, almost all the claims are based on experimental evidence. Second, with rare exceptions, SLA researchers never look at individuals, nor do they make claims about individual personalities. So here's another question for you to ponder. Why don't scientists look at individuals? Why do they base almost all their work on groups of people—usually comprised of very large numbers of subjects? (And isn't it a trifle ironic that researchers create experiments using "subjects" and yet claim to be "objective" not "subjective?") Or, to turn the question around, why do teachers often tend to remember only individuals, especially the "exceptional" students?

There are no easy answers to these queries, but it is important to stop every now and then to question the basis of our beliefs. And it is even more important to remember throughout your reading of this book that neither researchers nor teachers have any unique claims about why students succeed or fail in the language classroom; the evidence can be either experimental or experiential. Given the complexity of SLA, I think we need a lot of both before we can understand our students better.

Suggested Readings

Twenty years ago, it was fairly easy to keep up with any new publications dealing with SLA: There simply were not that many. This is far from the case nowadays! Two introductory texts that are fairly heavy reading but that offer a wide and balanced range of topics are Larsen-Freeman and Long's *An Introduction to Second Language Acquisition Research* (1991) and Skehan's more recent *A Cognitive Approach to Language Learning* (1998). For a short and sweet distillation of his much larger work (*The Study of Second Language Acquisition*, 1994), Ellis has written a very compact introduction, *Second Language Acquisition* (1997). To celebrate the 25th anniversary of TESOL, several experts were invited to write on various fields, and Larsen-Freeman contributed with an article for the *TESOL Quarterly* that briefly describes 10 major findings of SLA research ("Second language acquisition research: Staking out the territory," 1991). Finally, four books that have been specifically written to introduce the field to language teachers are Scarcella and Oxford's *The Tapestry of Language Learning* (1992), Lightbown and Spada's *How Languages are Learned* (1993), Cook's *Second Language Learning and Teaching* (1996), and Brown's *Principles of Language Learning and Teaching* (2000). The latter covers a broader range of topics and has been republished in a freshly minted fourth edition.

2

PEOPLE

A story about Oliver Wendell Holmes, the nineteenth-century American author and professor of medicine, tells how he happened to be walking along the beach one afternoon and spied a little girl playing in the sand. Prompted by a spontaneous childlike instinct, he decided to sit down and join in her play. They had a great time together, the distinguished jurist and the small child, but as the sun began to lower in the sky, the little girl realized it was time to go. As she got up to leave, Holmes became a bit more serious and instructed her, "When you get home be sure to tell your mommy that you played with Professor Oliver Wendell Holmes." Without a pause, the child responded with equal seriousness, "And when you get home, be sure to tell *your* mommy that you played with Mary Ann Smith!"

LANGUAGE AS A SOCIAL PHENOMENON

On the surface, this chance encounter seems linguistically unsophisticated, but if you examine the sociolinguistic context of the incident more carefully, you'll see that the young girl has learned a great deal about language as an instrument of social communication. Taken for granted is her already impressive skill in mastering English pronunciation, word choice, and grammar. From a very early age, native-speaking children like Mary can automatically use such complicated grammatical markers as *a* and *the* without hesitation. Our older ESL students, however, often find this skill very difficult to achieve. But reflect for a moment on Mary's social and linguistic skills in being able to carry on a conversation. Despite the fact that this adult is a complete stranger, she is immediately able to initiate, maintain, and conclude a conversation with him.

Although it is undertaken a myriad of times each day, carrying on a conversation is a complex sociolinguistic task. To perform this social activity, a young child has to acquire several skills. For instance, Mary has learned turn taking—when to start talking and when to stop and, more subtly, how to signal to Dr. Holmes, by language and body gesture, when she would like to intervene in their common discourse. She knows all about pre-closures—that we don't simply and abruptly end a conversation with good-bye; instead, we indirectly tell our interlocutor that it's time to bring the chat to a close. And in her final remark, Mary demonstrates a sophisticated knowledge of English address forms and appropriate register. Dr. Holmes gives his full name, intimating a formal, almost pompous tone, and Mary, recognizing this, matches him with her full name, knowing that in a situation such as this, it is necessary to supply her middle name, even though this form of address is rarely used in American English. The charm of this little story pivots around the fact that even a small child can intuitively understand how language both fuels and lubricates all kinds of social relationships.

All of this goes to show that at a very young age we learn the importance of communication with others—whether they are as familiar as our mothers or complete strangers whom we chance to encounter on a stretch of beach. Even if you don't feel the need to be in continual contact with other people as a source of social support and feedback, you probably still find it difficult to spend more than a few hours at a time without any communication with others.

A telling manifestation of this very human proclivity for social interaction is the loneliness we feel when we are in a strange country surrounded by people who do not know our native language. It is not just the direct contact with human beings that we miss, but the opportunity to converse with them. The following Learner's Account captures this need quite aptly and serves to introduce the role of social interaction with other people as a necessary criterion for successful language acquisition.

Learner's Account #6

I am an extroverted person. When there is an emptiness in my life, it is usually the absence of enough people around me to feed my self-esteem. When I need recognition for my existence, I search for it in the social world. It can be a friend lending advice, a group of classmates in study session acknowledging each other's input, or it can simply be a cashier at the gas station saying "two fifty" when I buy cigarettes. Particularly during the down times, my most common activity is to stride out into the world and seek attention, however slight.

In the language classroom, my extroverted personality seems most suited to an interactive method of learning. Indeed, during the term, I was happiest during interactive conversation sessions. At this level, the language was all very simple: greetings, small talk, direction-giving, buying things. But when a partner and I had an effective communication ("Where do you live?" "I live in the Sunset"), it was a good feeling. This was amplified when the partner was an instructor. I was speaking to a true Japanese, and her understanding me meant by association that all Japanese could understand and bond with me. It meant that an extra connection was being made that was not there before. It meant that we were recognizing each other on a level that I had previously been incapable of.

A Student of Japanese

Put tersely, without people, there are no languages. The first and perhaps most telling observation we can make about the use and acquisition of language is that it is a social phenomenon. Go anywhere around the world and observe people in any situation. When two or more gather together, lips, tongues, and jaws begin to move. If we were field biologists, content to sit quietly and observe this strange species called the thinking hominid, we would quickly conclude that humans are the most social and most linguistic of all animals, and we would immediately appreciate why a prominent psycholinguist entitled her study of human language *The Articulate Mammal* (Aitchison, 1989).

So common is conversation that when we encounter the two exceptions to our natural tendency to talk in social situations, we see that they are marked by highly unusual, even aberrant, contexts. On the one hand, if we find large groups of people not uttering even a word, it is almost always because of an exceptional situation (e.g., a congregation is silently praying in church, or a group of passengers is dozing at night on a trans-Pacific flight). In most cultures these circumstances are viewed as not representative of ordinary, everyday behavior.

The other exception involves just the opposite—a single individual, all alone, talking out loud. Again, in most societies, this is deemed atypical and sometimes even pathological. That is, when people speak without any interlocutors or respondents present, it is mostly viewed as unusual behavior (e.g., we mutter to ourselves, "Now what did I do with the keys?" as we are about to leave home, or even more aberrant, we see someone sitting on a park bench talking loudly to herself). As an aside, there is actually one instance where it is common to find people talking (often quite loudly) all alone nowadays: when they have cellular phones pressed to their ears. But thanks to the marvels of modern technology, in a very real sense, these speakers are not alone at all.

These two exceptions prove the rule. Speech is the social cement that binds people together, and because it is social, it rarely emerges in individual isolation. As several anthropologists have wittily observed, perhaps our species should be renamed. After all, when surveying the course of human history, there is little evidence that we are indeed the "thinking" hominid; there is rich evidence, however, to support the contention that we are Homo loquens, the "talker."

And we don't talk alone; the world talks with us. Whether introvert or extrovert or someone in between, like the learner of Japanese quoted above, we all share a common desire for linguistic intercourse; we need to hear and to be heard. Notice that in his Japanese class, this learner found satisfaction in the opportunities to converse in Japanese with his fellow students, but felt especially rewarded when conversing with his teacher because, unlike his classmates, she was a real Japanese, and his conversations with her seemed to represent a direct dialogue with Japanese society. Contrast his experience with the all too frequent occupation of many foreign language learners who spend hours memorizing grammatical paradigms or reviewing vocabulary all alone in their rooms. This is the opposite extreme, for there is no social contact and no direct access to the target culture. Even introverts find little motivation or utility in acquiring a new language by going from flash card to flash card instead of using the language socially, face to face.

2.1 *THE LANGUAGE OF CLASSROOMS AND KITCHENS*

When we were small children, we learned much of our mother tongue in a kitchen, especially if this was the room where we ate most of our meals. As adults, we continue almost always to use our native language at home and in the kitchen. By contrast, however, we frequently acquire our second or foreign language in a classroom and rarely use this other tongue in our kitchen (unless, of course, we live in a bilingual home). When you stop to think about it, the physical, social, and linguistic environments of these two places differ enormously, and this difference is not just between first and second language acquisition—these are two completely different places.

Get a sheet of paper and make two columns, the left-hand one for "kitchen" and the right-hand one for "classroom." Try to come up with a list of at least 10 contrasts between these two rooms that might in any way affect language learning. Here are a couple of differences that immediately come to my mind, especially when I think of my kitchen at home versus my ESL classroom at school.

KITCHEN	CLASSROOM
Pretty small—can seat about six people	Quite large—can seat about 40
Everyone faces each other at a table.	Everyone faces the chalkboard.
Lots of (nice) smells and sounds	No smells (at least no good ones!)

After you've recorded your 10 or so pairs, look back over this list. Consider the consequences of these differences on the process of language learning and teaching, especially the social ramifications of these contrasts. For example, in my kitchen, we have a round table, so no single person is in a physical position to control the conversation. However, when I'm teaching in my classroom, I'm always standing and my students are usually sitting in rows facing me, so by the very way the room is set up, I am inevitably in a position to control the discourse. Consequently, most language learning that goes on in my classroom is "teacher-fronted." What are some learning and teaching differences that you can think of based on the contrasts you have drawn between these two different environments?

A BEHAVIORAL MODEL OF FIRST LANGUAGE ACQUISITION

Before we look at how language learning is influenced by social factors, it is helpful to review some of the competing models of human behavior developed over the years by psychologists. After all, our views about how and why people talk to each other and how they learn languages are heavily determined by our ideas about how the human mind works. Historically, much SLA research was influenced by the initial work on **first language acquisition** (**FLA**), particularly the collaborative effort by Roger Brown and his colleagues in the 1970s (Brown, 1973). Their investigations of how little children acquired English focused especially on grammatical structures (such as the acquisition of /-ed/, the past tense suffix) and revealed that despite individual differences in rate of language learning, all first language learners seem to progress through the same distinct stages of acquisition. This emphasis on grammatical structures and stages of acquisition, as well as other processes, exerted a heavy influence on the then-young field of SLA for a decade or two. It is impossible, in fact, to appreciate modern SLA research without acknowledging the substantial legacy of FLA.

Perhaps the most significant impact of this on our field of SLA stems from the debate that surrounded the evolution of FLA research as a newly emerging discipline. This debate is the age-old argument between the behaviorists and the nativists, which goes all the way back to the Greek philosophers. Examine the contention between Plato, who believed that children were born with the ability to speak, and his student Aristotle, who held that children could acquire language only from their social environment. More than two millennia later, this debate continues to color our thinking about both FLA and SLA. Because it also shapes our views about how people, language, attention, cognition, and emotions all work together to create a place for language learning, it seems useful to reflect for a moment on a few contemporary variations of it.

Fifty years ago **behaviorism** was the popular model for all animal and human learning. We all remember learning about Ivan Pavlov's experiments with dogs, in which he demonstrated that it was possible to condition a dog to elicit a response (such as salivation) after repeated exposures to a conditioning stimulus (such as the sound of a bell each time the dog was fed). Although the classical model of behaviorism was extremely influential on studies of learning in the first half of the twentieth century, FLA was never really influenced by it, perhaps because psychologists could never quite overcome an initial reluctance to comparing toddlers learning their first words (especially if the infants were their own kids) with dogs wolfing down a bowl of food. But the study of child language acquisition *was* influenced by a revised version of Pavlov's model, developed by B. F. Skinner, and named **operant conditioning**. Skinner's contribution to Pavlov's original theory was the idea that it is not what happens *before* a response that is significant, at least in terms of learning theory, but what occurs *after* the response that shapes or "operates on" acquisition. Operant conditioning became the accepted model for developmental psychologists in the initial studies of FLA that began in earnest in the decades following World War II.

Following Skinner's theory, many psychologists believed that environmental influences were exceedingly important in determining the course and the success of language learning, because infants were encouraged to acquire new words and new rules based on what happened in their environment after they tried to speak. To cite a simplistic example, if a 10-month-old baby gurgles "ga ga" every time the mother picks the infant up, the mother may not provide much positive reinforcement to this perceived act of random babbling. But what happens when the infant babbles "ma ma" (as a baby invariably does, due to an intriguing mix of biological and environmental factors)? The mother usually responds with an ecstatic smile and an outpouring of positive reinforcement. According to Skinner, this kind of **shaping** operates on the baby's future behavior and encourages the child to discard "ga ga" in favor of "ma ma" in all subsequent vocalizations with caretakers (Skinner, 1957). So the initial interest of FLA research was directed to the way the environment shaped an infant's behavior to conform to the language used by the surrounding caretakers. It's helpful to remember that although this early behavioral model focused almost exclusively on the impact of the child's environment on mother tongue learning, it was not directly concerned with social interaction. That is, operant conditioning did not contend that people or social interaction were crucial for language acquisition; rather, it argued that the language that caretakers constantly used around children and their positive (or negative) shaping of infant behaviors each time attempts were made to communicate in the target language accounted for the successful acquisition of a mother tongue.

AN INNATIST MODEL OF FIRST LANGUAGE ACQUISITION

A second and very different perspective on language acquisition superseded the behaviorist model about four decades ago when Noam Chomsky (1957) first promulgated his ideas about linguistics. Because his views about language have had more of an impact on SLA theory and research than any other, they deserve a somewhat extensive introduction here. Chomsky's revolutionary **transformation-generative** (**TG**) approach differed substantially from previous views of grammar, which had tended to look at only the surface structure of language. That is, up until the introduction of TG grammar, linguists based their rules, quite plausibly, on the actual words people used in speaking or writing. But Chomsky (1965) proposed that these overt markers of language were only superficially indicative of how human language is structured, and that the essential rules of grammar lay hidden in the abstract deep structure of language. Although surface structure differences abound from language to language, the deep structure rules are universal and, according to Chomsky's early version of TG grammar, this is what characterizes the essence of linguistic communication.

An anatomical analogy might help make this surface/deep dichotomy a bit clearer. Although differences in skin color and other "surface structure" contrasts are immediately apparent when we look at people from different parts of the globe, it is obvious that all human beings share similar "deep structure" characteristics (e.g., all skeletal features are identical). Race, like beauty, tends to be largely skin deep. This means that any anthropological descriptions that are chosen to represent all humankind cannot depend upon superficialities ("everyone has bronze-colored skin and small noses") but must be based on more fundamental anatomical correspondences ("all humans have 33 vertebrae"). In like manner, Chomsky contended that even though the thousands of human languages differ enormously in their surface structure, they all share a common deep structure that can be called **universal grammar** (**UG**). UG rules are, by their very nature, extremely general and abstract.

Let's turn to a specific example of how UG facilitates the learning of a mother tongue. One illustration Chomsky and his supporters have cited is the observation that no language has a grammar rule that operates on how many words a phrase or sentence contains. That is, rules in any language always operate on a specific linguistic structure and not on how many words precede or follow that particular structure. Pretend, for the purposes of this illustration, to be a three-year-old child immersed in a sea of English. Every day you are inundated with hundreds of examples of English questions, and you are struggling, albeit unconsciously, to learn how to produce these difficult patterns. (Your task, incidentally, is not that much different from the job facing a beginning ESL student.) Now assume that you happen to hear the following questions in the space of a few minutes, and from this input, you attempt to come up with a "rule" about English question formation.

(1) Is he going?

(2) Has Daddy gone?

(3) Has your Daddy left?

A completely logical solution to the problem of how to ask these kinds of questions in English is to form a simple rule like the following: If you want to ask a question in English, count the first two words in any sentence you hear, then flip them so that the second word is first and the first word is second. (By the way, this is exactly the kind of logic a computer program would apply to this input to create a rule. This is how machines, but not people, learn languages.) This neat little trick works fine for many sentences, so that the questions in (1) and (2) do indeed come from switching the first two words of the sentences that underlie these questions. "He is going" changes to "Is he going?" and "Daddy has gone" converts nicely to "Has Daddy gone?" Of course, as you have already anticipated, this nice little rule quickly breaks down for the third question, because if this pattern were followed, the child would end up with the very un-English sounding "*Daddy your has left?" But because children can rely on an intuitive sense of language, thanks to UG, they never waste their time using this word-counting strategy to unpackage the patterns of their mother tongue, whether it is English or Ingush (a language spoken in the Caucasus). Eventually all kids end up with the correct structural solution. As all native speakers have intuitively learned, and as every ESL teacher has explicitly taught, questions are formed by finding the helping verb (whether it is the second or the twenty-second word in the sentence) and placing it in front of the subject.

*In this book, an asterisk is placed before a sentence to mark the sentence as ungrammatical.

In direct contrast to Pavlov, Skinner, and other behaviorists, Chomsky's innatist approach contends that it is not what the environment brings to the learner that is important, but what the learner brings to the environment. Unlike the behaviorists, who held that the mind of a newborn was a tabula rasa (a clean slate) upon which were written all of a child's experiences, the innatists believe that there is strong evidence for innate, preprogrammed linguistic competence in the form of UG. Children are born to be human—to think, to crave social interaction, to use an opposable thumb, and to walk. They are also born to talk, so to speak, so they speak. Of course infants are not born to acquire the specific language of their parents (just as they are not born to sway their shoulders when they walk, just like their dad). Nevertheless, Chomsky and many psycholinguists (e.g., Pinker, 1994; Boysson-Bardies, 1999) find strong evidence that children are born with innate linguistic abilities that allow them to anticipate and develop the rules and patterns of whatever language they are exposed to as infants, and from this claim has sprung the belief in UG. Granted, no child is born with the rule that adjectives must precede nouns (as in English), or that they must follow them (as in Thai). However, UG, the innate and abstract understanding that humans have about language, allows a child to intuitively realize that phrases have a central, important word, and that all modifiers can either come before or after this word. Infants growing up in an English-speaking household quickly realize that modifiers come first ("*good* baby," "*sweet* dreams"), whereas neonates raised in a home where Thai is spoken rapidly learn that modifiers come second (/tarok *dii*/, /fan *waan*/, the Thai equivalents to the English phrases above).

Beginning in the 1960s, developmental psychologists studying language acquisition began to reject operant conditioning and started to look at child language acquisition from a rationalist position. The pendulum swung dramatically away from scrutinizing what mothers and caretakers did or said to what babies appeared to be creating. Notice the double shift in perspective—from mother to child, and from externals to internals. Here, it becomes obvious that researchers studying either FLA or SLA were even less interested in social interaction than before, because their attention was diverted away from operant responses in the environment and toward the possible effects of innate factors, such as UG. Not surprisingly, much of the research that took place during this time attempted to show that it almost didn't matter what caretakers said or did; children followed innate stages of development and seemed almost impervious to the influence of their surroundings (Dulay, Burt, and Krashen, 1982). This rather extreme deviation from the earlier behavioral approach led, as you might already suspect, to the need for some counterbalance; slowly people began to muster evidence that neither the behaviorist nor the rationalist extreme was entirely satisfactory in explaining the complicated phenomenon of child language acquisition. The pendulum started to swing back to a more moderate position.

A Social Interactionist (Vygotskian) Model of First Language Acquisition

Ironically, it has taken developmental psychologists several decades of research to recognize what most parents almost instinctively apprehend and what the writer of our Learner's Account #6 insightfully discerned—that the foundation of all language learning is social interaction. This recognition does not directly contradict either the behavioral or innatist view of language learning, but nowadays, many psychologists are attempting to integrate these two earlier views into a **social interactionist** perspective.

This integrated theory is perhaps best represented by a model of learning promulgated by a former student of Pavlov, Lev Vygotsky (1962), who originated the notion that the most fertile environment for all early learning, including child language acquisition, is found in what he termed **the zone of proximal development**. This "zone" represents the difference between an individual child's level of linguistic and cognitive development and the potential level of development as shaped via interaction with adults or with peers. Put tersely, and paraphrasing Vygotsky's own words, "The relation between thought and word is a living person."

It is important to point out that Vygotsky's approach does not refute the behavioral claim that environmental conditioning affects learning. Because social interaction invariably focuses on our reactions to the people we come in contact with when we are infants, it upholds the behaviorist belief that a great deal of language acquisition comes from operant conditioning, especially the acquisition of pronunciation, vocabulary, and pragmatics, the branch of linguistics having to do with meaning in context.

At the same time, this view does not preclude innate human abilities. Infants invariably seek human interaction, not because it is present in the environment, but because they are born to do so. And in those exceptional cases when a child's genetic code is pathologically damaged (as it may be in many cases of autism), an infant ignores human contact right from the beginning, and consequently grows up with one of the rarest of human disabilities—it never fully acquires its mother tongue. If the need for human interaction is biologically programmed within us, logically and naturally, other human behaviors must be too—for example, UG.

But the social interactionist model is not content to be a mere synthesis of behavioral and innatist explanations; it offers much more. For one thing, a social interaction perspective challenges the conventionally stated rationale for language learning. Our common assumption is that we learn language in order to communicate, but the Vygotskian approach turns this proposition upside down. Children attempt to communicate and, in their attempts, learn language.

Let's go back to the kitchen for an example. An infant doesn't see a freshly baked cookie and think, "If I learn the word for that object, then I can ask for it" (the experience of any mother can attest to the frailty of this argument). No, the child reaches for the cookie, with or without comment, and is immediately shaped by a torrent of linguistic commentary from the caretaker, in which almost every other word is "cookie" or "cookies!" ("Don't touch the *cookies.* You can have a *cookie* after dinner. One *cookie,* OK? But no *cookies* now!"). Thanks to social interaction and the zone of proximal development, in this brief encounter the child very indirectly learns at least two things about its mother tongue (let alone about other lessons of life such as delayed gratification): The English word for that sweet thing that tastes so good is "cookie," and English is a funny language that marks plurals with an -s sound. In fact, it would be almost impossible for the child *not* to learn these two facts about English given the interaction just described.

This mini language lesson has taught the child both vocabulary and grammar, not because the child has been blessed with having a mom who is an ESL teacher, but because this brief interaction with an adult has allowed the child to acquire linguistic knowledge that the environment and UG alone would have been incapable of providing, even though both of these factors, of course, were present and are part and parcel of this Vygotskian approach to learning.

Another way social interaction helps is by creating many opportunities for children to acquire the pragmatic and sociolinguistic features of their mother tongue; they learn how to use speech in different contexts, and they acquire the ability to know what to say to whom, when, and where. Take the acquisition of various forms of requests. The zone of proximal development creates many opportunities for English-learning children to realize that a request like "gimme" can work with younger play-mates and some siblings but will definitely not achieve the desired results with mom and dad. And older children learn more complicated pragmatic variations of requests (e.g., "Wouldn't you like to…?" is a kinder and gentler way of asking "Wanna…?"). Again, though environmental shaping and UG are likely to play a role even in the acquisition of pragmatics, it is through the give and take of social interaction that so much of language is acquired and is acquired so well. People are the bridge between the world of children and their new world of language.

Quite recently several psycholinguists (e.g., Clark, 1996) have argued that too much of language analysis in the past has focused almost obsessively on language structure (what Clark labels "the product tradition") rather than on the entire communicative context (what he terms "the action tradition"). It seems apparent that the Vygotskian, social interaction perspective concentrates not so much on the final product as on this broader picture—on the entire "action" that is taking place during the communicative events that frame language acquisition. For all these reasons, then, it seems appropriate to adopt a social inter-actionist perspective for our study of how people play a significant role in the way we acquire a second language.

2.2 *FIND A BABY! (SOCIAL INTERACTION BETWEEN INFANTS AND CARETAKERS)*

Your task is to find a baby to observe with its mom, dad, or caretaker. If you do not have an infant in your own home or immediate neighborhood, it shouldn't be too difficult to locate one in a local park, shopping mall, or other public area. As long as you let the caretaker know that you simply want to observe and admire the little one for half an hour or so, even strangers will generally welcome the attention you lavish. It is helpful to use the following guidelines when you undertake this pleasant assignment.

(1) Try to observe an infant between the ages of about four months and twenty months. During this period of neonatal development, the baby is mature enough to be keenly aware of its surroundings, and yet dependent enough to spend a great deal of its life in the arms of older people or in close interaction with them. About 20–30 minutes is suffcient time to capture enough information to reflect on; this should amount to about 60 succinct comments.

(2) Of course, you can audiotape or videotape the proceedings if you have the equipment and the caretaker's permission, but a notebook, pencil, and an observant and unbiased eye will suffice. Try to be a good behaviorist and transcribe what the baby and the caretaker do and say, not what you *think* they are feeling or thinking. It is more objective to report, "M(mother) wiggles head toward B(baby) 3 times & says, You funny little pumpkin. B drools & smiles each time." When you record something like, "M teased the B until the B smiled," you are being more subjective and also a bit less precise.

(3) Try not to talk or participate directly in any activities during your observation period. As it is, you'll be busy enough transcribing your observation of a multitude of events. Besides, any intervention on your part, however slight, may affect the nature of the interaction. You should be disinterested, but not *un*interested.

(4) It's important to record everything you see, even if there is no overt linguistic activity. For example, the child might be nursing, and even when the mother is not speaking, there's still a great deal of interaction going on. What is the baby looking at? How does the baby respond overtly to sounds (speech or other noises)?

After reading over your notes, it is time to reflect on what you saw. Do any generalizations jump out at you? Even from the more diffuse, qualitative comments you have recorded, you are likely to reach a very elementary but profound conclusion. When caretakers speak to infants, the infants respond, albeit almost always nonverbally. If this is what you saw and recorded, your observation summarizes a great deal of recent research in the field of developmental psychology. From this rudimentary form of dialogue with its parent, the infant picks up a great deal about language.

For one thing, it learns that language is based almost entirely on speech and that speaking is intentional and meaningful. Unlike other oral sounds (belching, for example) speech is not random but purposeful behavior.

Babies also learn that conversation consists of timed responses on the part of the interlocutor and that dialogue involves turn taking. Their primitive reactions to speech encourage the caretaker to continue.

There are many other conclusions that could be drawn after considering the ways in which infants acquire their first language, but given that our interest is in how adults acquire a second language, what you saw when observing the baby should tell you something about the way "people" affect the nature and course of language acquisition—infant or adult, first language or second. One point should be made very clear, though; we do not want to conclude from all of this that the best way for an adolescent or adult to learn a second language is to recapitulate infancy and sit on the knee of a foreign language teacher gurgling after each phrase that is uttered! Having said this, it is apparent that the opposite extreme—sitting alone in a room and filling blanks in a grammar exercise or typing in verb forms in response to a computer program—is a radical departure from the social nurturing that same second language student received when picking up his or her mother tongue as a small child. The merit of this brief opportunity to observe and reflect on neonatal development is that this exercise makes explicit what all of us intuitively realize—there can be no language acquisition without people. Indeed, there can be no language.

SOCIOLINGUISTIC VARIABLES IN SECOND LANGUAGE ACQUISITION

Infants are blissfully innocent about the world in which they will soon mature, but since most second language learners are adolescents or adults, they have long passed the age of innocence and have learned, among other things, that their society is filled with people who are very different from their parents. They realize that the category "People" is not a homogeneous reflection of the faces of the family in which they grew up, but a conglomeration of different races, religions, and socio-economic classes. Even for language learners who live in a relatively uniform society such as Japan, where the vast majority of residents comprise one ethnicity and speak one language, social differences can be profound. And despite controlling for gender, and looking only at teenagers attending the same girls' high school, to take just one illustration, we still find that Japanese adolescents studying English in the same classroom can differ a great deal socially. Betrayed by superficial appearances, such as the students' uniforms, a foreign visitor might think that Megumi and Yuko are socially identical, but even in this comparatively controlled example, the girls could very well represent different social groups. Megumi's family might be much poorer than Yuko's, and she could speak a very different dialect, especially if she had just moved to the school from a different region of the country. When we examine the way our interaction with "People" affects our learning of a new tongue, we are immediately thrust into the field of **sociolinguistics**—the study of how social differences affect our use of language (Spolsky, 1998). Listen to the voice of an English-speaking Chinese-American student trying to learn Mandarin, and consider her concern about one significant sociolinguistic variable.

Learner's Account #7

And yes, I can't help but compare my performance to the performance of my peers. Sometimes I think it's unfair that native speakers of Cantonese are in the class. So I find myself intimidated by them. I'm also intimidated by the other native Chinese speakers of other dialects. The teacher enjoys calling on the non-Asian students. I get angry when the Asian students begin to laugh when a white or black student awkwardly tries to utter a phrase. But perhaps I'm silently laughing inside too. For it's a way to feel better about myself when I see other students who are "below" me.

A Student of Chinese

This learner's account illustrates that the most dramatic way in which we are forced to confront sociolinguistic variables in SLA is to consider the way we expect certain races and languages to match. As speakers of American English, we are taken aback when we see someone with a Chinese face who speaks English with a southern drawl, just as much as a visitor to North Carolina from Beijing is astounded when approached by an African American speaking fluent Mandarin. Naturally, most ethnic Chinese speak one of the Chinese languages as their mother tongue, but when we meet a Chinese-American person whose mother tongue is English, and who might stammer only a few words in Cantonese, we learn two important linguistic facts. First, and most fundamentally, we are immediately disabused of the notion that racial features might have something to do with our ability to speak a particular language fluently. Speakers of *any* ethnic background can learn how to pronounce any sound in any language, so it is opportunity, not race, that determines foreign accents. Second, and more pertinent to our focus on sociolinguistic variables, we all harbor presuppositions that the way people look determines the way they should speak. The nervous laughter in the classroom just described barely masks the racial stereotyping that is part of our social upbringing. In most communities, black and white faces aren't expected to produce articulate Chinese, but Chinese faces are, of course. Learner's Account #7 demonstrates, therefore, that the language that we carry around with us is not socially neutral; like the clothes we wear or the neighborhoods we happen to live in, speech is not just a mode of communication but a means of social identification.

THE ACCULTURATION MODEL

Some of the initial SLA research centered on the ways in which differences in socioeconomic class might impinge on the relative success or failure of certain groups of people to learn a second language. If we look at large groups of people in multilingual countries, we find some groups that are quite successful in picking up an additional national language, and other groups that are not. What might account for this difference? Certainly not race, which we have already ruled out, and surely not intelligence, since we have no anthropological evidence to support the misguided—prejudice which some people still harbor—that certain social groups (invariably their own) are intellectually superior to others (predictably those they dislike!). Schumann (1978) was the first to argue that socioeconomic differences between the language community of the learner and that of the target language played a significant role in determining the learner's success.

Contrast, for example, the successful French-German bilingualism found in many areas of Switzerland with the lack of bilingualism found in Southern California, where Spanish and English are spoken in roughly the same proportions as French and German in central Switzerland. According to Schumann, this differential success depends on the degree to which the two language communities **acculturate**, or adapt to each other, in each situation. In Switzerland, French and German speakers share the same socioeconomic status and easily acculturate to each other; hence, there is very little **social distance** between them. Conversely, in Southern California, because most English speakers retain a socioeconomic advantage over most Spanish speakers, there is socioeconomic distance between the two linguistic communities, and this social separation prevents acculturation from taking place.

Based on illustrations like this, Schumann posited an **Acculturation Model** of SLA, hypothesizing that whenever there is a substantial socioeconomic difference between two groups of people, those who come from the comparatively disadvantaged community will not acculturate to the advantaged and dominant majority language and thus will not be motivated to acquire the second language. In a place like central Switzerland, since the two linguistic communities are socioeconomic equals, the social distance between the two groups is small, acculturation is greatly enhanced, and fluent bilingualism prevails. Put tersely and formulaically, success in second language acquisition (SSLA) is inversely proportional to the social distance (SD) between the second language learning and target language communities.

$$SSLA = \frac{1}{SD}$$

Schumann supported his sociological explanation of SLA, not with demographic surveys of linguistic minorities, but via a longitudinal study of one Spanish-speaking immigrant to the United States. His research on this single subject showed, not surprisingly, that this immigrant failed to achieve much success with English, despite many opportunities to acquire the dominant language of the city to which he had moved. Because Schumann's hypothesis has not been applied to larger groups of learners, it stands as a thought-provoking model, open for reflection and verification.

Like most theories when they are first conceived and promulgated, the Acculturation Model seemed almost too ambitious in attempting to relate SLA success solely to socioeconomic factors. After all, there are obviously many exceptions to this claim that language learning is impeded by class differences or accelerated by class similarities. More important, as we have already seen from the PLACE perspective adopted by this book, language learning is much more than an economic or even a social phenomenon; it is more significantly determined by social psychological factors. This implies that "social distance" is better measured by internal measures, such as our attitudes toward the speakers and toward the society of the language we are attempting to learn, rather than by external variables such as socioeconomic class.

ACTON'S RESEARCH INTO PERCEIVED SOCIAL DISTANCE

Attitudes and feelings are much more difficult to quantify than socioeconomic status, which can readily be defined by family income and other economic and demographic measures, but this does not mean that we can't try to be objective about "subjective" behavior. There is a tendency for scientists to avoid studying phenomena that are difficult to quantify, however interesting they may be. Ulric Neisser, a psychologist respected for his research on memory, puts it even more strongly, claiming that "If X is an interesting memory phenomenon, psychologists avoid it like the plague" (1982:17).

But difficult though it may be to measure internal attitudes, social psychologists have, in fact, come up with a variety of ways to calibrate the feelings that one group of people has about another. Because our central concern is language learning, the social psychological research that most interests us concerns the way attitudes toward both the language and the culture merge together. Fantini (1997) calls this special nexus of culture and language **linguaculture**, a term that is particularly handy for describing the effect that people's perceptions have on the way they learn a new language.

Inspired initially by Schumann's concept of social distance, Acton (1979) decided to examine the role of **perceived social distance** in SLA, looking at the internal feelings learners hold about the linguaculture they happen to be studying. Since many of Acton's ESL learners came from Japan and Saudi Arabia, he decided to focus on contrasts between these two national groupings, and between both of them and Americans. He used a control group of native speakers of English, Americans of comparable age, as a contrast to the young Japanese and Saudi ESL students. To measure their internal social perceptions, Acton gave all of his subjects a questionnaire in which they were asked to rank their attitudes about certain concepts on a Likert scale (a numbered scale, usually around six points, ranging from very negative to completely positive). For example, the Saudi, Japanese, and American students were asked to rank their feelings about divorce, the assumption being that even though there are always obvious individual differences (some atypical Saudis might actually characterize divorce as slightly positive and give it a four on the six-point scale), the general tendency would be for the emergence of a consistent social consensus that would differ among the three groups and that would translate into a numerical scale, allowing the researcher to measure contrasts in social attitudes. Since the attitudes questionnaire was administered in the native language of each group (i.e., Arabic for the Saudis, Japanese and English, respectively, for the other two groups), Acton also sent the questionnaires back to Saudi Arabia and Japan so that the perceptions of matching groups of Saudi and Japanese students not learning ESL in the United States could be quantified. This experimental design allowed him to triangulate his data by contrasting the attitudes of his ESL students with those held by both the mother linguaculture (students back home) and the target linguaculture (American students).

Figure 2.1: Perceived Social Distance (Acton, 1979)

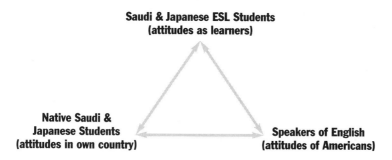

Saudi & Japanese ESL Students
(attitudes as learners)

Native Saudi &
Japanese Students
(attitudes in own country)

Speakers of English
(attitudes of Americans)

Very nice, you might say, but what does all of this have to do with SLA? Perhaps you can already anticipate the direction of Acton's design. Implicit within this comparison is the assumption that people's attitudes toward a target linguaculture affect, to some extent, their degree of success in acquiring that language. And the most transparent application of this assumption to SLA would be the hypothesis that the Saudi and Japanese ESL students whose answers on the questionnaires were most similar to the answers American students gave would be the students who would improve most during their intensive ESL course at the University of Michigan. Conversely, those ESL students whose answers were closest to the ones given by their counterparts in their own country would likely be the students who made the smallest gains in acquiring the new language. Perceived social distance would be the yardstick along which one could measure the potential for SLA success. Rather than finding an inverse correlation, as we did for the acculturation model, here we would expect a direct correlation between social distance and SLA achievement.

Acton needed one more piece of data before he could actually test his hypothesis. He obtained this by giving all his ESL students an English proficiency test (the Michigan Test) at the beginning of the semester and another at the end of the term, so that he could measure each student's improvement. By looking at the way each student's increase in English (as quantified by the two administrations of the Michigan Test) correlated with that student's perceived social distance from the target English-speaking culture (close if their scores were more similar to the Americans', distant if their scores more closely matched the scores of their compatriots back home), Acton came up with a surprising discovery.

The Saudi and Japanese students who showed the greatest gains in their Michigan scores (the best language learners, if we can be so bold as to extrapolate that claim just from two ESL tests) were *not* the ones whose answers on the attitudinal questionnaire most closely mimicked the attitudes of the American controls. Nor was the original hypothesis completely disconfirmed—the best language learners were also not the ones whose scores most closely matched the scores of the Saudis and Japanese back home. Instead, the ESL students who achieved the highest gains on the Michigan test were those whose attitudinal scores represented views about halfway between the attitudes of the mother culture and those of the target culture. Measured in terms of perceived social distance, it seemed that the optimal social distance for successful SLA is about in the middle between the two key cultures. Although correlations do not prove causality, Acton's early findings have been directly or indirectly confirmed by subsequent investigations into the ways in which learners' attitudes toward the target linguaculture might affect their acquisition of that target language.

LEARNERS' ATTITUDES AND THE TEACHER'S ROLE

It is all well and good to talk about how researchers can try to triangulate students' attitudes toward the new language and the culture they are learning about, but what role does the teacher have in all of this? More specifically, can teachers help change students' attitudes? Should they? And how is it possible to change people's attitudes anyway—aren't they pretty much fixed by the early cultural nurturing that all children experience? These are some of the questions that confront us whenever we deal with the mix of language and culture in our ESL classrooms, and they are the same questions that Mariko Okuzaki has thought about as an English instructor in Japan. Teaching younger learners in the northernmost island of Hokkaido, Mariko has often seen a reluctance on the part of her students to accept the linguaculture that accompanies the vocabulary she teaches in her English classes. Here is her rationale; following it is her activity in her own words.

In the Japanese-published and approved textbook for her class, there is a dialogue about eating sushi between an American girl visiting a Japanese boy, and Mariko's students were surprised at the girl's initial reluctance to try sushi. Some of them even felt that the American was "selfish" because she couldn't appreciate "the beauty of sushi." Mariko wanted her students to have more empathy for the target linguaculture, so she decided to create a situation in her English classroom where her students would go through the same kind of "culture shock" about strange food as that experienced by the American girl in the dialogue in their text. Once, when Mariko was eating in a cafeteria in the United States, she had seen someone eat an apple with peanut butter. For her, this way of combining foods was unique and unthinkable, but she purposely tried this odd combination to help overcome her own culture shock. Remembering this, Mariko thought she would introduce her students to the same experience to help put them into the American girl's shoes.

Mariko Okuzaki

It is natural to have feelings of denial, rejection, or even of ignorance at the first stage of exposure to a new language. The stronger the impact the teacher creates on the students' belief systems and their value judgments, the more questions about the stability of their values will be generated. Then, by reflecting on their belief system and value judgments as compared with the norms of the new culture, students will become aware of and then accept these differences. To help students encounter value conflicts and to help them shift their viewpoints, I often tell them of my experiences as an example and let them literally taste my experience in class.

I first saw an American friend eating an apple with peanut butter 17 years ago. My friend was in the school cafeteria, and at first I couldn't believe her sense of taste. I immediately judged her behavior as different and wrong! Peanut butter was only for bread. That was the belief I had held until then, and I couldn't believe that there could be any other way of eating peanut butter at the time. Later, I saw more foreign friends eating apples with peanut butter, and then I tempered my judgment and noticed it was not a matter of right or wrong, but a matter of different tastes. Although it took several weeks to try it myself, apple and peanut butter soon became one of my favorite combinations. I learned to cultivate an empathetic viewpoint and develop feelings for a new cultural experience.

In my class, I let my Japanese students simulate my experience with real apples and peanut butter. First I asked the students if they wanted to have an apple during the lesson. They definitely got excited about a chance to eat in class. Then, I told them there was one condition, and that was they had to eat something with the apple. They felt curious and started to ask me, "Is it honey, cream, jam, mayonnaise, or soy sauce?" Then, the whole class almost became chaotic when they saw me put peanut butter on the apple. However, after seeing me eat this, a few courageous students stood up, tried a piece, and told the class that it was wasn't so bad as they had first thought. I realized that gradually, the students had started to reflect on their feelings and rethink their own attitudes about food.

Finally, I encouraged the students to think about the feelings of foreign people by asking, for example, "How do foreign people feel when they see raw fish for the first time in their life?" My students realized that the same feelings they had had as their first reaction to the peanut butter and apples can occur to foreigners, and this reaction is natural and understandable. This activity of involving the students' sight, smell, and taste seems to work well in sensitizing their feelings to cultural differences.

Although her illustration is quite simple and does not seem to relate directly to language teaching, notice how Mariko was able to give her students a genuine acculturation experience without ever leaving the confines of that Japanese classroom. Note too that the use of smell and taste is one way of bringing a little of the "kitchen" into the classroom. How do cultural differences affect your students' learning of English? Do you recall any incidents like this that have hindered or helped your own struggles to acquire a new language? Can you think of a creative learning experience that you could incorporate into the materials and activities of your ESL classroom?

STAGES OF ACCULTURATION

We have seen that one way in which learners' attitudes toward a target culture might influence SLA is in the area of **acculturation** and **culture shock** (Furnham and Bochner, 1986). In today's world, due to such factors as improved transportation, the global economy, and—alas—the continued dislocation of large groups of people due to war and civil unrest, large populations of people are emigrating to new countries and often living as immigrants in these new places for long periods of time. Acculturation, the process whereby immigrants gradually become a part of their new community, is usually conceived of as consisting of four stages (e.g., Scarcella and Oxford, 1992): (1) a period of stereotypes and excitement, (2) a period of shallow comprehension and culture shock, (3) a period of deeper comprehension and anomie (distance from both the old and the new cultures), and finally (4) a period of empathy and permanent adjustment. Various researchers name these four stages differently (Brown, 2000), and there are also different interpretations on the ultimate nature of the final stage.

For example, some claim that acculturation should be distinguished from assimilation—the former referring to the happy maintenance of immigrant cultures within the larger host culture (the "mixed salad" metaphor), as opposed to the latter, which could imply that at this final stage, immigrant cultures blend into the homogeneous "melting pot" of the host culture. Notice that Acton's experiment suggests that if we look at acculturation in the same way as we look at language acquisition, as a longitudinal process, it is at the penultimate stage, the point of anomie—not the last stage—that SLA is most efficient. The social psychological explanation for this phenomenon, if it does indeed exist, is that learners are most open to acquiring a new system when they have progressed enough to be somewhat distant from both their mother tongue and the target linguaculture.

Or, to explain the phenomenon in another way, by the time individuals have acculturated to a new culture, since they have already adjusted and adapted to the new environment with whatever target language skills they have been able to acquire, they have no serious motivation to improve their linguistic skills any further. Thus, the final stage (the period of empathy and complete adjustment) is where the *least* language learning takes place, partly because the immigrant has had a great deal of time to acquire most of the language, but, just as important, because now the learner can get by with whatever second language skills have been acquired. It is not at all surprising that immigrants who have reached this final stage of acculturation—especially older immigrants—often speak a version of the target language that is fossilized, with many errors. An illustration of this is the many Asian immigrants to Los Angeles or London. They speak English rapidly and fluently, but they frequently omit articles and tense markers in their speech, and these errors seem to persist unchanged and fossilized even after many years of interaction with native speakers.

GILES' SPEECH ACCOMMODATION MODEL

Sociolinguists have identified another way in which the attitudes held by second language learners toward the target linguaculture influence the course of their language learning (Beebe, 1988). Based very much within the social interactionist approach toward language use, Giles (1980) proposed the **speech accommodation** model for accounting for social interaction in SLA. He postulated that conversations between speakers comprise three separate processes. They may tend to maintain their own individual dialect; or, depending on the circumstances, they may do just the opposite and make their speech even more distinct from the other interlocutor and diverge; or both speakers may try to adopt features of each other's dialects and thus converge. This linguistic divergence or convergence, according to Giles, generally parallels the social attitudes speakers harbor toward each other. In other words, to take the example of convergence, speakers who see themselves as "coming together" socially also tend to make their speech sound more similar to one another's.

A peculiar but not unusual manifestation of convergence is psychological convergence where speakers who really aren't genuinely familiar with the other speaker's dialect alter their speech in a superficial, and often inaccurate, attempt to display solidarity with the person they are talking to. Ironically, although the intention is to show convergence, this inappropriate attempt to display familiarity often ends up creating more social distance than if the speakers had simply maintained their own natural dialect! One example of psychological convergence that occurs frequently in SLA situations is the often misguided attempt by native speakers to "simplify" their mother tongue when speaking with nonnative speakers. This pidginized form is called **foreigner talk** (Ferguson, 1971), and although it is quite commonly used to indicate psychological convergence, because it is ungrammatical and stigmatized, it usually creates the opposite effect—a feeling of divergence on the part of the nonnative speaker.

Here is a brief excerpt from a conversation between a nonnative (but fluent) Nepali woman speaking English with an American tourist using foreigner talk. The conversation (as recalled and transcribed by the author of the book from which the example was excerpted) illustrates how this pidginized variety of speech can create negative reactions on the part of nonnative speakers of English.

> When I returned to the dining room, I approached the proprietress to ask for a beer. A small, graceful Sherpani, she was in the midst of taking an order from a group of American trekkers. "We hungry," a ruddy-cheeked man announced to her in overly loud pidgin, miming the act of eating. "Want eat po-ta-toes. Yak bur-ger. Co-ca Co-la. You have?" "Would you like to see the menu?" the Sherpani replied in clear, sparkling English that carried a hint of a Canadian accent. "Our selection is actually quite large. And I believe there is still some freshly baked apple pie available, if that interests you, for dessert." The American trekker, unable to comprehend that this brown-skinned woman of the hills was addressing him in perfectly enunciated King's English, continued to employ his comical pidgin argot: "Men-u. Good, good. Yes, yes, we like see men-u."
>
> *(Krakauer, 1997:43–44)*

Psychological convergence is evidenced by the use of language of both the participants in this episode, but it is apparent from this situation that, unlike the nonnative's choice of English, the American's decision to persist with foreigner talk, which was based on his misperceptions about the English competency of his Nepali interlocutor, created a feeling of disrespect and, ironically, of divergence. Giles' accommodation model is helpful, then, in showing that the language that speakers choose when they converse is a dynamic reflection of their sociolinguistic attitudes toward one another. It also helps to explain why a speaker's intention to demonstrate convergence may sometimes actually be perceived by the interlocutor as a demonstration of divergence.

HERMANN'S RESULTATIVE HYPOTHESIS

The final way in which a speaker's attitudes might affect the course of SLA is represented by Hermann's research into the way success or failure in second language classrooms encourages (or, sadly, discourages) learners to foster positive attitudes toward the new language and its speakers. Typically, social attitudes are viewed as a preexisting state of mind that precedes language learning (e.g., university students enter their first German class with either positive or negative opinions about what they are about to experience), but work by Hermann (1980), Genesee, Rogers, and Holobow (1983), and others indicates that things may be the other way around. For example, Strong (1983) investigated the results of SLA success on social attitudes in a group of Spanish-speaking children learning English as a Second Language (ESL) in California. His results corroborated those of Hermann, showing that pupils who had improved in their ESL competency displayed more positive attitudes toward Anglos. A study looking at a different age group (American university students) and a different language (French) adds further documentation that SLA success can affect social attitudes in a direct and positive manner (Lafayette and Buscaglia, 1985). The authors concluded their study by reporting that for most of these students, "…French was no longer an obstacle to be overcome, rather it began to assume the vehicular role that it plays among natives" (1985:335). In sum, it seems that all of these studies support Hermann's so-called **resultative hypothesis**.

One popular rationale for encouraging people to pick up a second language is the belief that learning a foreign language helps broaden a learner's mental horizons. Well-intentioned and intuitively attractive as this idea may be, this notion remains, at best, an unsubstantiated aspiration. Nonetheless, it is no exaggeration to summarize Hermann's resultative hypothesis about the effect of SLA on sociolinguistic attitudes with the claim that learning a new language might not change your mind, but it can change your heart.

LANGUAGE PLANNING—SOCIOLINGUISTICS AND THE WORLD AT LARGE

So far, all of the examples involving People and SLA that we have been looking at have been confined to brief conversations between speakers in a very restricted context, and except for Schumann's Acculturation Model, none of our discussion has involved the choice and use of languages that encompass entire nations of peoples. Nevertheless, because our social world is largely defined by the larger world of politics, an extremely important variable affecting SLA is the political system, which often dictates what languages should be learned, and by whom. The **Sociology of Language** or **Language Planning** is the study of how large institutions, such as national governments, control or influence the choice of languages to be learned in a nation; it can also incorporate the study of social, political, and economic forces that affect the choice of languages to be learned, even in the absence of overt government planning. To cite an illustration of the latter, for more than two centuries, children of immigrants who have come to the United States have automatically been immersed in a sea of English, and for a long time, it has seemed almost "natural" that anyone who was a citizen of the United States was, ipso facto, a native speaker of English. Listen to the voice of a typical immigrant—someone who emigrated from Italy to America with her parents as a young girl.

> My introduction to the American school system began when I entered a first-grade classroom not long after arriving in the United States at the age of six. Feelings of fearfulness at being separated from my family were heightened when I lost my way home on the first day of school. I wandered for what seemed miles in central Newark, New Jersey, crying until I was brought home by a policeman who lived in our neighborhood.
>
> During those first few months, the hours I spent in the classroom were a haze of incomprehensible sounds. I copied what the other children seemed to be doing, scribbling on paper as though I were writing; otherwise, I silently watched the behavior of teachers and students. Although I cannot recall the process of learning English and beginning to participate in the verbal life of the classroom, I know it was painful. I can remember, however, that within two years, I felt comfortable with English and with the school community—how it happened I do not know. I suspect that a combination of factors worked in my favor: a close-knit family, personal motivation, good health, sympathetic teachers, peer acceptance, and who knows what other intangibles of time and place. When it finally began to happen, I remember the intense joy of understanding and being understood, even at a simple level, by those around me.
>
> *(Rosalie Porter. 1990. Forked Tongue. NY: Basic Books, pp. 14–15)*

What is remarkable, but by no means unique, about this young immigrant's achievement is that she went on to become a native speaker of English, was awarded a Ph.D., and became a published scholar. In fact, this anecdote comes to us in her own words, as an excerpt from a book she published about bilingual education. But expectations about the learning and use of English in the United States, Canada, Australia, and the United Kingdom have changed in the decades since World War II, and many sociolinguists interested in language planning have questioned the "immersion" tradition that predominated in the past. They have studied and even promulgated new alternatives to the role national languages play and the way they should be learned. Because language planning has such a profound impact on what language(s) people will learn in school and how they will learn them, we cannot conclude this chapter on People and SLA without a brief look at the big picture and the sociology of language.

THE THREE CIRCLES OF WORLD ENGLISHES

The conflagration of World War II had a profound and irrevocable effect on the politics of language in many countries around the globe, and the United States, despite its geographical isolation, was no exception. Because America was forced to mobilize and deploy hundreds of thousands of personnel over a period of years to two separate and diverse theaters of war, the world and its languages came to the United States with unprecedented impact. Thanks to the efficient work of many linguists marshaled by the war department for this purpose, tens of thousands of Americans began to learn not only Japanese and German, the languages of the Axis powers, but the varied tongues of their Allies, languages as diverse as Czech and Chinese.

But America, and American English, also came to the world. A large part of the linguistic legacy of that international conflict was a rearrangement of world languages—a kind of unplanned language planning at a pan-national level. English grew to supersede all other international languages, including French, and became the lingua franca of the modern world. Granted, many other factors account for the rise of English, and the legacy of British colonialism remains the single most powerful influence for its spread, but World War II was the political watershed that marked the flood of English around the globe as the most taught and most widespread language on the planet (Crystal, 1988).

Some sociolinguists consider this phenomenon an inappropriate consequence of socioeconomic imperialism (Phillipson, 1992; Skutnabb-Kangas, 2000), particularly in those situations where the rise of English might be linked to the demise of certain indigenous languages. Be that as it may, no matter how we deal with the fact that English is now the only world language, the learning of English has become a massive educational undertaking for most countries and has created an extensive commercial market for publishing companies. Today, English links nations and peoples together by land (via the majority of newspapers, magazines, scholarly journals, and books), by sea (as the international maritime language, and as representing three-quarters of the world's surface mail), by air (via BBC and CNN and by serving as the international language of air traffic control), and now by fiber-optic cable (carrying most of the world's e-mail). And though insignificant in its comparative importance to all these other enterprises, not insignificantly for books like this, English language teaching has spawned and supported most of the research done in SLA over the past few decades.

Figure 2.2: The Three Circles of World Englishes

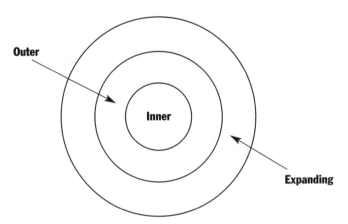

Until recently, the teaching of English has been split into two supposedly very different situations: English-as-a-Second Language (**ESL**), where it is taught to nonnative residents in English-speaking countries, and English-as-a-Foreign Language (**EFL**), where it is taught as a nonindigenous language—as it is in most nations on earth. Given the heterogeneity of English usage that has emerged from nation to nation since World War II, however, Kachru (1985) has come up with a trinary categorization that is a more accurate characterization of the new world order. Countries where English has had a long tradition as the majority language are called **inner circle** nations. Clearly, New Zealand, the United Kingdom, and the United States are apt representatives, but so too are lesser known places such as Belize (the former British Honduras). The **outer circle** is represented by a large number of nations scattered around the world, almost all of them former colonies of England. In none of these nations was English an important language before colonization, but today, English is either a national language or functions as one of the primary languages for commerce, education, and government. Nigeria, Zimbabwe, Malaysia, the Philippines, and Vanuatu are a few of the many countries that fall into this category. Finally, the largest sweep of nations comprise the **expanding circle**—from Afghanistan to Zaire (now the Congo) alphabetically, and from Iceland to the southern tip of Chile, going from pole to pole. Notice that the inner and expanding circles are generally equivalent to the ESL and EFL categories, respectively, leaving the outer circle nations as a new classification flanked by the other two.

More significant than this simple redesignation of the use of English are Kachru's claims about the consequences of looking at this linguistic diffusion with fresh eyes. Notice first of all that the title for this final subsection pluralizes the proper noun English into **Englishes**. This is neither a typo nor bad grammar, but an attempt to signify that, from a contemporary sociolinguistic standpoint, "English" is not a single, homogenized standard emanating from one prestige area—traditionally exemplified by Received Pronunciation (RP) from London, or Standard American English from San Francisco. Rather, the term World English*es* implies that, viewed more broadly, the language contains international dialects that are just as acceptable and legitimate varieties of the language as geographical dialects in the United Kingdom (e.g., Yorkshire English) or sociolinguistic dialects in the United States (e.g., African American English Vernacular). Seen from this perspective, a resident of New Delhi telling a friend in the retroflected pronunciation characteristic of many Indian speakers and substituting /p/ for /f/, "Shabash! (Hindi for "Congratulations") I am peeling happy por you," is no less an "English" sentence than the nonstandard but exceedingly common use of double negatives among English speakers in inner circle countries ("Look, I don't got no money!"). The pervasive use of English internationally has, according to Kachru, encouraged linguists to broaden their definition of what constitutes "standard" English. Is it fair, to cite just one of many potential contradictions, to claim that Joseph Conrad's novels are masterpieces of "native" English literature, even though he never won a Nobel Prize in Literature (nor was he a native speaker of the tongue) but, in the same breath, to commend Wole Soyinka's works simply as excellent examples of "nonnative" English, even though this Nigerian author did receive the Nobel prize for literature in 1986? In sum, the spread of English around the globe has challenged many of our long-held sociolinguistic expectations and has forced us to rethink what it means to be a "native" speaker of a language. Because of the tremendous changes that have overtaken the world in our lifetime, English is no longer "owned" by the inner circle; it has expanded to every corner of the globe and must be shared as a mutual resource among all the inhabitants of our planet.

2.3 *WHO'S BETTER—A NATIVE OR A NONNATIVE ENGLISH TEACHER?*

For many decades, most people in the English teaching profession believed that the best teachers were native speakers. So strong has been this belief that native speakers with almost no pedagogical experience were often hired over non-native speakers who were highly trained and experienced! After all, so the reasoning went, if you were living in Australia and wanted to study Arabic, who would you prefer as your teacher, a native speaker of Arabic or an Australian friend who had learned Arabic at university? But given the global spread of English and the growing diversity of contexts in which it is being taught, many TESOL professionals are rethinking this assumption that native speaking teachers have an automatic advantage over nonnative teachers of English. Consider these situations.

(1) If you owned a large English language school in an expanding circle nation (let's take Indonesia as an example), what advantages would you face by hiring teachers from countries like the United States or the United Kingdom?

(2) Now, in the same situation, what advantages would you enjoy by hiring Indonesian English teachers (and let's assume that your school always hires a few native speaking teachers so that your faculty isn't completely Indonesian).

(3) If your school was in an outer circle country (let's say Kenya), would your reasoning change?

(4) What if your school was in an inner circle country (e.g., a private school for nonnative speakers in a large English speaking city, like Dublin)?

(5) Go back to the first two situations, where you are in a position to hire English teachers for an institution in an expanding circle nation. From a student's perspective, what advantages are there to being taught by a native speaker of English? What advantages are there to being taught by someone just like you (say, a native speaker of Bahasa Indonesia)? After considering the relative merits of native and nonnative English teachers in these different global contexts, would you now feel comfortable with the claim that, all things being equal, native English speakers are almost always the best teachers?

THE EFFECTS OF LANGUAGE PLANNING ON THE TEACHING OF FOREIGN LANGUAGES

Sociologists of language are particularly interested in the impact of language planning on language teaching in individual countries. At some point in virtually every nation's history, this influence has been easy to determine, even in the many places around the world where there is no government-sponsored academy to regulate the national language(s). France, for example, has experienced several well-publicized campaigns in which the government in power, through the national academy, has tried to regulate and legislate English loan-words out of the French language, or at least off billboards and storefronts; however, these somewhat superficial attempts at linguistic engineering have met with little success. Less well-known perhaps, but by far much more influential, have been the decisions various governments have made about the choice of a national dialect (Norway), the creation of a new national language (Israel), the selection of official national languages (Nigeria), the decision to simplify the writing system (China), or the decision not to simplify (Taiwan).

These and many other examples of language planning involved the national language(s) of the country cited, but language planning can also include decisions about the prioritization of foreign language teaching. When the Soviet Union successfully launched the world's first satellite in 1957, the United States responded with a post-sputnik flurry of legislative and budgetary support in order to accelerate progress in science and technology. Included in this wave of patriotic fervor was the National Defense Foreign Language (NDFL) Act, which suddenly poured millions of dollars into support for foreign language learning and teaching. This infusion of support encouraged an unprecedented develop-ment of materials, methods, research, scholarships, and teaching personnel, and was especially effective in promoting the teaching of less common languages. Although the United States, like all the other inner circle English-speaking nations, has no government-sanctioned language academy, the way the NDFL bolstered foreign language teaching demonstrates that even without an academy and clear-cut language policies, governments can very rapidly promote changes in the teaching of foreign languages in any country.

One of the most dramatic examples of this kind of linguistic engineering took place in the People's Republic of China (PRC) during the years following its foundation in 1949. Up until 1949, China, like most of its Asian neighbors, had prioritized English as the most important foreign language to be taught in schools and universities. However, because the Chinese communist government had been influenced by Soviet models of development, in the early 1950s the PRC made Russian top priority among all foreign languages to be taught in the nationally controlled educational system (J. Scovel, 1982). Tens of thousands of English teachers were retrained as Russian teachers, under the naive belief held by many of the linguistically unsophisticated bureaucrats in Beijing that all European languages, since they didn't have tones or use characters, were rough-ly equivalent. After a blitzkrieg of summer seminars and frenzied study of the Cyrillic alphabet, these dedicated teachers tried desperately to begin anew as competent teachers of Russian. At that time, English didn't even rank second on the government's priority list but was supplanted by Spanish, which was pro-moted because of its potential to create Chinese liaisons with the burgeoning people's revolutions in Central and South America. (For some peculiar reason, the artificially created "universal" language, Esperanto, was also promoted at this time.) After being the major foreign language for over a century, thanks to this new, draconian government policy, English quickly became a minor player among the languages taught in the world's most populous nation.

Of course all this has changed radically in the past 50 years, and because of many dramatic reversals in Chinese government policies since the early 1950s, there has been a top-down government promotion of English in the PRC as well as a bottom-up popular enthusiasm to learn the language for a score of years. Indeed, so ardent is the determination to learn English among the some 1.2 billion Chinese that there are probably as many learners of English in China as there are native speakers of the language in the United States. What we learn from this short review of second language planning is that governments can and do make decisions that drastically affect which foreign languages are to be taught, and how. Because of their mammoth import, these national decisions are far more significant in their effect on language learning in any given country than such relatively trivial classroom issues as what methods should be used or what materials should be chosen. Not that what teachers and learners do is unimportant, but from a sociolinguistic perspective, no force is more consequential to the teaching of languages in a society than the consequences of language planning (or the lack thereof).

SLA AND BILINGUAL EDUCATION

A final example of the way that People and language learning interact with each other is the controversial topic of bilingual education in the United States, especially as advocated as an alternative to the "English only" movement. Many have written about this topic, but few (e.g., Hakuta, 1986) have done so fairly and wisely. This is because the sociology of language is not confined to just a single classroom (a second-year Spanish class) or a few people (a teacher and her students), but includes competing philosophies about public and private education, political forces and parties, allocation of state and federal funding, and laws and lawsuits. Debates about language teaching methods and models of SLA, though sometimes trenchant, rarely evoke anger or tax tempers, but the stakes are much higher when SLA issues are brought to the political arena.

Another reason for this emotional ardor, at least in the United States, is that this issue is not so much about the teaching of foreign languages (Japanese, German, and French), but deals with how nonnative speakers (virtually all of them immigrants) should acquire English, the "official" language of the United States. It is easy to be dispassionate about someone else's language, but our passions are quickly aroused when it comes to our mother tongue. Bilingual education is about the only area of SLA that is debated in legislative assemblies, argued about on the op-ed pages of newspapers, and even reaches the highest altar of the collective American consciousness, the evening news on television!

In essence, the debate is between two different routes for assisting the non-English-speaking children of the many immigrants who come to America to acquire fluency in English. The traditional route that most immigrant children have taken, and most nonnative pupils still take, is the submersion approach; this is the one most favored by the "English only" lobby. The quote from Porter cited earlier in this chapter represents this path. Children are free to use their mother tongue at home with friends and family, but once they enter a public school, they are immersed in a sea of English. A modern variation of this approach that has been used by many school districts over the past few decades is for the school to provide ESL "pull-out" classes for the children, usually during their first year or

See p. 33 for the excerpt, which describes her experience learning English through the submersion approach two of schooling. The basic justification for this supplemental instruction is that the additional help students receive in these special classes, which usually focus on essential communicative competence in English, can help the children with their comprehension of the subject matter they are trying to acquire in their other classes. Note, however, that even with supplemental ESL instruction, submersion programs are monolingual, not bilingual, education.

The alternative and more controversial route is the **bilingual education** approach. Within this program, non-English-speaking children who enter an American school, either as kindergarteners or as older students entering one of the higher grades, begin most of their classes in their native language, but gradually shift over to take more and more classes in English as they progress from grade to grade. Typically, classes in math and science are among the first to be taught in English, whereas classes in social studies and, of course, "foreign" languages, are taught in the child's mother tongue for several grade levels. Schools adopting a **maintenance** program support the teaching of the child's mother tongue throughout the child's tenure in school, but at least in the United States, most bilingual programs are **transitional**; within a usually short span of time (e.g., within two years of the child's enrollment), mother-tongue instruction is dropped since it is assumed that the pupil's English skills are good enough to compete at grade level from then on (Lessow-Hurley, 1990).

The fundamental premise of bilingual education, whether transitional or maintenance, is that it is very difficult for children to understand concepts in a foreign language if they have not already learned these concepts in their mother tongue (Cummins, 1994). It also seems difficult to understand how children can develop literacy in a second language if they have not become literate in their first. A third justification for this approach is the way bilingual education programs in public schools appear to validate minority children's home language and culture, especially in countries like the United States, where so many of the socioeconomic values of the popular culture seem closely tied to a monolithic and monolingual Anglo norm. And yet another argument for these programs is that, from a language planning perspective, it seems odd to support educational policies that, in effect, encourage children to become monolingual in grade school (i.e., few primary pupils have the opportunity to learn a foreign language) but supposedly promote bilingualism in secondary and tertiary schooling (e.g., many colleges still require a foreign language as a general education requirement). Although we will look more intensively into the relationship between age and SLA in Chapter 5, intuitively, it seems odd to discourage bilingualism in primary school, at the very time when children seem chronologically equipped to acquire a new tongue.

Another version of bilingual education that has become quite popular in Canada and has even been adopted in a few U.S. schools is an **immersion** program (Genesee, 1987). Here, to take a typical Canadian example, an English-speaking child will enter a school in which all classes are taught in French, except the "English" class. The child will progress through all grades (if it is an "early" immersion program) with this same linguistic ratio of instruction. The difference between this and the typical "submersion" situation is that students always receive at least one class in their mother tongue, and so immersion programs are still a form of bilingual education. Note, too, that unlike most bilingual education programs in the United States, which are transitional, these programs follow a maintenance model because the child's mother tongue is actively taught throughout the student's schooling. One difficulty U.S. advocates of bilingual education face in trying to promote immersion programs in the United States is that, unlike its southern neighbor, Canada is a bilingual nation by history, by culture, and by law, and although there is vigorous debate about the use of English and French in every province, and views vary dramatically depending on whether you live in Quebec in the east or Alberta in the west, bilingualism is not an alien concept for the average Canadian. For many Americans, however, especially those who are the most assiduous supporters of the "English only" propositions that many states have now passed, "real" Americans are monolinguals—and, of course, they are monolingual speakers of English, not Spanish or Arabic!

Given the advantages just listed in favor of bilingual education, why are so many Americans opposed to this apparently useful approach to language planning? Though not grounded in educational or sociolinguistic principles, the most popular argument for the traditional English submersion method, and one that has also been invoked by supporters of the "English only" movement, is the claim that the English language is one of the key elements in forging national unity in a nation of immigrants. Especially in contrast to the "Old World" in both Asia and Europe, from where most Americans have emigrated, English has helped to identify Americans by their citizenship rather than their nationality. In other words, unlike so many other countries of the world, for many U.S. citizens, it is your second language (English), not your first, that identifies you as an American. In many other parts of the world, by contrast, if the language of your home and family is different from the national norm, it is difficult to be recognized as a true "citizen" of a nation, even if you are fluent in the second or "national" language. There are tens of thousands of Hungarian speakers, for example, who have been born and raised in Slovakia. Even though most are fluent speakers of Slovakian, they are identified as "Hungarian" in their nationality and have been treated historically as second-class citizens. Not that prejudice in many forms does not fester in America, but legally, you can be a full-fledged citizen of the United States without being able to speak a word of English. (Indeed, every single American born in the United States is an example of this claim—at least for the first year or so of life!) For symbolic reasons, but even more significantly for social and economic ones, virtually all U.S. citizens learn English. But even the "English only" lobby would not claim that English must be a citizen's *first* language, so English as a second (or third) language is an emblem of citizenship, and in the United States, unlike the "Old World," citizenship is of far more consequence than nationality.

By the way, it may seem whimsical to any disinterested observer of this debate over bilingual education that the strongest argument propounded by the proponents of "English only" is the observation that throughout the history of the United States, English has served to unite all immigrants as Americans. Ironically, of course, the phrase that captures this nationalistic sentiment best is emblazoned on the national seal in *Latin*, not English ("e pluribus unum")!

There are several limitations to bilingual education, however, and partly because of these, bilingual education was recently dismantled in California by a voter initiative. One strong argument against bilingual programs is their relative cost, especially in the many school districts around the country that enroll children from a large variety of language backgrounds. In many districts in California, for example, the student body can represent several dozen different home languages. Even if it were possible to find qualified bilingual teachers for each language, the funding required for facilities, materials development, and scheduling would be prohibitive. Because of these logistical and economic constraints, bilingual education programs in most schools where many different tongues are represented tend to allocate their bilingual resources to the majority language (in most cases Spanish) and tend to place the many children speaking other languages (e.g., Hmong, Russian, Amharic, etc.) into ESL classes. Thus, in effect, all the benefits argued in favor of bilingual education tend to accrue only to children who come from Spanish-speaking homes, and are often denied to students who speak other languages.

Besides the practical and economic constraints of trying to promote bilingual education in school districts where there is great linguistic diversity, some have argued against the premise that children are at an educational disadvantage if they are forced to learn new subject matter in a new and second language (Porter, 1990). Again, based partly on the assumption that young children can acquire languages very rapidly, opponents of bilingual education claim that even under "submersion" conditions, young immigrant children especially can quickly catch up with their native English-speaking peers and achieve academic success. Telling evidence for this argument comes again from states such as California, where in addition to millions of native speakers of Spanish, there are substantial numbers of Asian immigrants. Although languages like Chinese and Korean exhibit much more linguistic difference from English than does Spanish, when one looks at the academic achievement of non-English-speaking students in California, Chinese and Korean speakers are far more successful than Spanish speakers, suggesting that factors such as socioeconomic class and sociocultural expectations about academic achievement are more important than language planning as criteria for academic success.

CONCLUSION

In sum, it is easy to see why discussions of bilingual education can be confusing and even contentious. But because language is the social cement that binds us together as a society, this debate, and all the other social issues discussed in this chapter, demonstrates the way so much of language learning is shaped by the personal and political traditions that have been created by People. Whether we are political leaders debating what languages children should learn in every school in the country, or a little girl choosing what words to say when she bids good-bye to a stranger on the beach, it is clear that without People, there is no language.

Suggested Readings

When we start thinking about all the material people have written about People, we may feel like the mosquito that happened to find a nudist colony one summer evening—you hardly know where to begin! Anthropologists and sociologists have studied humans and their cultures intensively, but in recent years, much of the academic work that has been more directly relevant to SLA has been undertaken by ethnographers and sociolinguists. Two short, readable, but comprehensive books that deal with most of the topics discussed in this chapter are found in the Oxford Introductions to Language Study series: Spolsky's *Sociolinguistics* (1998) and Yule's *Pragmatics* (1996). Another small but comprehensive introduction to many important cultural and social aspects of SLA is Van Lier's *Introducing Language Awareness* (1995). A linguist who is quite well known in the United States and who has studied a topic not directly discussed in this book is Deborah Tannen. Among her many publications, *Gender and Discourse* (1996) contains a collection of essays on differences and similarities between the language of women and men. Crystal's *English as a Global Language* (1998) is a solid summary of the reasons for and the consequences of the emergence of English as the most international of all languages. For readers with an interest in the teaching of English in outer circle countries, specifically China, Parry has edited an insightful collection of essays dealing with all sorts of sociolinguistic and pedagogical topics (*Culture, Literacy, and Learning English*, 1998). Bialystok and Hakuta's *In Other Words* (1994) is an excellent introduction to many of the themes discussed throughout this book, but two of their chapters—Chapter 5, "Self," and Chapter 6, "Culture"—look specifically at the ways People interact with SLA.

For those who wish to read more about bilingual education, Hakuta's *Mirror of Language* (1986), Lessow-Hurley's *The Foundations of Dual Language Instruction* (1990), and Irujo's *Teaching Bilingual Children* (1998) offer differing but illuminating viewpoints. For a summary of research on bilingual education in American schools, August and Hakuta's *Educating Language-Minority Children* (1998) serves as a comprehensive reference. The "English only" movement and its relationship to bilingual education in the United States is critically examined in a recent anthology edited by Gonzalez (*Language Ideologies: Critical Perspectives on the Official English Movement*, 2000). Many TESOL professionals are now interested in the ways in which larger perspectives, such as critical theory, might inform the way we view English language teaching. An entire issue of *TESOL Quarterly* (1997) entitled "Language and Identity," edited by Norton, has been devoted to these broader sociopolitical viewpoints. Finally, for teachers of younger ESL learners, Genesee has edited a comprehensive anthology that addresses sociolinguistic and pedagogical concerns (*Educating Second Language Children: The Whole Child, the Whole Curriculum, and the Whole Community*, 1998, sixth edition), and Samway and McKeon have written *Myths and Realities: Best Practices for Language Minority Students* (1999), a short work addressing many pedagogical and administrative issues.

3

LANGUAGES

Professor Eleanor Jorden is well known for her role in developing materials to teach Japanese to university students in America. On one of her first trips to Japan many years ago, she arrived at her hotel in Tokyo exhausted from jet lag and the long flight across the Pacific. Because she had an important engagement the next morning, she asked at the desk for an early wake-up call. After she had fallen into a deep sleep, the phone rang sharply by her bed at what seemed to be the middle of the night. Groggily, she groped to answer and heard her name: "Professor Jorden?" "Yes," she responded, still only half conscious. She was startled by the soft but intent Japanese-accented voice that announced, "Your time has come!" Granted, we tend to alarm easily when our slumber is punctuated by a middle-of-the-night call, but even under more felicitous circumstances, most of us would find it disconcerting to have a stranger announce that our time has come!

What caused this miscommunication? This amusing incident is a particularly revealing example of the linguistic complexities that arise when we attempt to become fluent in a second tongue. It demonstrates, among other things, that the problems a nonnative speaker of English faces in acquiring the new language don't always stem from the learner's mother tongue. The problem with "your time has come" is not that it is a direct translation of Japanese. Actually, the phrase is perfectly acceptable English—and that's part of the problem. Indeed, experienced ESL teachers would be proud of any student who could come up with a phrase like this, for it shows that the student has acquired the present perfect tense (a bugaboo of English grammar that has bedeviled many an ESL student). So the difficulty with this phrase is not that the nonnative-speaking hotel worker made an error in pronunciation, word choice, or grammar. How then can there be an error in language learning when, seemingly, there is no mistake?

From the perspective of SLA, the problem here is an error at the pragmatic level. Although the Japanese English speaker was quite competent in his second language (actually, we could almost say *because* he was competent in English), the phrase he chose did not convey the meaning he intended. A native speaker would have chosen any one of a number of utterances to convey the intended meaning: "It's time to wake up," "This is your morning wake-up call," and even "Good morning, Professor Jorden. Have a nice day!" So from the viewpoint of SLA and of an ESL teacher, the miscommunication did not stem from the Japanese language or from an overt error in English, but from ignorance of the pragmatics of English usage. Put bluntly, when we say that someone's "time has come," we are saying that it's time for that person to die. But this is an especially difficult idiom to pick up because the same hotel worker could call Professor Jorden and inform her that her fax, friend, taxi, or airport limo had come, and it would mean exactly what he said. But when he called to tell her that her *time* had come, the phone call had a very different ring. So in addition to the complexities we reviewed in the previous chapter about how People affect the course of SLA, here we will consider the many ways in which Languages can intervene as well.

Investigations

3.1 *AREN'T ALL JAPANESE FACTORIES "BORING"?*

I once asked my ESL students to introduce themselves to their new classmates on the first day of class. The only Japanese student enrolled in the course stood up, announced his name, and told us that he was a businessman who worked for a boring company. Spotting the quizzical look on many of his classmates' faces, and harboring a bit of curiosity myself, I asked the new student what kind of "boring" company he worked for, commenting that many jobs can be boring. Equally confused, he replied with some insistence that it was a boring *company. Now quite muddled, I persevered with my initial question, "Yes, but what* kind *of boring company?" Quite exasperated at this point, the student responded with an illustrative sweep of his right arm as if he had just guided a ball down a lane. "We make* boring *balls!" he exclaimed. "Ah," I replied, my face lighting up with the rest of the class, "a* bowling *company!" As a beginning student, not only was he bowled over by the classic /l/ vs. /r/ problem in English, he also had trouble pronouncing the contrast between the two different back vowels in these words.*

Certainly, there was some miscommunication between my student and me (and the rest of the class as well) because of his mispronunciation of this one word, but consider the following possibilities. Did the student understand my question? Did he try to respond in English, his second language? Did he attempt to continue communication despite the initial breakdown? Did he try to use a different communication strategy when speech failed? And so, overall, was this Japanese student really *that* limited in his ESL abilities?

Now, get together with another person who teaches or tutors ESL students. Each of you should think of an "error" anecdote similar to this one to share with the other person. After you describe the example, try to narrow the error down. Was it a mistake in word choice, pronunciation, grammar, spelling? Was it a confusion with another word in English, or did it stem from the student's native tongue? Would the error be correct if it had been spoken (or written) in a different context (like "your time has come")? After you've completed your little linguistic analysis of each other's example, go back to the five quick questions I asked above after my "boring" illustration. Overall, was your student (or tutee) really that limited in English?

INTERFERENCE: NEGATIVE TRANSFER

Those of us who are native speakers of English and who tend to make light of pronunciation errors by our ESL students shouldn't feel quite so smug. We encounter exactly the same interference when we ourselves start to study a new tongue, as illustrated by this ESL teacher's account of her first attempts to speak Korean.

Learner's Account #8

Last night our instructor (our *new* instructor—the old one is gone) gave us another eleven vowel sounds! ELEVEN! As if I didn't have enough sounds to keep me occupied. The worst part about it is half of them sound like /wa/, but they're supposed to be different somehow. She stood stiffly at the front of the room and told us to listen carefully. Then she said, "Wa...wa...wa...wa. Can you hear the difference?" Nope, not at all!

A Student of Korean

Examples like the ones just cited led applied linguists to believe that the most important linguistic factor affecting the course of SLA for any second-language learner was the **interference** of the mother tongue with the new language. In many ways, interference in SLA can be seen as simply another manifestation of the way older habits of behavior intrude into the way we attempt to learn anything new; that is, interference is based directly on behavioral psychology. If we have been driving a car without automatic brakes, we tend to brake too abruptly the first couple of times we drive one equipped with them. If we're used to a certain area code prefix when we dial a telephone number, we often begin with that wrong prefix when we switch to a number with a different area code. And if a woman has dated a man named Don for a period of time and then finds a new boyfriend named Dan, she can be forgiven for calling her new beau Don (although probably not by Dan).

Interference in language learning is similar. It is the **negative transfer** of linguistic behavior in the mother tongue to the new linguistic patterns of the second or target language. Notice that interference arises only when the structures differ, as in the examples above. If the linguistic structures of your mother tongue are identical with those of the target language, there is **positive transfer**—and thus virtually no interference. Interference can occur with any type of structure, and since a couple of phonological examples have already been cited, a simple syntactic illustration might be useful here.

Consider two different groups of ESL learners: students whose mother tongue is Arabic, and those whose native language is Spanish. If we take just one syntactic structure, say the passive voice, we can see from the three following statements that Arabic differs from both Spanish and English because it doesn't have a syntactic passive. Take the English sentence "The cat chased the dog."

(1) Arabic (–passive: a close equivalent is given in English translation)

"As for the cat, the dog chased it."

We would expect interference (negative transfer) from the student's mother tongue to interfere with the English passive.

(2) Spanish (+passive: note that the translation is identical to English)

"The cat was chased by the dog."

Since there is positive transfer from the student's first language, we would not expect any first language interference in English.

(3) English (+passive)

"The cat was chased by the dog."

SLA researchers have documented, just as predicted in (1) and (2) above, that many Arabic ESL students have trouble producing the English passive, whereas Spanish speakers have not, although a bit later, we'll learn about an intriguing exception to this claim (Kleinmann, 1977). Just as an American tourist finds it easy to adjust to traffic patterns in countries like China or the Czech Republic because they drive on the right, and this allows for "positive transfer" of traffic expectations, Spanish speakers can quickly pick up the English passive because of its similarity to Spanish. But Arabic speakers trying to learn the passive in English are like American tourists visiting Japan or the United Kingdom, where all traffic flows on the left, and because of this the transfer is negative and there is interference, at least initially.

Almost 50 years ago, most linguists believed that interference caused almost all of the problems second language learners encountered, and most of their research was based on what they called **contrastive analysis** (**CA**). Although it can be—and has been—used for other linguistic applications, for the most part, CA was applied to SLA, where it was claimed that if you described all the relevant linguistic structures of the student's target language (e.g., English), and contrasted them with all the relevant structures in the student's mother tongue (e.g., Arabic), any gaps in the latter when compared to the former would result in errors and in learning problems for the second language learner.

Although several prominent linguists in both Europe and North America contributed to the development and evolution of CA, one of the earliest and most ambitious attempts to apply CA to ESL is the work of Lado (1957). Lado gave examples of how negative transfer from the student's mother tongue interfered with the acquisition of the target language at all levels of analysis—phonology, morphology, syntax, pragmatics—and even at the cultural level (in fact, his book is entitled *Linguistics Across Cultures*).

This early work using CA to help applied linguists predict first language (L1) interference in the learning of the new or second language (L2) has fallen into disfavor nowadays, however. It has been largely superseded, or, to be more accurate, supplemented by several additional explanations about SLA over the past four decades, so much so, that some researchers claimed that virtually no SLA errors came from L1 interference! Dulay, Burt, and Krashen (1982) asserted that the majority of learners' errors stem from reasons other than L1 interference, a statement based on an earlier, and much stronger, claim that less than five percent of all mistakes made by children acquiring an L2 were actually triggered by the children's mother tongue.

This is an astounding statement and one that is virtually impossible to substantiate empirically. For one thing, if we are talking about pronunciation, it is extremely difficult for adult L2 learners to acquire the phonology of another language after puberty without the interference of their L1 as a "foreign accent" in their speech (Scovel, 1969). At the phonological level, therefore, it is indisputable that negative transfer is occurring almost 100 percent of the time. Even if we look at another level of linguistic analysis, for example, the acquisition of grammar, where there are often many explanations for L2 errors that seem to have nothing to do with L1 interference, it is impossible to rule out negative transfer completely. An example of this is the omission of the third person singular, present tense suffix "-s" in English, one of the most pervasive errors ESL students make, and one often cited by researchers such as Dulay and Burt as a prototypical illustration that other factors, not interference, create learning difficulties in SLA. Any ESL teacher will immediately be familiar with grammatical errors such as the following.

Teacher: So you like to go to movies. What does your sister like to do?

ESL Student: *My sister <u>like</u> to go to movies too.

Later in the chapter we'll explore several of the reasons why mistakes like this are so prevalent in both the speech and writing of English learners, but one possibility for the student saying (or writing) *like* instead of *like<u>s</u>* is that she or he is making the answering task as easy as possible by taking the teacher's cue *like to go to movies* and simply substituting *my sister* in the subject slot, thus coming up with the safe but incorrect response *my sister like to go to movies too.*

Based on explanations such as this, SLA researchers like Dulay and Burt claimed that negative transfer could not be a factor in motivating this error. But, candidly, we simply don't know. CA predicts that speakers of virtually any L1 will have problems picking up the present tense "-s" suffix in English because no other language has a tense system quite like English. Speakers of L1s like Chinese or Korean will have trouble because these languages have no suffixes at all for present tense. Based on negative transfer from their mother tongue, therefore, such students will delete the "-s" in English. Even speakers of languages like Spanish, which does mark verbs with present tense suffixes, will delete the "-s" because in Spanish, "-s" marks the second person singular (e.g., you "likes" movies) but has no suffix for the third person singular (e.g., she "like" movies). Going back to the very plausible explanation that the student may simply be modeling the response on the teacher's cue, proponents of CA might very well agree, but add that the reason ESL students tend to do this is because negative transfer completely confuses them about what to say when it comes to the third person present tense ending in English. As result, they are motivated to copy the teacher because of negative L1 transfer. All told, interference is clearly at work at some levels, for example at the level of pronunciation, and is difficult to rule out completely at other levels of analysis (e.g., syntax).

Although we will be investigating alternative SLA explanations in a moment, it is helpful to summarize the ways in which the early work on interference about a half a century ago has left a profitable legacy for those of us involved with contemporary issues in language learning. First, this early work on the way an L1 has an impact on the learning of an L2 was the first formal research into SLA; the use of CA, beginning around the conclusion of World War II, to study and predict the role of interference in language learning, marks this beginning. It also signals the birth of applied linguistics, the use of linguistic insights and analysis to better understand the use and the influence of language in society.

A second observation worth making is that there is strong evidence that the mother tongue interferes with the acquisition of a new phonological system, especially when we learn that new system as adults. As soon as we start to speak an L2, native speakers of that language recognize that we are "foreigners," even when our L2 is fluent, highly educated, and socially appropriate. Native speakers might lack the kind of international experience or exposure to foreign accents that enables them to identify exactly which country a nonnative speaker comes from, but any native speaker of American English, for example, can instantly tell that former Secretary of State Henry Kissinger was not born and raised in the United States, even if he or she were unable to trace his national origins from the negative transfer of his native German into his exceedingly fluent English. The permanent persistence of foreign accents brought about by the interference of the mother tongue on any second language learned after puberty is the foundation for the **critical period hypothesis** and suggests, as already pointed out, that at least for pronunciation, mother tongue transfer for adult L2 learners leaves a salient and perhaps indelible imprint (Scovel, 1988).

Finally, even at other levels of linguistic analysis, such as the acquisition of new words or the learning of new grammatical patterns, the influence of the L1 can be strong and cannot be summarily ruled out. We have already seen how hard it is to discount the role of negative transfer for syntactic patterns like the third person singular present tense suffix "-s," despite the clear evidence that there are several reasons that have nothing to do with interference to explain why this suffix is problematic for ESL students. It appears that these explanations, valid though they may be, do not preclude the possibility of CA helping to explain why errors are made. More likely, these explanations supplement the observation made many decades earlier that the L1 plays a powerful role in determining the course of SLA.

NOT ALL ERRORS ARE MISTAKES

Before we take a look at alternatives to the CA explanation for why L2 learners may experience difficulties acquiring a second tongue, it might be useful to step back and define exactly what we mean by "error." As early as 1967, Corder made the useful observation that it was important to distinguish between "mistakes" and "errors." Up to this point, these two terms had been used interchangeably as synonyms, as they usually are in everyday speech, but Corder was wise enough to see that SLA research was better served if the words were defined to describe two different types of linguistic misbehavior. **Mistakes** are any inaccuracies in linguistic production in either the L1 or L2 that are caused by fatigue, inattention, etc., and that are immediately correctable by the speaker (or writer). A classic example of mistakes is the spoonerism, named after the British scholar and cleric William Spooner, who became notorious for the slips of the tongue that flavored his lectures and sermons (Fromkin, 1973). Spooner once addressed a group of coal miners in a sermon as "you noble tons of soil," and at another time referred to Queen Victoria as "our queer old dean." Mistakes like these might be interpreted from a psychoanalytic perspective as Freudian slips (Freud, 1904), but irrespective of their underlying psychological origin, mistakes are clearly miscues in **performance**, a term Chomsky (1965) introduced to refer to the overt production of language as either speech or writing. Native speakers frequently make mistakes in speech (calling a person by the wrong name, as cited earlier) and in writing (typos are clear examples of mistakes made by fingers flying too fast), and it should not be forgotten that L2 learners can make mistakes as well.

All of us have experienced the frustration of trying to answer a teacher's question in our foreign language classroom, and almost as soon as the word comes out of our mouth, we stop in embarrassment and say, "I mean...!" The essence of this category of miscue, according to Corder, is that a mistake demonstrates no misunderstanding of the correct, underlying linguistic structure. Spooner knew, for example, that Welsh coal miners are "noble sons of toil" and that Victoria was his "dear old queen," just as a woman knows that her current boyfriend's name is really Dan and not Don, and just as we know what the correct word to use in our foreign language class was or what the correct spelling was in the word we mistyped on the computer. Mistakes, then, reveal nothing about the underlying competence a language user has about language structure (Chomsky, 1965).

This is why **errors** are so insightful for SLA research, because they are goofs in competence. Taking Corder's dichotomy to an extreme, we could go so far as to state that native speakers never make errors, only mistakes, but nonnative speakers not only make mistakes, they commit errors. That is, because native speakers have almost full knowledge of the linguistic structure of their mother tongue, when they do come up with a linguistic goof, they almost always immediately correct the mistake; however, because L2 learners have an incomplete understanding of the target language, they are unable to correct many of their L2 miscues, and these errors thus reveal a lack of competence in the language they are trying to acquire. Of course, like all dichotomies, especially those that are defined too rigidly, this one starts to get fuzzy, and it can be argued that native speakers do occasionally commit "errors," but only in a few instances (e.g., the writing of compositions for a university class) or for a few linguistic structures (e.g,. it seems to me that nowadays, many native English speakers are using "less" instead of "fewer" in phrases like "*Less* people are reading newspapers nowadays"). Be that as it may, Corder's distinction seems to hold up the vast majority of the time.

The "original sentence" in the example on the next page contains a common error made by beginning ESL students. Native speakers of English rarely make a mistake like this, and when they do, they rapidly repair their miscue by providing the correct version (a) because they have the competence to understand, at least tacitly, that English grammar requires the indefinite article *a* in this context. Learners of English, on the other hand, especially beginners who are still struggling to understand the complex way in which English marks noun phrases with articles, will frequently "correct" their original error, when it is pointed out to them, with yet another error, (b), demonstrating that they lack linguistic competence in this new grammatical system. This contrast illustrates why Corder's distinction is so illuminating. L2 errors serve as the window to the developing competence of L2 learners, and because of this, they are the data that make up much SLA research.

Original Sentence: *My friend is chemistry teacher.

(a) Target Sentence: My friend is <u>a</u> chemistry teacher.

(b) ESL "Correction":   *My friend is <u>the</u> chemistry teacher?

INTRAFERENCE: INTERLANGUAGE, OVERGENERALIZATION, AND CREATIVE CONSTRUCTIONS

It's appropriate now to return to an earlier error example: "*My sister like to go to movies too." Why do miscues like this pepper the conversations and the compositions of all ESL learners, and why do the learners themselves find it so difficult to correct these errors? Native speakers with no training in SLA find these questions particularly vexing because errors like this seem to crop up most frequently with the "easiest" components of English grammar. "Everyone knows," an English speaker might protest, "that you say *my sister likes* and not *my sister like*," or "Little words like *a* and *the* are so simple; why can't ESL students pick up the easy stuff?" Cook (1996) makes the sage observation that we generally look at ESL learners in a completely wrong light. Most often, we judge them solely by their ability in the language that is *our* L1 but *their* L2, and so we consider them *in*competent. Worse yet, some might even believe that ESL classes are nothing more than a form of remediation. But it is instructive to remember that *all* ESL students have proven themselves excellent language learners; after all, they have acquired their mother tongue perfectly, and many of them are studying English as their third or fourth language.

This has prompted Cook to characterize all L2 learners as "multi-competent" (1996:7). In addition to full competence in one language (their mother tongue), these students have growing competence in one or more additional languages. Consequently, the errors that pop up and persist in a learner's new language, particularly at the beginning level, do not stem from stupidity! Nor do these miscues come from lack of attention or motivation, because the students have already proven they have learned a great deal about English. It's just that certain grammatical patterns appear to give them a lot of trouble and continue to pervade their performance in their L2 for a very long time, sometimes even right up to when they have become fluent bilinguals.

Two key points emerge therefore. First, L2 learners make many errors despite the fact that they have the aptitude and the motivation to master the new language; after all, if a person can become fluent in both spoken and written Japanese, why would English be any more challenging? Second, the errors that do occur appear to be mostly confined to only a few L2 structures; they are not simply random goofs that emerge haphazardly (e.g., you never find ESL students who consistently make one error for every sentence or commit an error on every seventh word). How can SLA explain these two phenomena?

Inspired by Corder's initial exploration into the etiology of learners' errors, beginning in the 1970s, SLA researchers began to adopt a new approach to answering questions like those just raised. Part of the rationale for developing this new and different perspective to error analysis came from the growing influence of cognitive psychology which, at least in the field of linguistics, had begun to replace the behavioral model that had predominated for many decades. As a consequence, applied linguists were more reluctant to attribute L2 errors to the interference of L1 "habits," and more motivated to interpret them as attempts by L2 learners to create their own explanations of how structures in the new language were patterned. Researchers like Selinker (1972) argued that SLA could most insightfully be viewed as a longitudinal process, similar in many ways to a child's acquisition of a mother tongue. He hypothesized that errors were best understood as part of the learner's **interlanguage**, a term he introduced to refer to the developing competence of L2 learners, from an initial stage of very limited knowledge about the new language to a final stage of almost complete fluency in the target structures.

This new perspective on errors created a new interpretation about their origins, an interpretation that rejected the previous CA explanation attributing most errors to interference. You will recall that according to the proponents of CA, errors arise from the mismatch between the grammatical habits of the students' L1 and the new grammatical patterns the students must acquire in the L2. Using this approach, "easy" grammatical patterns such as articles or the third person singular present tense suffix can become quite difficult for learners if there is interference from the mother tongue. But we have already seen that the interference explanation goes only so far, and that other forces, besides the students' mother tongue, might be at work. Further, if the CA explanation is correct, how does it account for the fact that virtually all ESL learners have trouble with certain grammatical patterns when it is obvious that learners of English speak many different native languages? To take a specific example, why would an ESL student who speaks Spanish, a language that has a system of tenses much more inflected and complex than English, have almost the same trouble in remembering to use the "-s" in *My sister likes*... as an ESL student who speaks Chinese, which has absolutely no tenses whatsoever? CA would predict that the Chinese speaker would make many more errors with this structure in English than the speaker of Spanish, but this is simply not the case, as demonstrated by a great deal of SLA research summarized by investigators like Dulay, Burt, and Krashen (1982). They discovered that Spanish-speaking and Chinese-speaking ESL pupils tended to have an almost equal amount of difficulty picking up the third person "-s" suffix. Conundrums like this prompted SLA researchers to challenge the CA model of interference and propose an alternative explanation, one that I call *intra*ference.

Intraference is the confusion a language learner experiences when confronting conflicting patterns *within* the structure of a newly acquired language, irrespective of how the target language patterns might contrast with the learner's mother tongue. Like interlanguage, it is a term that can also apply to a young child's nascent attempts to acquire a mother tongue, but because our primary focus is on second language acquisition, especially among adult learners, we will confine our attention to intraference in SLA. Why do virtually all ESL students have trouble learning the third person singular suffix? Intraference claims that much of the problem comes from the conflicting information about verb suffixation that English itself presents to any learner. Contrast the classical Latin conjugation of verbs in the present tense with the English equivalent. Although some English speakers might hold the very mistaken belief that their mother tongue originated in some shape or form from Latin, it is immediately apparent that unlike its classical counterpart, which has six different suffixes appended to the root *ama-*, modern English has almost no inflections (i.e., there is only one suffix, "-s").

	Latin		**English**	
	singular	plural	singular	plural
first person	*amo*	*amamus*	*(I) love*	*(we) love*
second person	*amas*	*amatis*	*(you) love*	*(you) love*
third person	*amat*	*amant*	*(she/he) loves*	*(they) love*

Regardless of whether your native language is Spanish or French, which are modern models of the Latin system of conjugation, or a language like Chinese or Vietnamese, which have no verb conjugations whatsoever, a major influence on your acquisition of English is not so much the interference you might experience from your mother tongue, but the intraference that English itself creates. That is, within (from Latin, "intra-") English itself, there is a pattern that "pierces" ("-ference") any attempts to learn the tense system, creating the assumption that, at least for the present tense, English does not use any suffixes.

Look at this English paradigm another way. Supposing you were an ESL student learning the English present tense. Based on the examples just cited above, you would come up with the very accurate observation that out of six opportunities to mark the verb root with a suffix, unlike Latin, which marks the root each time with a different suffix, English has only one suffix ("-s"). Now if you are writing sentences in your new language, or even more challenging, trying to carry on a conversation in English, if you are quickly forced to guess whether or not a new subject, like *my sister,* requires a suffix on the verb, you are likely to guess that there's no suffix and come up with something like **My sister like to go to movies.* In other words, if you are gambling with a six-sided die, and you know that five sides are blank and only one has an -s on it, you would certainly be foolish to assume that when you rolled the die, the -s would appear. L2 learners may not be gamblers, but like everyone, they are opportunistic, and again and again, according to this newer approach to SLA, it is *intra*ference and not so much *inter*ference that leads them to make intelligent guesses about grammatical patterns in their new language. These inferences are sometimes correct and sometimes lead to errors, like the common one just cited, but in essence, errors demonstrate that learners are active and creative participants in the SLA process and are not simply responding from the habits they acquired while picking up their mother tongues.

Intraference leads to **overgeneralization** as the predominant strategy for L2 learners, although, as we'll see in a moment, it is not the only way that intraference is manifested in a learner's interlanguage. Overgeneralization means that whenever learners encounter a new rule or pattern in the target language, they assume that the rule or pattern operates without exception. Again, notice the difference between the way this strategy works and the way mother tongue interference works. The student's tactic is not "when in doubt, retreat to how it works in my native language," but is more like "when in doubt, retreat to the last thing I learned about this new language."

To define the difference from a behaviorist's perspective, *inter*ference is based on old habits; *intra*ference is based on new habits. Consider the following examples of some of the errors my ESL students have made in their writing assignments, and notice that in each case, it's not even necessary to do a CA between the student's L1 and English to ascertain that the errors come from overgeneralization of what the students have already acquired about the structures of English and not from L1 interference.

(1) *At Ota Fuku Tei, a customer is *severed* in a very nice, traditional Japanese way.
(2) *They use alcohol to *narcotize* themself.
(3) *Alcohol makes you *disfunctioned*.
(4) *In the lowlands we raise *wheats*, and in the mountains we raise *corns*.
(5) *The stranger *gave to him a gift*.

All of these are probably errors and not careless mistakes, because they come from the students' writing and, presumably, my students took time to look over what they wrote and edited out any mistakes they were able to catch.

At least in these examples, it is quite clear that none of the errors come from the students' native languages. This is immediately apparent in example (1), in which the (Japanese-speaking) student obviously mixed up *served* with *severed*, and has humorously evoked an image of a crazed samurai warrior "severing" customers left and right in a very classical manner! (1) could thus be considered an illustration of lexical overgeneralization, although we cannot rule out the chance that it is simply a mistake in spelling. (2) and (3) are both examples of morphological overgeneralization; that is, the two students were confused by the highly irregular derivational morphology of English and added the wrong suffixes to the words they were trying to create. Again, it is obvious that these errors are not a mistranslation of their mother tongue, but are overgeneralizations from English. If English speakers can derive *criticize* from *critic*, why can't an ESL student derive *narcotize* from *narcotic*, and if *functioned* is the past tense of *function*, why can't *disfunctioned* be the adjectival participle of *disfunction*? (4) is a beautiful example of how the target language often sets the student up for overgeneralization errors—in this case, miscues involving grammar. Observe how the student has cleverly, but probably unintentionally, matched the plural nouns *lowlands* and *mountains* with symmetrical plurals in the English uncountable nouns *wheat* and *corn*. L2 errors often evoke whimsical images because of the unintended meanings generated by their overgeneralizations. (In this instance, we could accept at least the second half of this statement as being accurate, because with all the hiking people are forced to do in the mountains, they probably do "*raise corns!*" on their feet!)

The last example, (5), unlike the others, introduces a rather complex illustration of syntactic overgeneralization. The correct English target is clearly *The stranger gave him a gift.* The problem here once again does not originate from the student translating this sentence word for word from the mother tongue, but from the way English provides two different patterns for direct and indirect objects. Notice how we can alternate between a pattern like *gave him a gift* and a pattern containing a completely different word order (but with the same meaning) *gave a gift to him* or even *gave a gift for him.* It is this alternation that befuddles many ESL students and encourages them to overgeneralize one pattern into another and thus come up with, in this case, the unacceptable *gave to him a gift.*

We can see from these miscues that overgeneralization is a powerful force in shaping a learner's interlanguage, especially in the areas of word formation and syntax. Native speakers might not be sensitive to the complexity of these patterns, and we'll see in the final section of this chapter that ESL students who make errors with patterns like this are actually motivated by a very valid and universal linguistic principle about the structure of human languages.

Applied linguists studying intraference found examples and explanations like these so winsome that it led them to believe that rather than being reactionary, and relying almost completely on their L1, L2 learners were actually revolutionary, because they were creating new rules and patterns in an attempt to pick up their new language. Dulay, Burt, and Krashen (1982) coined the term **creative construction** to describe this innovative view of learner errors. Like children, who acquire their mother tongue by creating new words and new rules (e.g., "goed" for went) (Reich, 1986), adult L2 learners create new L2 constructions from their overgeneralizations of what they have acquired in the target language. A concrete illustration should make this point more convincing. The following problem will give you a chance to enter the mind of an ESL student and see how clever he was in "figuring out" English grammar, even though, in the short run, his "creative construction" did not improve his performance in class because his own rules for English had nothing to do with English grammar. Nevertheless, this example should demonstrate to any teacher who believes that errors are nothing more than symptoms of a student's laziness or lack of intelligence that, from the perspective of SLA, L2 errors usually reveal just the opposite. This student might have been weak in English, but he was diligent and creative—perhaps a bit too creative for his own good.

Investigations

3.2 *A Thai Student's Creative and Clever Rule for English Grammar*

Many years ago, when I was teaching English at a university in Thailand, I was asked to give my students exercises in translating Thai passages into English. Because most of the students in my class were quite weak in their second language, I chose one fairly simple Thai passage about monkeys for them to translate. Here is an approximation of what one student wrote. (I do not have his original composition and have had to rely on informal notes I made many years ago.) At first, these errors seem completely chaotic and random, but if you look at the data closely, you might be able to figure out the resourceful creative construction that this student invented in his attempts to master the mysteries of English grammar.

(1) *In Thailand have many kind and type of monkeys.*
(2) *Monkeys like to eat many kind_ of fruit.*
(3) *But the monkey likes most to eat coconut_.*
(4) *They gather coconuts from coconut tree_.*
(5) *Because of this, people raise monkeys to gather coconut_.*

1. Just look at the use of the "-s" suffix. In this illustration, the "-s" has two grammatical functions: It is used to mark noun plurals as in (1) *monkeys*, and it also signals the problematical third person singular present tense suffix as in (3) *likes*. For the purposes of this exercise, ignore any other errors; for example, a better translation of (1) would be "*There are many kinds of monkeys in Thailand.*" (Incidentally, my best student, who was completely bilingual in Thai and English—and should have been teaching the class instead of me!—came up with, "*In Thailand, monkeys come in all shapes and sizes.*") From these five sentences, make two lists. The first list should contain all the correct examples using "-s" in the data, and the second should list all the incorrect uses. I've made your task even easier by underscoring all uses and omissions of this suffix in the data. Even from these two short lists of a few words, it's easy to conclude that this Thai EFL student committed many simple errors in English and yet, at the same time, demonstrated that he had learned something about English grammar. So even though we are concentrating on this student's errors and trying to explain their etiology, let's not forget that he is multi-competent—his Thai is superb, and he has learned at least some English.

2. The first part was easy—now comes the hard part! Try to figure out the creative construction that this student came up with to account for his translation from the original Thai passage into the strange English that forms our data. At first, it seems as if the student is simply guessing, following a strategy many students use when answering multiple-choice questions on a test when they have no idea of what the real answers are. To some extent, his choice of where to place the "-s" suffixes *is* random guesswork, but there is a method to his mad mess. Before you continue on to 3, look back at your two lists and at the five short sentences and see if you can come up with the student's "rule." (As his teacher, I have to admit that at the time, I thought his errors were haphazard and lacked any system, but in a conference session with him when we were reviewing his work for the class, I stumbled across the fact that he had actually created his own rule in English from the explanations he gave me about why he chose to add "-s" to certain words.)

3. Now let's look at the solution to this challenging little SLA problem. All five sentences share one major similarity—there is only one "-s" suffix in each sentence. This is not accidental: it turns out to be this student's "rule" for English grammar! To an English speaker, this creative construction might sound crazy, but put yourself in the student's sandals. You are a Thai EFL student, struggling to learn all this new information about a language that is spelled in a totally different orthography and is completely

unrelated to your mother tongue. Remember too that Thai has absolutely no plurals or tense markers. Your English teacher's explanations about count and non-count nouns, singular and plural, first person and third person, present tense and past tense, etc., etc., etc., (to quote the King of Siam from *The King and I*) sounds hopelessly confusing! Because you encounter this strange "-s" at the ends of words all the time, you could be forgiven for dreaming up the idea that every English sentence has to have one word that ends with "-s." This is the rule my student created. But he went further and refined it in a clever way. According to him, you could put the "-s" on the subject of the sentence, on the verb, or on the object, but the choice was pretty much random, reflecting the tentative and dynamic nature of his interlanguage as an English learner. His creative construction worked pretty well, especially when he got lucky and chose the generic noun, *the monkey*, for his translation of (3).

Of course, even an English speaker with no training in grammar can see that this student's "rule" has nothing to do with English syntax, but from an SLA perspective, this is irrelevant. What is relevant is the fact that the student is an active learner, and is almost desperately trying to overgeneralize from the little English he has acquired. He has not simply chosen to retreat to a strategy of translating his native language into the target L2.

AVOIDANCE

These illustrations of intraference in SLA are convincing reminders that mother tongue interference is not the only or even the major factor influencing the course of a learner's interlanguage, but fairly recent work in the field has had an odd effect: It has indicated that in heretofore unnoticed ways, a learner's mother tongue can actually play a surprising and decisive role in the acquisition of a new language. The surprise is not in the errors that arise, but the very opposite—the fact that errors are never committed! Let an English speaker introduce this new topic as she describes her attempts to learn Spanish.

Learner's Account #9

I do find that when I speak Spanish or when I am writing in Spanish, I tend to avoid using verb tenses that are hard for me. For example, my professor assigned an essay for us to do on December 3rd. We just had to write a simple paragraph about what we did for Thanksgiving. I kept my essay very simple, and I only used the past tense to make sure I did not use the other tenses incorrectly. She wrote on my paper, "Very good, but we have studied many more verb tenses that could enrich your essay." I had to agree with her comment. I tend to avoid using anything that I feel is difficult. I wrote in my journal that day that I wanted to start challenging myself more and use the harder tenses even if I feel very uncomfortable.

A Student of Spanish

Because avoidance is a subtle and sometimes misunderstood phenomenon, it is advantageous to spell out the conditions under which it appears. First, we are only considering avoidance in the use of a second language, even though we can certainly talk about "avoiding" certain words or subjects in our first language. Second, as is implied from the description just shared, we tend to avoid structures that differ from our mother tongue; consequently, as already intimated, this phenomenon forces us to reconsider the role of CA and interference in SLA.

Third, and perhaps not quite apparent from the Learner's Account excerpt, there is always an alternative way of expressing the L2 structure in the target language. In the Spanish learner's case, she could describe her Thanksgiving vacation all in the simple past tense (which is similar to the use of the past in English) and avoid the complex preterit tense in Spanish which differs from English much more than the past tense. Here is an analogous situation for ESL students learning English. Imagine an ESL student writing about her Thanksgiving vacation using sentences like the following.

> I _did_ go to Portland for Thanksgiving. I _did_ see an American family while I was there, and they _did_ take me sightseeing during my stay. On Thanksgiving day, they _did_ give me a traditional dinner, and I _did_ eat lots of turkey....

Although the student's description sounds a bit odd—overly assertive and almost defensive in tone—there are certainly no errors in her writing, and this is a unique signature of avoidance in SLA; frequently, it can lead to virtually error-free L2 production. But the ESL student in this illustration is doing exactly the same thing as the English-speaking learner of Spanish; she is avoiding more difficult tense patterns in the target language by choosing an alternative structure, in this case, the use of _did_ for all verbs in the past tense. By choosing the _did_ alternative, she is able to avoid all the irregular past tense forms that prove so difficult to acquire for beginners (e.g., _went, saw, took, gave, ate_, etc.).

A fourth and final observation that should be made about avoidance is that, from the point of view of SLA, it doesn't matter whether learners are completely unaware of their L2 avoidance or whether they have intentionally chosen it as a strategy; it still influences interlanguage significantly and, as already mentioned, it is hard to pinpoint because its very use ensures that almost no errors will be committed. Based on these observations, we can define **avoidance** as the tendency for L2 learners not to use grammatical structures that would normally be used by native speakers in that context because those L2 structures contrast significantly with the grammar of their mother tongue.

The fact that avoidance creates few miscues in an L2 learner's speech or writing creates problems for SLA researchers both in terminology and in experimental design. Avoidance really can't be classified as a part of "error" analysis, since few if any errors are committed. Partly for this reason, researchers like Larsen-Freeman and Long (1991) prefer to call the study of interlanguage "performance" analysis because, as they rightly observe, the focus of SLA research should be on the entire repertoire of a learner's L2 performance and not just on the errors. Notice too that by examining all of a learner's output, we value all that the student has acquired and do not just concentrate on what the student has problems with, underscoring, once more, Cook's (1996) admonition to respect the multi-competence of all L2 learners. And the relative lack of errors creates quandaries for experimentation as well, because SLA researchers, like psychologists, make their living off the mistakes of their clientele!

The predicament researchers face is best illustrated by the remark once made by the humorist Robert Benchley: "You can't prove a platypus doesn't lay eggs by taking a picture of it not laying eggs." How can you prove ESL students are avoiding a certain structure simply because they don't use it in a particular situation? Going back to the earlier illustration, we can see that there are a couple of explanations for the lack of irregular past tense forms in the ESL student's composition about Thanksgiving vacation which have nothing to do with avoidance. (1) The student may intentionally use *did* to emphasize that she indeed went to Portland, saw an American family, etc. In other words, she may have intentionally chosen this form of the past to sound assertive. (2) The student may have never learned the irregular past tense forms in English. We can't avoid something we have no knowledge of. Although no one has ever heard me utter even one word of Albanian, this does not "prove" that I have avoided speaking this language. Although the first alternative is more plausible than the second (after all, it is hard to imagine a student who has acquired enough English to write an essay about her vacation but has never learned any irregular past tense forms), to be responsible scientists, we have to account for both of these variables in any attempt at experimentation. Due to these general difficulties, therefore, it took a substantial amount of time before SLA researchers were able to successfully demonstrate that avoidance is a significant factor in shaping the course of interlanguage. The first experiment to do this (Kleinmann, 1977) is well worth reviewing in some detail.

To help him get around some of the potential problems just discussed, Kleinmann decided to look at two different groups of language learners. Fortunately, he was teaching in an ESL program that was represented by two nicely contrasting language groups: Arabic speakers and Spanish speakers. With the help of linguists who knew these two languages well and were able to make contrastive analysis comparisons with English, he isolated several English structures that were absent in either one or the other language. In order to simplify his rather complicated experiment, I am isolating only two of those structures for illustration here. As already mentioned, Arabic lacks a grammatical structure found in both English and Spanish (the passive), and, as is further illustrated by the depiction below, Spanish lacks one that is present in both English and Arabic (the use of the infinitive complement following verbs like *ask*).

English	**Arabic**	**Spanish**
Passive: The cat was chased by the dog.	*Not Present*	*Present*
Objects of *ask*: He asked me <u>to go</u> home.	*Present*	*Not Present*

Significantly, English has equivalent expressions for both the Arabic and the Spanish alternatives to these structures, so that it is possible for an Arabic or a Spanish speaker to say almost the same thing in English without using the structure that would cause problems for the ESL student. For example, an Arabic speaker can say (2) instead of (1), and a Spanish speaker can use (4) instead of (3), and both Arabic and Spanish speakers will be understood by English speakers. (And, as a matter of fact, most English speakers would never realize that the ESL students were avoiding anything at all.)

(1) The cat was chased by the dog.

(2) As for the cat, the dog chased it. (Arabic equivalent)

(3) He asked me <u>to go</u> home.

(4) He suggested that I <u>should go</u> home. (Spanish equivalent)

Because there are English equivalents to the way these students express themselves in their own language, it is easy for these students to avoid the target structures in English that cause them difficulty, and this is why avoidance usually leads to errorless L2 performance. In other words, Arabic-speaking students who say or write sentences like (2) and Spanish-speaking students who use sentences like (4) are generally viewed as very competent in English. Despite all this, note that in some sense they are not using English at all; they are simply providing the English equivalent of their mother tongue! Remember that the strategy of avoidance is usually not a conscious one; these students automatically gravitate toward the English equivalents whenever the linguistic conditions allow them to.

To prove that his ESL students actually knew these English structures and were not "avoiding" them out of ignorance, Kleinmann gave them a grammar test and confirmed, from the high scores the students received, that they had studied these English structures. Because they were a high intermediate level class, their competence in English was quite good, and it was no surprise to see that, when given enough time, both the Arabic-speaking and Spanish-speaking students were able to display their knowledge of passives and the use of infinitives after *ask* in a test.

The more difficult challenge, however, was setting up a situation in which these structures could be used in a normal, communicative context. In other words, Kleinmann couldn't conduct an accurate experiment simply by asking his students directly, "tell me if you avoid these structures in English." It is hard enough for a native speaker to answer metalinguistic questions like this, and besides, because avoidance tends to be an automatic and unintentional response, it is tougher for ESL learners to provide an honest response. For these reasons, whenever possible, SLA researchers attempt to measure the effects of the variables they are interested in indirectly, by observing L2 language behavior, especially when it happens within a communicative context.

To achieve this objective, Kleinmann set up a simple oral test that very cleverly ascertained whether or not his Arabic-speaking and Spanish-speaking ESL students were trying to avoid the respective structures in English with which they encountered difficulty. He interviewed the students individually, and to assess the use of the passive, he presented them with a picture, for example, a depiction of a traffic accident where a man driving a bus clearly rams into the back of a car driven by a woman. He then asked, "Tell me, what happened to the car?" Eliciting an infinitive complement after *ask* demanded a more complicated protocol. He had a friend present during the interview, and, in order to set up the appropriate communicative situation, he asked the friend to go over and open a window (presumably because the room was too stuffy), and then turning to the ESL student being tested, he said, "Tell me, what did I just say?"

To make certain that English speakers used the two target structures naturally and spontaneously in the two situations just described, Kleinmann field tested this part of his experiment with several colleagues. Sure enough, in response to the query about the car accident, native speakers responded with a passive ("The car *was hit by* the bus") or a passive-like structure ("The car *got struck by* the bus"). Similarly, when asked to recount his request about opening the window, they replied with an infinitive complement, ("You asked him *to open* the window"). Altogether he set up four opportunities to use a passive, and four opportunities to use the infinitive, and the native speakers of English provided the appropriate structures virtually every time because, of course, they had no motivation to avoid them.

With all the conditions for accounting for avoidance behavior controlled for, the stage was set to begin the experiment. a) Native speakers freely used these structures, so if the ESL students did not use them in this little test, it was probable that avoidance was taking place. b) Because of the contrast analysis Kleinmann had undertaken on the three languages involved, if the Arabic- and Spanish-speaking subjects avoided the English structures that were absent in their respective mother tongues, it would be clear that L1 interference was behind this avoidance behavior. c) The students had an alternative way of expressing the structure they were avoiding in English. And finally, d) Kleinmann designed his experiment without presupposing that the ESL students were consciously aware that they were trying to get around structures in English that differed from those in their mother tongue. In fact, for everyone who participated in the experiment, the situation seemed to replicate a typical language proficiency interview and did not seem to be an artificially contrived test to ferret out avoidance. After interviewing each of his students and recording all of their responses in the two varying linguistic situations, Kleinmann collated his results and was able to make a reasonable judgment about whether or not the subjects had exhibited avoidance behavior in their use of English. These results are simplified and summarized in the following table (Table 3.1).

Table 3.1: Avoidance Behavior in Adult SLA (based on Kleinmann, 1977)

English Structure	L1 Group	N	Mean Score	Std. Dev.	Test of Sig.
PASSIVE	Arabic	24	1.58	1.35	3.98**
	Spanish	15	3.20	1.01	
INF. COMPL.	Arabic	24	2.88	0.34	5.24**
	Spanish	15	1.53	1.19	
					** $p < .01$

p<.01 means that the result is statistically significant.

Don't be put off by this table if you are easily daunted by numbers, because statistical information such as this gives a clear and crisp peek into the heart of any experiment. Besides, I have greatly simplified the data that Kleinmann detailed in his original article in order to center the focus on the central question: Can we prove that these ESL students avoided English structures that differed markedly from their mother tongue? Moving from left to right, we observe, first of all, that the data have been divided into two pairs of rows. The top pair tells us about how much the subjects tended to use the passive, and the bottom two rows reveal how much they tried to use the infinitive complement construction.

Moving to the right, the next column divides the students by their mother tongue, and immediately to the right of that, the "N" refers to the number of students involved. Kleinmann had 24 Arabic speakers and 15 Spanish speakers participating in this experiment, and, as we would expect, the same number of subjects participated in both the passive and the infinitive complement tests. Ordinarily, it is crucial to have the same people participate in all parts of an experiment. On seeing that the two language groups were not equally represented in this experiment, you might wonder whether or not this difference in the N might skew the results of the study. Since the numbers are neither too small nor disproportionate (e.g., our worries would indeed be valid if Kleinmann had tested only three Arabic speakers and only one Spanish speaker), but for this type of experiment the difference is irrelevant, and the N simply reflects the fact that he had a larger number of Arabic-speaking ESL students that semester, and further, that he did not want to exclude anyone in his classes from participating. It is well worth noting that his goal was not just to explore avoidance behavior as a researcher; as an ESL teacher, he also wanted to assess his students' ability to communicate in English in a seminatural context.

Now we come to the very heart and soul of the experiment—the descriptive statistics that tell us whether or not avoidance actually exists as an SLA phenomenon. Recall that for each English structure being tested, there were four opportunities to use the target form. Also, you should remember that this is not a study of errors. The figures cited in the "Mean Scores" do not refer to correct or incorrect scores: they are the average number of times the Arabic-speaking or Spanish-speaking subjects tried to use the structure in question, not whether they made any errors. As already noted, native speakers of English averaged just about perfect "fours" when they were tested; they almost always used passives and infinitive complements in the situations that had been set up to elicit these structures. So here, in the middle of Table 3.1, we have direct evidence of avoidance. The Arabic speakers chose the passive (a structure their mother tongue didn't have) less than half of the time (only 1.58 times out of the four), whereas the Spanish speakers used the passive twice as often (fully 3.20 times out of four chances). The widely different patterns of usage between the two language groups seem interpretable only in terms of avoidance behavior, given the context of the experiment. This difference is also validated by a test of significance, which confirms that there is a probability of less than one chance out of a hundred ($p < .01$) that the students would have responded in this manner purely by chance.

Here, it is helpful to digress a moment into the field of descriptive statistics (Bailey, 1998). Based on some fundamentals from this area of applied mathematics, SLA researchers such as Kleinmann use the term **significance** in a restricted and special manner. Significance, when used as a statistical term, refers to the notion that when data from an experiment like that shown in Table 3.1 are fed into a statistical formula (a "test of significance"), the number obtained must reach a probability level of at least 5 out of 100 (p<.05). That is, significant results, in this technical sense of the word, are results that have almost no chance of being random. Put another way, if you were told that X behavior occurs 50 percent of the time in the presence of Y (p<.50), you wouldn't put much credence in X as a causal variable; after all, many things have a roughly fifty-fifty chance of co-occurring. But if X co-occurs with Y 95 percent of the time (or, as in the case of Table 3.1, 99 percent of the time—p<.01), it would seem that there is a definite link between the two phenomena.

Two further observations about significance are worth mentioning here. Even statistically significant correlations do not prove causality, or certainly not the direction of causality. On a very stormy day, you could probably demonstrate, to a p<.01, that people open their umbrellas when they step out into heavy rain, but this doesn't prove that opening umbrellas causes it to rain. Second, and just as important, research can reveal *significant* results, but they may not be *relevant*. Only after researchers have carefully crafted an experiment and are able to interpret the results in a reasonable manner based on a thorough knowledge of their field can the power of statistical significance illuminate a particular study.

There is one column remaining that I haven't explained, and that is the one that lists the standard deviation in the responses of both language groups. This is a figure used in descriptive statistics to measure the degree of variance in the responses of a group of people: the larger the standard deviation, the wider the variance, and vice versa. For example, if every single one of the 15 Spanish-speaking ESL students had tried to use the passive three out of the four times, their mean score would have been 3.0 and their standard deviation would have been zero, since there was absolutely no variance—everyone made exactly the same choice. Usually, experimentalists want to see low standard deviations; they want their subjects to behave in a predictable manner, and, they hope, in a manner that predicts that the researchers' original hypothesis is correct. But the standard deviation figures in Table 3.1 are quite high compared to the mean scores, and they are definitely higher for the Arabic speakers than the Spanish speakers for the passive (1.35 vs. 1.01), while the situation is reversed for the infinitive complement data (0.34 vs. 1.19). Though not nearly as essential to the results as the contrast in mean scores, the standard deviation figures tend to further buttress the results evolving from this study. After all, we would expect more variance for the Arabic speakers in using the passive, because this is the structure that is so different from their L1. Conversely, we would also anticipate more variance from the Spanish speakers trying to use infinitive complements, since this is the structure that differs most from their mother tongue.

Now, let's go back and review the data for the infinitive complements. The same two groups and the same number of subjects remain, of course, and again the key figure is the difference between the two means, the reverse this time of what we saw for the passive. Although the results are not quite so convincing (the Arabic speakers didn't use infinitive complements twice as frequently as the Spanish speakers: 2.88 vs. 1.53 out of a possible four chances), what is important is that the statistical validation remains just as significant (i.e., the test of significance once more results in a p<.01). Even though this was a fairly modest study, involving relatively few students, and despite the fact that I have only summarized a few of the essentials of the experiment, the evidence is convincing. When the appropriate conditions are present, L2 learners tend to avoid structures in the new language that are not found in their mother tongue, so in some ways, interference does play a salient role in SLA, even in the acquisition of syntax.

Avoidance in the ESL Classroom

Because avoidance research is fairly new and has not received much emphasis either in SLA or in pedagogical circles, many teachers may not be aware of the phenomenon in their ESL or foreign language classrooms. We might even make the claim that avoidance has been avoided! One of my former graduate students, Lisa Morin, has taken the opposite tack and thought about tackling avoidance directly. Here she shares her thoughts with you.

Lisa Morin

> I had learned about avoidance in graduate school, so when I started teaching advanced grammar for writing at the university level, I could already see an area of potential conflict. Students in my grammar class are graded on how accurately they use target grammar structures in compositions they write both in and out of class. Since they write their own compositions (as opposed to doing controlled grammar exercises), they have control over how often they use the target structures and whether or not they use the most challenging ones. Good students who try to use the most challenging structures in order to practice and learn them will probably make errors, but if they make errors, their grades will go down.
>
> I wanted to find a way to deal with this Catch-22 situation. How could I encourage my students to take risks in grammar, to stretch beyond their comfort zone? How could I quantify their risk-taking so that I could reward students fairly for trying to master the more difficult grammar structures? And how could I give them useful feedback on the success of their risk-taking efforts?
>
> First, I knew that if I made risk-taking a grading criterion, the students would begin to take more risks—calculated ones, I hoped. I decided to tell the students that a paper that avoids the more complicated grammar structures we're studying will get a lower grade (even if it's error-free) than one that contains a few errors but does use the target structures (as long as the student has demonstrated that he or she can use the structures consistently and accurately most of the time). I hoped that this would relieve some of the students' anxieties about errors.
>
> Then, I had to find a way to evaluate the students' performances accordingly. To do this, for each assignment, I created a simple tally system for counting the number of correct and incorrect attempts made at the target structure. For example, when the target structures for an assignment are verb tenses, I count the number of times a student used each verb tense correctly, making a tally mark in the "correct" column next to the name of the verb tense on a feedback sheet. I do the same for the number of incorrect attempts. (These are one- to two-page compositions, so I can do this very quickly.)

With the feedback sheet, the students and I can all see clearly whether they are playing it safe by using just simple structures, or whether they are stretching themselves and taking more risks by using some of the more complicated structures we're covering. If, for example, a student attempts to use the past perfect tense four times and succeeds in using it correctly twice, that fact is worthy of notice and praise, for it shows that the student is attempting to enlarge the number of grammar structures in his or her repertoire.

By using similar evaluation techniques for the other assignments in the course, tailored to the various grammar points we cover in class, I am able to assess risk-taking and avoidance patterns and give the students feedback on whether or not they are taking appropriate risks with language.

Although Lisa is addressing the thorny and perennial problem of how to correct ESL assignments in a fair and fruitful way, her concerns extend far beyond error correction, avoidance, and language. Her voice is peppered with phrases like "risk-taking," "comfort zone," "students' anxieties," "playing it safe," and "stretching themselves," terms that deal more with emotions (the topic of Chapter 6) than with language and linguistics. Reflecting on the concerns Lisa just shared, think about your students and how you respond to their ESL errors. How do you give them credit for their total performance without grading them solely on their accuracy? How do you wriggle out of this Catch-22 dilemma?

UNIVERSAL GRAMMAR (UG): PRINCIPLES AND PARAMETERS

In this chapter, we have retraced the history of how SLA researchers have investigated interlanguage by first examining the role of mother tongue interference, then the consequence of the target language transfer (intraference) via overgeneralization and creative constructions, and, in the preceding section, we have just reviewed the difficult-to-measure but definitely discernible effect of avoidance. This leaves us with the final and most recent application of linguistics to SLA research, the potential influence of linguistic universals on language acquisition.

For many decades, linguists have been fascinated with the notion that the approximately 10,000 languages spoken in the world today are more similar to one another than they are different. But it was essentially the work of Chomsky (1965) that codified many of these ideas into a coherent framework, especially in terms of presenting them in an abstract and formal manner. Several scholars have subsequently tried to investigate or discuss the relevance of this work to SLA (White, 1989; Cook, 1993). In essence, universal grammar (already introduced in Chapter 2) is the theory that all natural human languages, from Abau to Zuni (but not systems like calculus, BASIC, or even possibly Esperanto) share an abstract, underlying foundation. Most linguists agree with Chomsky that because this UG is innately specified only in our species, it plays a key role in encouraging virtually every human infant to acquire a mother tongue, while, at the same time, it ensures that even the most ardent and prolonged attempts to teach intelligent primates a human language (e.g., recent work with bonobo chimps, Savage-Rumbaugh, Shanker, and Taylor, 1998) will be doomed to failure (Pinker, 1994). According to Chomsky, UG consists of a set of core rules (principles), common to all languages, surrounded by a peripheral set of parameters that provide optional choices among the languages of the world.

Going back to the sample sentences used to introduce Chomsky's idea that all languages are based on UG, you may remember the claim that no language has rules that are based on numbering words in a sentence. That is, for the three simple questions—"Is he going?" "Has Daddy gone?" and "Has your Daddy left?" the English rule for asking questions isn't, "take the second word in any sentence and put it in front of the first word." As already pointed out in the previous chapter, this "rule" works for the first two questions, but not for the third—or for thousands and thousands of others! Here then is an illustration of a fundamental principle of core grammar for UG: All syntactic rules must operate on linguistic structures, not on the linear position of a word in a sentence. In other words, one of the ways English creates questions out of statements is to take the verb and move it to the sentence initial position. This rule holds whether the verb is the second word in the sentence or the twenty-second word. Going back to the creative Thai ESL student who invented his own, highly elaborate explanation for "-s" in English sentences, notice that even his crazy rule was structure-dependent: He hypothesized that you could place the "-s" on parts of speech like the verb or the object as well as on nouns. Nonetheless, he never dreamed of a pattern in which this suffix could be placed on something so weird as any even-numbered word (counting off from left to right beginning with the first word of the sentence). The Thai student's attempts to learn a language were very human because they were channeled by UG. In a very genuine way, structure-dependent rules can be viewed as part and parcel of our humanity; they exemplify a core principle of any natural human language we speak or any that we attempt to acquire.

So much for core grammar and principles; what about peripheral rules and parameters? Here, let's investigate a slightly different situation. Contrast these two conversations between two friends, one in Thai and the other in English. I've purposely made the English exchange a direct translation of the first to make your CA a bit easier. In part because the conversation in English is an attempt to replicate the one in Thai, one salient distinction between these two texts is that the English version is wordier. I've also provided a simple glossary of the Thai words to help you pinpoint the difference between the two languages more effectively. Looking at these data then, what are some major linguistic differences you can spot between these two languages?

	Thai		**English**
Somjit:	pai nai?	Sam:	Where are you going?
Somsee:	pai tiaw.	Sue:	I'm going out for some fun.
Somjit:	pai duaikan mai-1?	Sam:	Can we go together?
Somsee:	mai-2 dai!	Sue:	No, we can't!

Glossary:	pai = go	mai-1 = question particle
	nai = where	mai-2 = no, not
	tiaw = (for some) fun	dai = can
	duaikan = together	

(Note: Thai is a tonal language, but tones are not marked in this transcript, and that is why there is a "mai-1" and a "mai-2." The first has a rising tone, sort of like the way we'd pronounce *my* at the end of the sentence, "Did you say *my*?" whereas the second word has a falling tone, like the *my* in "Yes, I did say *my*!" This tonal difference is just as significant in Thai as the contrast in vowels between the two English words *my* and *may*.)

Your brief attempt at CA surely disclosed a number of differences between these two languages—word order, for instance. Sometimes the Thai phrases seem to reverse the typical English word order (e.g., "go...where" instead of "where...go" or "not...can" instead of "can...not"). Also, as described earlier in this chapter, English uses inflections more extensively than Thai (e.g., just "go" in Thai instead of "are going"). But I hope yet another difference caught your eye. There's a whole set of words that English uses in this little conversation but that are completely absent in Thai. The Thai phrases have no pronouns and no subjects. More concisely and precisely, they have no pronominal subjects (e.g., "mai dai" instead of "No, *we* can't"). Now this doesn't mean that the Thai language doesn't use pronouns at all. All languages have pronouns—another example of a core principle of UG. As a matter of fact, Thai actually has many more pronouns than English (Cooke, 1968). For instance, you may find it hard to believe, but there is a special "I" that is used only when you address the king. So the major difference between the two languages here is not lexical but syntactic. Thai, to adopt a term from linguistics, is a "**pro-drop**" language, and English is not. In other words, when the pronominal subject is clear (in this case, it is specified by the context), you can drop the pronoun in Thai utterances, but in English, even when the pronominal subject is clearly understood by both interlocutors, you are not allowed to delete it. Accordingly, English is not a pro-drop language, and we are forced to say "you" and can't get away with a kind of Thai equivalent "*Where are going?" As already indicated, this has nothing to do with how many pronouns the language might contain, but everything to do with how the grammar of the language works.

The Thai example just cited is a classic instance of peripheral grammar. We wouldn't want to specify that pro-drop is a core principle, because obviously not all languages are like Thai (and Spanish); there are many languages like English (and French) that require utterances to use pronominal subjects. So pro-drop is a parameter, an optional feature of UG that is usually represented in a binary fashion. If we liken it to the two-way switching in a computer program, parameters are originally set in a "normal" default position—in this case as +pro-drop. But if a language learner is immersed in a sea of –pro-drop input, because this feature is a part of the periphery of UG, the innate, linguistic "switch" can easily be turned off to allow the learner to acquire the obligatory use of pronominal subjects. Unlike principles that are unchangeable because they are innately specified as part of core UG, parameters can be influenced by environmental input (in L1 learning and possibly SLA too) and can be switched to the alternative position. Spanish-speaking and Thai-speaking children grow up with +pro-drop unaltered, because their mother tongue input does not provide pronominal subjects in many contexts; on the other hand, French and English-speaking children quickly learn to reset the pro-drop parameter to "minus" because the constant L1 input they receive tells them that these languages require pronominal subjects. In sum, UG is based on an innately specified system but it is not impervious to relevant influences of the learner's linguistic environment.

THE ROLE OF UG IN SECOND LANGUAGE ACQUISITION

Everything that has been said about UG so far pertains only to mother tongue learning. Chomsky was not and is not interested in multilingualism, and yet, as many linguists have observed (Cook, 1993), given the prevalence of bilingualism around the globe, the proper goal of linguistics is not to explain how the mind acquires a solitary language, but how it picks up languages. This leads us to the complicated question that is of central concern to current Second Language Acquisition (SLA) research: To what extent does UG affect SLA, if it affects it at all? The issues and the research that swirl around this question can be most clearly summarized by three logical alternatives.

(1) UG plays no role in SLA (at least after puberty).
(2) UG plays the same role in SLA as it does in L1 acquisition.
(3) UG plays a partial role in SLA.

Although there are linguists who argue for each of these positions and attempt to muster support for each of the three, there is presently no clear consensus about this support, to some extent because it is difficult to quantify something so abstract as UG principles and to measure them under experimental conditions. By and large, grammaticality judgments have been chosen as a popular testing instrument, but it is not at all certain that this experimental methodology is ultimately accurate or insightful (Schutze, 1996). Of the alternatives enumerated, the third seems to have garnered the most support (e.g., Bley-Vroman, Felix, and Ioup (1988), and it unquestionably fits into the overall approach taken in this chapter: the idea that the linguistic forces influencing the course of a learner's interlanguage are many and diverse.

Go back for a moment to an earlier example in this chapter, the error involving the incorrect use of an indirect object in English ("*The stranger gave to him a gift"). What are some plausible linguistic explanations for such an error? We've already reviewed two. First, the learner could be translating from the mother tongue, so it's possible that interference (negative transfer) is partly responsible for this miscue. Second, because English uses two different patterns for indirect objects ("gave him a gift" vs. "gave a gift to him"), the student could have easily overgeneralized from the latter to the former and come up with "*gave to him a gift."

But there is a third possibility. If UG plays at least a partial role in adult SLA, this type of error (which is ubiquitous among ESL students, irrespective of their mother tongue) could crop up because L2 learners of English are motivated by a principle from UG. The UG principle involved says, in effect, that the noun following a verb that is closest to the verb is always perceived as the object of that verb. If there are two nouns following the verb, the closest noun is, of course, the direct object, and so the next noun will be the indirect object. Because English has two completely different word orders for describing most indirect objects, a peculiar problem arises. For one alternative ("gave a gift to him"), English obeys this UG principle and sequences the two nouns in the expected order (Verb + Direct Object + Indirect Object). But for the other, English actually violates this UG principle by placing the indirect object, not the direct object, right after the verb ("gave *him* a gift"). (As a historical aside, it's interesting to note that this latter, non-UG pattern, is the earliest, "Old English" form of the dative, and the "gave a gift *to him*" sequence is historically more recent.) You might want to quibble here that if at least one language (English) uses at least one exceptional pattern like this, we can't claim that the principle is "universal." However, nature tolerates exceptions, so we don't want to discount the "universal" observation that birds fly simply because penguins don't. Returning to the main point then, from a UG perspective, one would expect ESL students to come up with the "*gave to him a gift" pattern because it marks the indirect object with "to" thereby signaling the fact that this is an unusual or remarkable exception.

Assuming that UG plays at least a partial role in the development of SLA errors, we can conclude that there are at least three plausible causes for the "*gave to him a gift" error—interference (negative transfer from the L1), intraference (overgeneralization from one target language structure onto another), and UG (the need to mark structures that appear in an unexpected position in a sentence). When two or more forces can play a role in error creation, we call this **multiple effects** (Selinker, 1992), and we expect multiple effect errors to easily fossilize. Fossilized errors are miscues that are very difficult for the learner to overcome and that tend to persist even after many years of exposure to and use of the L2. In fact, they may endure as a permanent emblem of the learner's status as a nonnative speaker of that language. (Recall that according to the critical period hypothesis claim, foreign accents can be viewed as an example of fossilized interlanguage.) The troublesome third person singular "-s" that we discussed earlier in this chapter is another example of an error that has multiple explanations for its etiology and that, as all experienced ESL teachers will recognize, is also very difficult to eradicate.

CONCLUSION

We have seen from the material reviewed in this chapter that errors spring from the active and creative response of learners to the multiple and varying linguistic forces that shape their interlanguage. Nevertheless, both as language students and as language teachers, although we recognize the importance of linguistics in SLA, we readily acknowledge that language is only part of second language acquisition. What about the acquisition component of SLA? What about psychology? More specifically, what is the role of memory and of consciousness in the acquisition of a new language? Like Professor Jorden, our time has come, so for us, it's time to leave linguistics and turn our attention to attention.

Suggested Readings

Although they are now quite dated, some of the early writings on contrastive analysis and error analysis are still worth going back to, for they are readable and insightful in many ways, even for today. Lado's *Linguistics Across Cultures* (1957) is instructive both as an explanation of contrastive analysis and also as an early reference to intercultural studies. Corder's short but seminal article, "The significance of learners' errors" (1967), remains a lucid introduction to error analysis. It has been reprinted in both Richards (ed.) *Error Analysis* (1974) and Schumann and Stenson (eds.) *New Frontiers in Second Language Learning* (1974).

For readers who have no training in linguistics but are interested in learning more about a field that is so intimately related to the business of learning and teaching languages, I recommend two very different introductions written for the layperson. Pinker's *The Language Instinct: How the Mind Creates Language* (1994) is a fairly lengthy, opinionated, wide-ranging, and entertaining review of modern linguistics. On the other hand, Widdowson's *Linguistics* (1996) is a more succinct and impartial volume. Nowadays, many of the research articles and textbooks that deal with the application of linguistics to SLA focus almost exclusively on the relationship between UG and SLA. If you have done any reading in linguistics and are interested in this more narrow branch of SLA, Braidi's *The Acquisition of Second Language Syntax* (1999) is a recent and readable introduction. For a wider view of how linguistics and even psycholinguistics relate to SLA and to language teaching methodology, Cook's *Linguistics and Second Language Acquisition* (1993) is instructive, as are the first six chapters of *Second Language Learning Theories* (1998) by Mitchell and Myles.

This chapter has given you a brief glimpse of the use of statistical data in SLA experimentation, and since so much of contemporary SLA research involves statistical procedures and analysis, it is helpful to have at least a minimal degree of numerical literacy. Bailey's *Learning About Language Assessment* (1998) provides this in an accurate but painless manner! A sequence of two articles by J. D. Brown (1991, 1992) published in *TESOL Quarterly* gives a crisp and friendly introduction to statistical data: "Statistics as a foreign language—part 1: What to look for in reading statistical studies" (1991), and "Statistics as a foreign language—part 2: More things to consider in reading statistical studies" (1992).

4

ATTENTION

" A " is the first letter of the alphabet, and so "Attention" is first among all the psychological ingredients that go into the alphabet soup of human learning. It is no accident that the "A" for "Attention" is also the middle letter of PLACE, the acronym chosen to represent both the outline of this book and the model that molds the views about SLA presented here. No wonder that this psychological construct should be so predominant, for after all, attention is the centerpiece of learning. Indeed, it frames our entire experience. And because attention occupies the very center of the PLACE model, its central position symbolizes attention as the bridge between the outside world of People and Languages (PL-) and the internal realm of Cognition and Emotions (-CE). Thus, as we reach the halfway point in this introduction to SLA, we are starting to move away from all the multiple stimuli that the external surroundings bring to our senses, and begin instead to examine the myriad responses created by our internal environment.

Attention is the thoroughfare for many connections: from stimulus to response, from seen to unseen, from external to internal, and from social to individual. It should come as no surprise, then, that this pivotal construct is so difficult to define and to understand, for in it are packaged not only the sum and substance of learning and teaching, but also the essence of psychology. An additional complication is the problem that it's often hard to separate attention from other salient constructs such as memory and task difficulty, as the following story about an overly pompous professor attests.

It seems that a famous professor had assigned his students a lengthy term paper to be handed in at the end of the semester, and having a large class, he wanted to guarantee that they would all submit their assignments on time. "They must be turned in no later than 4:00 p.m. on the last day of class. No exceptions!" he had warned them sternly, and he had gone on to admonish, "I won't accept a single paper submitted after that time, even if it's a minute late!" As luck would have it, one poor student with the inevitable problems that seem to crop up with word processing had trouble printing up her final draft, and she was even more delayed by traffic and parking problems. She sprinted from the car to the professor's office but, alas, she had gotten there a bit too late. He had already locked the office door and was striding purposefully down the hall when she almost ran into him clutching her precious assignment. "I'm so sorry," she blurted out, "I had all these problems with my computer, and the traffic, and with parking. Here," she begged obsequiously, "please take my assignment. I'm so sorry!" The illustrious scholar glanced irritatedly at his watch and sniffed, "It's already a quarter after four, so I've waited even past my deadline. I can't make any exceptions, my dear. Sorry!" Grabbing his huge pile of papers in both arms, he wheeled to go, but the student was persistent. "Excuse me sir," she pleaded, "Do you remember my name?" At this the professor became even more agitated. "Do I know your name??" he repeated almost mockingly. "Young lady, I'm a full professor with an international reputation. I go to scores of conferences and am constantly in touch with hundreds of scholars from around the world. The undergraduate course you're in has over 40 students. How on earth can I pay attention to all of my students' names when I have so many other important things to worry about? Of course, I can't remember who you are!" "Good," she retorted with a sudden smile, and she quickly slid her late paper into his huge stack of assignments and bolted down the hallway back to her car.

SIFTING THE "EMIC" FROM THE "ETIC"

The first problem that we encounter in dealing with attention is trying to decide what exactly to attend to when we are faced with new information. Using a metaphor that has been popularized by psychologists in the past, attention can be viewed as a searchlight that sweeps the dark to illuminate all those areas of our total environment that we reckon to be important at that moment. The problem, however, is how do we know precisely where to aim the light? We have all been in situations in which we have confronted a new skill, and when that skill is demonstrated to us for the first time by someone who is more proficient, we are at first completely puzzled.

Suppose, for example, that I am seated at a piano next to a competent pianist trying to learn a few new chords, and she deftly plays a progression of three for me. If I am a beginning student of the keyboard, I am likely to protest in a mixture of amazement, admiration, and frustration. Before I even try to figure out how she moved her right hand, I'm asking myself, what did she do with her left hand—with each finger of her left hand? Why is it that I didn't even notice that she depressed the sustain pedal with her right foot for each chord change? In brief, where do we shine the searchlight? With so much to distract our attention, what exactly do we pay attention to?

Learning a new language, especially during the initial stages, is a perfect example of a high-level skill that can absorb and confound our attention. Decades ago, the linguist Kenneth Pike (1954) coined a handy pair of terms that help to sort out the difference between the new information that learners need to pay attention to and all the stuff they can afford to ignore. These terms delineate the contrast between the wheat and the chaff of attention. Information that is relevant or meaningful in a communicative situation is **emic**, a suffix that appears at the end of the linguistic term "phon*emic*," referring to a meaningful or relevant sound in the phonological system of a specific language. In contrast, **etic** refers to all the redundant information in any situation that is not directly useful or relevant for communication (hence, the term "phon*etic*").

To cite a phonological illustration from linguistics, the distinction between the vowels /u/ in *cooed* and /U/ in *could* is "emic" in English because if you mispronounce these two sounds, you change the meanings of these two words. Conversely, it doesn't matter whether or not you pronounce the /u/ as a nasalized vowel (as in *noon*) or without any nasality (as in *dude*), for nasal vowels are "etic" in English. (Pronouncing *Hey dude!* with nasal vowels doesn't change the meaning of this greeting.)This phonological situation is the reverse in French, however. The /u/ vs. /U/ distinction is not phonemic in French; as a result, French learners of English (as well as speakers of almost any other language) have trouble pronouncing the word *could* without sounding as if they're saying *cooed*.

However, in French, the contrast between a nasalized and nonnasalized /o/ is "emic" (*beau* and *bon* are both pronounced /bo/ but the /o/ in the second word is nasalized). Because of this, English speakers have trouble with the phonemic contrast between nasal and nonnasal vowels in French. Therefore, when they are learning to pronounce the French word for *good (bon)* they tend to pronounce the final /n/ (which is actually silent in French), in order to produce a nasalized /o/. To French ears, it sounds as if the learner is saying the English word *bone* and not the French word for *good*.

Understanding this fundamental contrast between "emic" and "etic" is vital to comprehending the role of attention in learning, and is just as crucial in appreciating the problem all language learners face when trying to acquire a new tongue. It demonstrates that the key challenge for learners and teachers isn't that ESL students aren't paying attention—often, they are. No, the basic problem is that learners don't know what to pay attention to; they can't sift the "emic" wheat from the "etic" chaff. The allocation of attention isn't just an obstacle in the acquisition of phonology. Look back at Learner's Account #3 in Chapter 1. You will see that allocation of attention can pervade the learning of vocabulary and syntax as well.

4.1 *"Now Class, Pay Attention!"*

When eyes start to wander during class, how many times have we heard teachers say, "Now class, pay attention!" At moments like these, teachers have intuitively picked up on an insight that experimental psychologists have investigated intensively—our eyes are usually a sure sign of where our attention is allocated. In many ways, the eyes are the searchlights for the brain's attention mechanism. So when teachers see their students looking here and there but not at them or at the lesson, they give out the "Pay attention!" command. But to what extent can teachers, or anyone for that matter, control attention?

Here are a few classroom vignettes that deal with attention and, concomitantly, with memory. Why did the students attend so assiduously (or apparently did not do so in one case)? Do you think the teacher intentionally tried to create attention by using certain techniques? Did attention always depend on what the teacher did? Do you think the students paid attention and remembered because whatever happened was important? Finally, are there certain common variables that all these situations share?

(1) An adult remembers only one thing from his elementary school geography class. He recalls the teacher walking slowly up to one of four globe lights on the ceiling, tapping it lightly with a long wooden pointer, and saying in a normal tone of voice, "In Argentina, they eat what they can, and they can what they can't." The teacher then proceeded to each of the next

three lights and did the same thing at each one, repeating this phrase three times. The adult can still remember the "ping" sound of the pointer striking the light globe just before the teacher repeated this phrase.

(2) A group of 26 ESL students is given a dictation practicing, among other things, the use of the third person present tense marker –s, which they have just reviewed in class. The teacher reminds the students that all of the six sentences they hear will be in the present tense, and several of the sentences will require the use of the –s suffix on the verb. The teacher is surprised and frustrated to find that seven of the students forgot to add the –s suffix on at least one of the sentences, even though the teacher repeated each sentence slowly three times for the dictation. Obviously, the students weren't paying attention—or were they?

(3) Decades after he attended medical school, my father was able to remember his anatomy instructor striding to the lectern in the school's amphitheater to begin a lecture on the anatomy of reproduction. He began by standing stiffly with his legs together, his head bowed down on his chest and his arms extended straight out with both hands drooping limply downward. His first sentence was, "My body is the uterus, and my arms are the fallopian tubes!"

(4) In a beginning college French class, the teacher asks a rather timid student sitting toward the back of the room what page of their text has the answer she is looking for. She interrupts the student when he starts to respond with "*sur* la page…" ("*on* page…") and repeats, "Non, *à* la page, *à* la page." (In French the expression is "*at*," not "*on*" page so and so.) The teacher must have gotten the student's attention because for more than 40 years, the student has remembered this difference between English and French.

ATTENTION AND NEUROPSYCHOLOGY

The introductory anecdote about the pompous professor should help underscore how complicated it is to try to define attention, because any definition is inexorably linked to other psychological constructs. Cowan (1997) devotes an entire book to summarizing the many experiments and models psychologists have constructed over the years to account for attention and its role in shaping memory, and he goes so far as to include a chapter on the research that explores the potential sites for attention in the brain. His book is a grave reminder that because attention is so central to psychology, it is almost hopeless to expect psychologists to come up with a single, uniform definition and model of it, especially in the way it governs memory. This contentious lack of agreement looms large when Cowan wryly sums up the attempts to integrate psychological and neurological research in the final chapter of his highly technical text: "There are some real differences in the world views of researchers using different types of research methods, and more mutual understanding seems imperative" (Cowan, 1997:273).

Further obfuscating the picture is the recent popularization of ways in which possible neuropathological deficits might diminish the attention of otherwise normal children and young adults and create learning problems for them. Teachers in schools and universities in the United States, for example, are well aware of a newly recognized but very common learning disability called Attention Deficit Hyperactivity Disorder (ADHD), and although many teachers, parents, and school systems automatically assume that the learning and behavioral problems of children who have been labeled ADHD stem from a neurological problem tied specifically to the children's attention system, many neuropsychologists who have studied this phenomenon are uncertain about its diagnosis and even less clear about its neurological etiology (Spreen, Risser, and Edgell, 1995). The reification of "attention disorder" as a specific disability with the accompanying assumptions that it has a definite neurological origin, and that it can be treated with drugs (e.g., Ritalin and Dexadrine), makes it all the more difficult for teachers, and the general public as well, to appreciate the true complexity of attention and its role in human learning.

Disorders such as ADHD have been so popularized and politicized that they have cast much more heat than light on our understanding of how attention regulates learning, but this doesn't necessarily mean that research in neuropathology cannot contribute to our study of language acquisition. To cite just one area of research in this domain, work in neurolinguistics over the past several decades has greatly improved our understanding of how the brain processes language, and most of these insights have come from clinical studies involving brain-damaged patients (Scovel, 1998). Because this book is devoted to SLA and to how the fortunate majority of us who experience no brain damage acquire a new language, neuropathology is beyond the scope of inquiry; nevertheless, one brief illustration of the work in this area can serve to exemplify the contributions that have been made by **neuropsychology** (the study of normal and pathological brains in order to better understand the functioning of the human mind).

One type of neuropathology that is directly tied to language is autism, a fortunately rare affliction that severely limits all language acquisition and is also accompanied by social and psychological pathology. A form of autism was depicted in the movie *Rain Man* in which the lead character, played by Dustin Hoffman, was an **autistic savant**. Autistic savants are patients who suffer from a less severe variety of autism and who display certain supernormal, but highly restricted, skills. As the name of the condition implies, patients are far below normal in language and interpersonal relationships, but are extremely precocious in certain very narrow skills.

A group of neuropsychologists has recently studied autistic savants with exceptional calculating skills and have postulated that their subjects' condition might be explained in terms of defective attention processing (Casey, Gordon, Mannheim and Rumsey, 1993). The 10 autistic patients they examined all had an amazing ability to immediately answer any questions about dates on the calendar. Despite their autistic disabilities, these patients could still rapidly name the day of the week for any date in the past or future, even if the date were several centuries ago! Astounding as this feat may appear, especially for someone suffering from a severe neuropsychological deficit like autism, the phenomenon can actually be explained quite easily. The calendar that we use repeats itself every 28 years, so as long as you can memorize this single 28-year span, you can account for any day in human history or in the years to come. Granted, this in itself is no easy task, but Casey et alia claim that because autistic patients have an attention deficit, they are able to perform this remarkable trick. Autistic patients tend to fixate on certain activities and find it nearly impossible to switch their attention to a new and different task. In an experiment contrasting 10 autistic adults with 10 control subjects, the authors were able to demonstrate that this unusual skill to calculate calendar days could actually be explained as a kind of pathology: The autistic savants were able to recognize the presence of new stimuli but, unlike the controls, they found it very difficult to transfer their attention away from the calendrical calculation task to that new activity. Ironically, then, this brief foray into neuropsychological research demonstrates that "paying too much attention" can lead to learning and behavioral disorders! So much for neuropsychology, at least for the moment.

Tomlin and Villa's Model of Attention

Even if we were to confine this introductory discussion of attention to SLA research only, we would be beset with a variety of problems. For one thing, the SLA researcher who has probably written the most, and the most insightfully, about attention has used at least three different but overlapping terms for this construct: "consciousness," "noticing" (Schmidt, 1990), and "awareness" (Schmidt, 1993). And as we have already seen, attention has played a central role in several of the SLA models that have been formulated. Krashen (1985) contends that if L2 learners become conscious of and pay attention to the linguistic structure of their L2 input instead of concentrating just on the meaning, natural "acquisition" will turn into unnatural (and ultimately unsuccessful) "learning." Notice that with this model, attention can almost be viewed as having a negative effect on SLA; students who pay the most attention, at least to linguistic form, will become the least accomplished in L2 performance.

In an issue of *Studies in Second Language Acquisition* devoted entirely to the cognitive foundations of SLA, Tomlin and Villa (1994) examine the role of attention in language learning from the perspective of cognitive science. Like Schmidt (1990), Gass (1988), Scovel (1995), and several other scholars, the authors hypothesize that attention is divided into several stages. And again, like many others in the field of SLA, they also draw heavily from previous research in psychology, especially experimental psychology. For Tomlin and Villa, **detection** is the essence of attention, and they define this as "the process that selects, or engages a particular and specific bit of information" (Tomlin and Villa, 1994:192). Detection is the goal of all attention, but, according to their model, it is not the only component, for learners also utilize awareness, alertness, and orientation.

The first term, **awareness**, is used to describe both an overt demonstration that the learner has acquired some new skill or knowledge and the ability to report subjectively about this experience. For example, we can claim with some confidence that ESL students are "aware" of the /u/ vs. /ʊ/ vowel contrast in English when (1) they are able to identify this contrast consistently on a "same or different?" listening task, and (2) they can offer a subjective reflection about this ability (e.g., if asked how they were able to tell whether the vowels they had heard were the same or different, ESL students might say that they felt that somehow one sound was longer than the other). It is worth pointing out here that even without awareness, learners can attend to a task and achieve detection.

Alertness is used in a meaning virtually identical to the ordinary definition of the word, and so it refers to a learner's overall readiness to confront new stimuli in a task. Alertness can help enhance orientation, but like awareness, it is not dependent on the other constructs and is not a necessary condition for detection.

Lastly, **orientation** deals with the general expectations a learner may nurture about a new linguistic task. In experiments on word processing, to cite one illustration, a certain response can be encouraged by priming. If you were asked to add a fourth word to a sequence like *hand, land, grand, ?*, you would probably continue the rhyming scheme and say something like *band*. But supposing you started with the same original word but followed it with a different sequence— something like *hand, arm, head, ?*, you most probably would name a body part such as *leg*. Although the first stimulus word is identical for both lists, our orientation influences what we expect to attend to in the two tasks. Once again, like the other terms, detection can be independent of the other components, though, as already noted, alertness can amplify orientation effects.

Based on these four constructs and on their experimental findings, Tomlin and Villa have come up with the following model for SLA, depicted below in modified form (Figure 4.1). Observe, first of all, that the three terms just defined are

Figure 4.1: **A Model of Attention in SLA** (adapted from Tomlin and Villa, 1994: 197)

bracketed by parentheses, indicating that they are not obligatory components of this model. In other words, L2 learners can pay attention without awareness, alertness, or even orientation, but attention in SLA cannot exist without L2 input or without detection. However, all three of these optional components can be present at any time, in any combination, when a learner is paying attention. The key implication of this model for SLA is that attention can be enhanced when the three optional constructs are present in a learning situation. Consequently, the primary application of this model to the L2 classroom is that when teachers (and learners) can augment L2 input with activities that encourage awareness, alertness, and orientation, the chances are greatly increased that learners will detect this input and use it to make hypotheses about the language they are acquiring. Tomlin and Villa's model was designed primarily to help explain the role of attention in the learning of grammar, but it seems plausible that it can apply equally well to the acquisition of other L2 skills, such as pronunciation, vocabulary, and pragmatics. Useful as this model is, however, remember that it is only one representation among the many that have been posited by SLA researchers.

McLaughlin's Model for Attention and Processing

McLaughlin (1987) is one of several scholars who have been highly critical of Krashen's hypotheses about SLA and of his claim that the natural "acquisition" of language cannot take place if learners pay attention to linguistic structure. In collaboration with others, McLaughlin has developed a model in which attention plays a central and positive role in the process of acquiring a new language (McLaughlin, Rossman, and McLeod 1983; McLeod and McLaughlin, 1986; and Nation and McLaughlin, 1986). McLaughlin bases much of his SLA model on the earlier scholarship of cognitive psychologists, especially that of Schneider and Shiffrin (1977). According to this psychologically based approach, SLA is viewed as pairs of cognitive activities. The first and primary division is between **incremental** and **gestalt** learning. The former refers to any task that is linear and is performed in a step-by-step manner. Learning to bake bread and learning the alphabet are nonlinguistic and linguistic examples of typical activities that are usually acquired via sequential instruction. In contrast, gestalt learning tends to happen all at once, usually after repeated exposures or attempts, and is difficult to break down into individual sequences. Learning to ride a bicycle or acquiring the ability to know when to call people by their first name are illustrations of this other type of learning. Notice that for gestalt activities, it's difficult to break the task down into chronological sequences (e.g., first you do X and then you do Y), nor do you gradually progress from incompetence to competence. Learners work and work at the task and then, quite suddenly, are able to ride a bike without falling down or, if they're English learners, become very accurate in sensing when it is appropriate to start using a person's first name.

Incremental learning is then subdivided into two types: **controlled** and **automatic**. As its name implies, the first involves the learner's intentional vigilance to the task, and demands a great deal of time. The second, by contrast, is quick and routinized. Anyone older than 10 has learned how to tie a shoelace by relying on automatic processing, but if we observe a young child trying to pick up this skill while still in the controlled processing stage, we are suddenly reminded of the complexity of the task that we now so easily accomplish. Incremental SLA is no different. As beginning learners of an L2, we are astounded at the remarkable automaticity that native speakers of that language display in their ability to accurately and efficiently process and produce L2 sequences. They, in turn, are often puzzled at why our controlled processing of these sequences is so laborious and inefficient. There is some irony in the fact that these native speakers tend to consider us just as "childish" as little kids struggling to tie a recalcitrant shoelace.

By now it may be apparent that attention seems to play a vital role in helping to define the difference between controlled and automatic processing. Again, based on the literature of psychology, McLaughlin posits two different forms of attention: **focal**, referring to the direct and central focus of a learner at a new task, and **peripheral**, describing the marginal and secondary vigilance of the learner. Going back to the Investigation 4.1, if we follow the eyes of learners when they are trying to pick up a new skill, whatever they are staring at is their focal attention; whatever they happen to notice in their peripheral vision occupies their peripheral attention.

Although McLaughlin, Rossman, and McLeod (1983) specify that focal and peripheral attention are represented both in controlled and in automatic processing, I am simplifying McLaughlin's model with respect to this claim in order to better accommodate his approach to SLA into this present discussion of attention. For the purposes of our discussion here, then, I suggest that most of the time, controlled processing requires the learner's focal attention, and automatic processing demands only peripheral attention. This oversimplifies the complex interaction between attention and processing in general, but I believe it makes McLaughlin's model more relevant to our understanding of attention and its role in language acquisition and in classroom instruction.

Now to return to the original dichotomy, what about gestalt learning? Since it is all-or-nothing and usually occurs suddenly and unpredictably, like learning how to ride a bike or how to swim, we obviously can't describe it with the same terminology that we have just employed for incremental learning. Gestalt psychology was introduced in Germany, so the term itself comes from the German word for form, shape, or figure, implying that the gestalt approach requires a holistic perspective. The learner must attend to the *whole* form, the *entire* shape, and cannot focus on individual parts. For this reason, gestalt learning cannot be viewed as either controlled or automatic, and, even more important for our discussion here, neither can it be seen in terms of focal or peripheral attention. When you are trying to learn how to ride a bike or decide whom to call by their first name, there is no single thing, not even a set of activities, to which you must direct your attention. It's not that attention isn't necessary for gestalt learning, it's simply that, unlike incremental learning, it's extremely difficult to pinpoint what aspects of the task to be learned are being attended to.

Again, drawing from psychological research, McLaughlin introduces a new pair of contrasts for this type of holistic learning: tuning and restructuring. **Tuning** is what is taking place when learners make an assumption or a hypothesis about what is happening from the ocean of gestalt information they are immersed in, even if parts of that information don't seem to fit the learner's hypothesis. **Restructuring**, on the other hand, is what occurs when learners are so flooded with information that goes against their initial hunch that they eventually decide to abandon the hunch altogether for a new hypothesis to explain the gestalt. To cite an illustration from SLA, supposing Carlos, a new, teenage immigrant to California, is trying to figure out the "rule" for using first names in American English. Based on what little English he has heard and seen in his first few months in the United States, he makes the assumption that when you meet an English speaker who is an adult female, unless that person has a very prestigious job or is quite elderly, you can call her by her first name. But if the person is male, you always use his family name. This hypothesis works fairly well for Carlos because, for one thing, all his high school teachers happen to be male, and the only female adult he has talked to at the school is the principal, but because of her obvious prestige, he uses her family name too. But one day his science teacher is sick and the substitute is a 30-year-old woman. Following his intuitive rule, Carlos calls her "Joan" in class. From the substitute's overt reprimand, and from his classmates' tittering, Carlos realizes that he must tune his hypothesis to assimilate this new information. So he comes up with the amendment that you must always use the family name for all high school teachers, even if they are women, and his revised hypothesis will work for a while. Eventually, however, Carlos will be forced to restructure his hypothesis and realize that using first names in American English is not directly related to gender. His new hunch might be that he should never use first names with anyone older than 20, irrespective of gender or position, and this new hypothesis will, or course, be eventually tuned and restructured again.

You can see from this example that because there is no single set of rules or sequences to follow, gestalt learning involves a series of sudden revisions until eventually the learner simply "gets it." Like incremental learning, there is no clear-cut end point where the learner can claim 100 percent mastery, so she or he is always an active hypothesis-tester when it comes to learning. Second language acquisition is no different.

For gestalt learning, students begin with a hunch, constantly tune it to assimilate new information, at some point restructure their hunch to accommodate a better explanation about this information, and then proceed all over again to begin tuning this newly formed hypothesis. The following figure summarizes the discussion of McLaughlin's model and depicts the way these different aspects of SLA are distinguished from each other.

Figure 4.2: McLaughlin's Model of SLA in Simplified Form

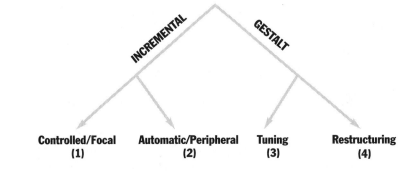

Here are some examples of the four different ways learners attend to and acquire the L2:

(1) Carlos learns how to spell new names in English (e.g., "J-o-h-n")

(2) Carlos knows how to spell "John" and starts to do so in a dictation, but as his peripheral attention is on spelling, his focal attention (and what he's trying to control) is on a sound contrast—did the teacher say "John" or "Joan"?

(3) Carlos decides that it's OK to call women who are not very old or do not hold prestigious positions by their first names, but when he calls his substitute teacher "Joan," he is reprimanded, so he revises his hypothesis to "Don't call any high school teachers by their first name."

(4) Carlos is criticized for calling his neighbor's wife by her first name, so he constructs a completely new hypothesis: It doesn't matter whether it's a man or a woman, in America, call anyone older than 20 by his or her family name!

Clearly, McLaughlin's model of SLA demonstrates the major tenet of cognitive psychology: Learners are always active and intelligent participants in the acquisition of a new language. This model also helps to show the importance of attention in SLA and the way that it is interrelated with other psychological processes.

4.2 *CLASSIFYING LEARNING ACTIVITIES*

Listed below are four language learning experiences that many ESL students encounter at some stage of their interlanguage. Match each of the experiences listed below to the four-way system just described and adapted from McLaughlin. Using the numbers 1–4 from Figure 4.2, write the number of each of the four categories listed in the figure in front of the experience you think it matches. After you've written down your responses, compare them with the ones I've provided at the end of this exercise.

Controlled, Automatic, Tuning, or Restructuring?

__a) A fifth-grade ESL student is told to use *an* before all words beginning with a vowel and *a* before those beginning with a consonant. The child writes phrases like "*a* hour" and "*an* university," but the teacher tells her that it's not the way the word is spelled, but how it sounds. Quickly, the child picks up the appropriate form of the article (e.g., "an hour," "a university").

__b) The teacher asks an ESL kindergarten class to sing "Happy Birthday" for one of the students and to point to that student each time they sing "you" and the student's name during the song.

__c) Students are taught how to form the passive by breaking it down into four transformations (e.g., first switch the subject and object, then add the verb "be" in the appropriate tense, etc.).

__d) An Arabic speaker learning English, partly influenced by his L1, always introduces English passives with "As for…." In a composition, he wrote "As for Islam is often misunderstood by Americans," but his teacher told him this sentence sounded odd, so the student "corrected" the sentence in his second draft to read, "As for Islam is misunderstood often by Americans."

Your responses may not match mine in every case, but this doesn't mean your classifications are wrong. There is no indisputable system for categorizing behavior as complex as human language acquisition. When there are mismatches between your responses and mine, it's likely that we are using slightly different criteria in classifying that particular activity or that our attention is directed to slightly different parts of the situation. The point of this investigation, like all the other investigation sections in this book, is not to check whether or not you've comprehended the material we've covered but to prompt reflection about what you've just read.

My responses were:

(a) 4 It appears as if the teacher's prompt ("It's not how it's spelled but how it sounds") has caused the child to restructure the old rule (use *a* if the word begins with a consonant letter and *an* if it begins with a vowel letter) to a very different hypothesis—*a* and *an* depend on listening, not on reading.

(b) 2 Here, the students can produce a chunk of English automatically (the "Happy Birthday" song), so they can devote their focal attention to a new activity (pointing) while their peripheral attention is still allocated to singing.

(c) 1 This appears to be a distinct example of focal attention being devoted to a linear learning of a set of rules—a very typical approach to teaching SLA.

(d) 3 Recall that Arabic speakers are prone to avoid the English passive; this learner seems to be following this avoidance strategy. So, when asked to correct his error, he tunes his answer by changing the position of the adverb, thinking that this might be the reason his sentence is wrong.

Now that you've gone through a couple of my examples of these four different language learning strategies, try coming up with your own illustrations. It is easier (and more fun) to do this with a partner. One opportunity for this, if you are a teacher, is during a discussion you have with someone after they have had a chance to observe your class (or after you have had the chance to observe another teacher's). Which of McLaughlin's four categories are illustrated by the examples you and your partner have chosen? What does this tell you about the instructor's teaching style? What about the student's style of learning? Are student(s) and teacher paying attention to the same thing?

ATTENTION AND MEMORY

You don't have to have studied psychology to see that there's an obvious link between attention and memory. The anecdote about the pompous professor that opened this chapter pokes fun not just at his pomposity, but also at his inadequate memory and inappropriate attention. Attention and memory mix together every day in the life of ordinary people. "Pay attention, I want you to remember this," parents, teachers, and bosses frequently enjoin their charges. And every one of us can admit to failing to remember something because we simply weren't paying attention. This intuitive belief, that attention and memory are joined at the hip like Chang and Eng, the original Siamese twins, is well documented by current psychological research, so it's not remarkable that many psychologists have developed models of cognition that depend on the interrelationship between these two constructs (Cowan, 1997). Because there are so many models, because most of them are so complex, and because all of them are designed to deal with the general use of attention and memory in daily life rather than with the specific task of trying to learn a new language, they are outside the domain of this book; still, it's sobering to realize that there is no unanimity among cognitive scientists on how human attention and memory work, when they do!

We will spend more time looking at memory in the next chapter, when we examine the effects of cognition on SLA, but because we are attending to attention here, it's helpful to look at one way in which attention and memory are interwoven. One highly unusual but dramatic demonstration of the way the two are linked comes from the results of a special kind of damage to the brain. Traumatic injuries to the brain, like those to any other part of the body, can be very diffuse (as in Alzheimer's disease, which affects the entire brain) or quite local (as in a minor stroke, which usually affects a small area, like the left half of the occipital lobe), and it is often this latter type of more circumscribed pathology that has guided neurologists over the past century or so in localizing how the brain controls specific cognitive functions.

One pathology that is well documented results from trauma to either the left or right side of the brain in the **parietal lobe**. This is a large surface of the brain that covers an area just above and behind either ear and that is a primary sensory area for processing faces, places, spaces, and mazes. For reasons known only to Mother Nature, the entire left hemisphere of the brain is largely responsible for the right side of the body and vice versa, so if you were unfortunate enough to have suffered a stroke in your right parietal lobe, one consequence of this traumatic event is that you would have a great deal of trouble processing perceptual stimuli on the left side of your body.

What does this have to do with attention and memory? Interestingly enough, this one-sided perceptual disability is often associated with a condition called **visual field neglect**, where the patient tends to completely ignore the side of the body on the other side from the affected half of the brain (Kapur, 1997). This means that if you were a patient with a right parietal lobe stroke, you would tend not to attend to the left side of your body. Amazingly enough, you would "forget" that there was anything on your left side! At meals, you would be inclined to ignore using a fork (if it were placed on the left side of your plate), and you would not drink any beverage (were the glass placed to your left). All this would happen not because you didn't use forks or weren't thirsty, but because you wouldn't "remember" that there were objects in your left visual field. If asked to draw a picture of a person, you would tend to draw only the right side of the body and leave the left side of the picture relatively blank. In fact, professional artists who have suffered from a right-sided parietal stroke have sketched faces where the right side of the portrait is just as detailed and perfect as their pretrauma art work, but the left side of their sketches contains only a few details. (Gardner, 1975).

This single example of neuropathology underscores two things. First, if the perceptual part of our attention is severely damaged, we are unable to "pay attention" to external stimuli, no matter how salient and obvious they may be to others. Second, if we cannot direct our attention to outside information, we are, of course, incapable of remembering it, even when we "know" this information is present. Parietal lobe patients continually "forget" they have an arm or a leg on the opposite side from the damaged hemisphere, even though they have lived all their lives with those limbs. Surely this demonstrates the truth of the expression, "out of sight, out of mind!" This is just one example of the kind of evidence that cognitive scientists can muster to demonstrate the complex way in which attention is interwoven with other cognitive processes such as memory.

ATTENTION TO L2 INPUT

Not even the most strident critics of classical or operant conditioning would dare to claim that the role of the environment is so minimal in language learning that UG and other innate factors alone are sufficient to promote successful SLA. Albanian children grow up speaking Albanian, and Zulu children mature into native speakers of Zulu. The linguistic environment counts, and if there is no input, there is nothing to pay attention to; hence there is no learning. For this reason, the role of target language input has been a central concern of SLA; for some researchers, it is the very foundation of their theories about how adults can best learn a second language (Krashen, 1982: Brown and Palmer, 1988). And because the founders of the early Audio-Lingual method based their teaching on the premise that "listening precedes speaking, speaking precedes reading, and reading precedes writing," attention to target language input has been a tradition in L2 teaching for more than half a century (Fries, 1945).

Krashen has been the most ardent and persistent advocate for the primacy of input in SLA, and among his many publications is a book titled *The Input Hypothesis* (Krashen, 1985). Like many others of his works, this volume introduces and argues for his model of SLA, which includes the input hypothesis as one of five central components that together comprise his model. The title is a bit inappropriate, therefore, since the book is devoted to all five of his hypotheses about SLA and not solely to the role of input. Put tersely, and in his own bold words, Krashen claims that "humans acquire language in only one way—by understanding messages, or [that is] by receiving comprehensible input" (Krashen, 1985:2). Like many linguists and laypeople, Krashen contrasts the apparent ease, efficiency, and accuracy with which most people pick up their mother tongue with the effort, labor, and lack of success frequently encountered by adults learning a second language, especially in a school setting. The kitchen vs. the classroom! Krashen argues that successful adult SLA depends largely on replicating the conditions under which children "naturally" acquire their L1, and the key ingredient for this "natural approach" (Krashen & Terrell, 1983) is exposure to comprehensible input in the target language.

Advocates of this input approach to SLA theory and to L2 pedagogy claim that L2 learners are no different from children acquiring their mother tongue: They "naturally" attend to input that they can comprehend and that they find interesting. Children are successful first language learners because attention is automatically directed to the massive amounts of comprehensible input that they receive. Adult (or child) second language learners are, according to the input hypothesis, no different, and because they can and do pay attention to meaningful L2 input, they, like mother tongue learners, can acquire a new language easily, pleasantly, and successfully.

Although all SLA researchers agree that exposure to a language is a necessary precondition for SLA, most of them disagree with Krashen's contention that it is also a sufficient prerequisite. A stark contrast to the input hypothesis, for instance, is the long list of "conditions" for second language learning posited by Spolsky (1989). Of the 74 described in his book, only one (Condition 71) explicitly deals with comprehensible input, and just as telling, Spolsky does not identify this condition as one of the 31 that he deems "necessary" for successful acquisition. Simply stated, comprehensible input is just one of more than 70 factors for Spolsky, and it doesn't even rate among the top 30. While he is certainly not trying to assert that L2 input comprises only $1/74$ of all the conditions necessary to become an accomplished language learner, Spolsky's stance regarding the impact of input on SLA diverges dramatically from Krashen's. In doing so, this position reflects the popular belief among a majority of researchers that input is a necessary but far from sufficient criterion for SLA achievement.

Many have reacted to the "strong" or overstated version of Krashen's input hypothesis. Over the years, these criticisms have ranged from the guarded (Larsen-Freeman and Long, 1991) to the grudging (Brumfit, 1994), and from the tart (McLaughlin, 1987) to the testy (Gregg, 1984). These researchers, and many others in the field, agree with Spolsky that many other conditions besides comprehensible input are needed for L2 learning to be a success. For one thing, L2 input needs to be simplified in order to be used effectively by a learner to fuel successful acquisition. Krashen accounts for this by stating that the difficulty level of the L2 input must be slightly higher than the learner's level of L2 comprehension, which he has symbolized with the equation "i + 1." Learners constantly improve because they pay attention to the mismatch between the input they understand (i) and the slightly more difficult input they are getting (+ 1). As many have pointed out, the trouble is that Krashen provides only this formula and does not explicitly define how input can be appropriately modified for language learners.

In contrast, Larsen-Freeman and Long (1991) summarize the many studies that have been done on how modified input can be beneficial to a second language learner. In brief, this research shows that modified input to L2 learners functions in much the same way that **child directed speech** (**CDS**) functions as input for infants acquiring their mother tongues (Berko-Gleason & Ratner, 1993). Because CDS (also referred to as "baby talk," "motherese," or "caretaker talk") is characterized by exaggerated intonation patterns, simplified vocabulary and syntax, and a focus on "here and now" discourse, psycholinguists believe that these linguistic features enable infants to acquire their mother tongue much more rapidly than if their input was confined solely to the kind of speech adults use with one another. All this is a way of reiterating the importance of social interaction in any kind of language acquisition.

The SLA equivalent of CDS is **foreigner talk** (**FT**) (Ferguson, 1971), a term introduced in Chapter 2 that does not refer to the language of "foreigners" but to the simplified register that native speakers use when speaking to non-native speakers. Like child directed speech, foreigner talk consists of simplified vocabulary and syntax and can include pronunciation changes as well (e.g., an increase in volume), but unlike CDS, which is almost always grammatical, FT often includes pidginized simplifications of the target language that create ungrammatical utterances (e.g., "Jose! *You no move these, OK?"). The advantage of this modified form of input with nonnative speakers is that it helps make comprehension easier for these learners (Gass & Varonis, 1994). The disadvantage, of course, is that FT, especially when it contains pidginized ungrammatical utterances, can be viewed as demeaning and disrespectful to the adult learners trying to acquire the new language (Meisel, 1980).

For a discussion of foreigner talk, see p. 31.

Ellis (1997) finds the distinction between input and **intake** useful when looking at how learners pay attention to new linguistic information:

> The learner is exposed to input, which is processed in two stages. First, parts of it are attended to and taken into short-term memory. These are referred to as intake. Second, some of the intake is stored in long-term memory as L2 knowledge.

This contrast between input and intake highlights the role of attention in SLA, for without attention to L2 input, there can be no intake, and, to follow the sequential processing which Ellis is describing here, without intake, the learner cannot store new knowledge about the target language. In the alchemy of language acquisition, therefore, attention is the reagent that transforms external input into the internal intake necessary for successful learning.

ATTENTION TO TYPES OF DISCOURSE IN CLASSROOM SLA

Up to this point, we have been reviewing only psychological, neurological, or SLA explanations about attention; with few exceptions, we have not investigated the specific kinds of language that ESL students and other language learners must pay attention to. In other words, we have been concentrating on the searchlight but have ignored the direction of its beam. As classroom teachers, we are constantly vying for our students' attention, and rarely does even an hour of class time pass without us exhorting our students to "Listen up," or to "Pay attention!" Fortunately or unfortunately, we cannot get inside our students' heads, but we can exert some control over what aspects of the second language our students pay attention to (when they do).

What kinds of language serve as linguistic input? Richards (1990) has devised a two-by-two matrix that divides the target language material into categories that appear to be particularly useful when considering what language learners should attend to. One pair of contrasting tasks a language learner has to contend with is the distinction between **top-down** and **bottom-up** processing (Carroll, 1994). In top-down processing, a learner's attention is directed toward the big picture, focusing on the general gist of whatever is being heard or read. "What are they talking about?" or "What's the author trying to say?" are typical top-down questions. In listening comprehension, topic sentences ("Here are two reasons why you should buy this product") or introductory discourse markers ("Once upon a time…") are excellent cues for top-down processing. As this directional metaphor implies, bottom-up is when the flashlight of attention shines on the fine details of spoken or written discourse: "What does *prolepsis* mean?" or "Did she say she *two* or *three* people are coming for dinner?" In conversation, we can usually interrupt with requests for clarification in order to secure the bottom-up details we seek. In reading, we can stop and reread a passage when the specific details prevent immediate comprehension, or we can turn to a dictionary if an important new word impedes our understanding.

Notice that language learners, like native language users, are constantly allocating their attention to linguistic comprehension, but sometimes the attentional searchlight is directed to more general, top-down information, whereas at other times, very specific bottom-up data are spotlighted. It is unfortunate that educators frequently get caught up in an either/or argument over which of these two processing modes best facilitates language acquisition. Long and fruitless have been the debates, for example, between whether to employ top-down strategies like whole language or bottom-up tactics like phonics in the teaching of reading. New readers, like competent ones, must ultimately rely on both modes to ensure proficiency. Similarly, both modes must be included if we wish to capture the full range of language that learners should attend to.

The other pair of contrasts Richards uses to frame his matrix is the difference between transactional and interactional communication (Brown and Yule, 1983). **Transactional** language is language that functions primarily to communicate information, usually for commercial, vocational, or educational reasons. As the term implies, **interactional** language is for interpersonal communication. Lectures, instructional manuals, and news broadcasts are examples of the first type; personal e-mails, postcards, and jokes are examples of the second. A similar dichotomy that is often used to characterize the different functions of language among bilingual children is the contrast Cummins (1981) has drawn between **Cognitive Academic Language Proficiency** (**CALP**), which refers exclusively to the transactional functions of language, and **Basic Interpersonal Communicative Skills** (**BICS**) which, of course, characterizes the interactional functions of communication.

Again, as was pointed out with the first distinction between top-down and bottom-up processing, language learners, like native speakers, must be able to communicate using both modes, transactional and interactional, although, depending on their situation, second language learners might rely less on the interactional functions of English than would native speakers. A group of Russian engineers learning English in Novosibirsk, to cite just one illustration, would be much more attentive to transactional/CALP functions of English than to the interactional use of BICS. Richards uses these two pairs of contrasts to create a two-by-two matrix forming four cells, each representing a linguistic goal for learners to attend to.

Figure 4.3 Richards' Language Teaching Matrix (Richards, 1990)

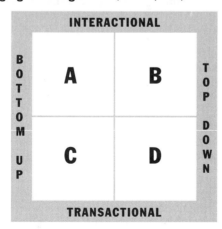

Wendy Levison and Margaret Grant have taught ESL classes with me at San Francisco State University. They have done more than just think about attention and language learning; they've actually tried to develop some classroom activities to help their students attend to the English structures that are an important focus of the lower-level ESL classes we jointly teach. Here they tell about some of their experiences.

Wendy Levison
and
Margaret Grant

We're sure many teachers have noticed how adept students can be at proofreading a controlled exercise in class and clearly articulating the rules (for instance, that a modal is followed by the simple form of the verb or that the article "a" is followed by a singular noun), when they are given an exercise selecting those features. However, they don't seem to apply these rules to their own speech or writing. After reading about some of the SLA research, we were intrigued with the work done on attention and tried to help our students notice what was going on in the language used in the environment around them as a way to reinforce the grammar lesson and to show the connection between class-work and real-life language.

Our first attempt yielded some very interesting results. We asked our students in a college-level grammar class to listen to native-speaker English in several settings (a college lecture, a television or radio program, a conversation between two native speakers, etc.) and to record instances of the use of the present tense. We asked them to write the sentences in which they heard the present tense and then explain why it had been used. The first thing we noticed was that students couldn't really identify the present tense. For example, in the sentence, "Don't just think about it, do it," one student mistook the imperative for the simple present.

When they did recognize the tense, they showed little understanding of why it was used. One student said of the sentence, "I want to buy a jacket," that *want* was a simple present because it was habitual. When explaining an example of the present progressive, one student said that in the sentence "I'm eating lunch later," the present progressive indicated that the person was eating right now!

We quickly realized that students needed to understand the purpose of these assignments and had to be taught how to "pay attention," so we developed a more explicit approach. First, we introduce each new grammar structure with an activity both to arouse interest and to practice the skill of paying attention. Then, we assign homework in which the students pay attention to form. Finally, the students together analyze the samples they have collected and formulate rules for the structures.

The results have been gratifying, but even more important for us is the fact that our students have discovered that they can learn English by "paying attention" and using this strategy actively. Our experience has shown us that students can really benefit by focusing attention, but they have to be taught how to do it. Here is one student's evaluation of this approach. "When I was doing this homework, I found that the rules our teacher taught us in the class appeared in articles in the newspaper. It was natural, and I was excited. In these articles, the things we had already been informed about changed from 'a' to 'the.' It is difficult for me to forget this knowledge because it was accompanied by emotion."

4.3 TEACHING PRINCIPLES AND THE ROLE OF ATTENTION

Look back over this Teacher's Voice and think about the ways these two experienced teachers have tried to create contexts in which students are encouraged to attend to the linguistic tasks the teachers have chosen.

Now, consider the following teaching principles that seem to be the basis for the exercise you just read about.

1) Students are active participants in selecting examples and describing rules.

2) Learning takes place outside as well as inside the classroom.

3) Students are not simply asked to "pay attention."

4) They get very specific tips on what to pay attention to and how to do it.

5) Examples don't come from the text but from the radio, TV, or magazines.

What do activities like this tell us about the role of attention in SLA? What do they tell us about the role of the teacher in SLA? Looking at your own teaching, what are some activities or experiences you can think of that have helped your students "pay attention"?

CONCLUSION

It may be clear by now why the "A" for attention is central to the PLACE perspective on how people acquire a second language. Because it represents the gateway between the outside world of people and linguistic input, and the internal realm of thoughts and feelings, it is a construct that affects and is affected by almost every aspect of language learning. For this reason, we have seen that it is hard to separate attention from such disparate variables as consciousness, memory, perception, linguistic input, and linguistic form. Like the professor struggling down the hallway with an armful of term papers at the end of a week, a language learner's attention seems to be constantly overloaded with too much input and too little intake. Fortunately, despite its salience in SLA theory, learners do not have to depend solely on attention. All of them can rely on one of nature's most magnificent creations to help them with the daunting task of acquiring a new tongue—the human mind. It is time then to turn our attention in the next chapter toward the role of cognition in SLA.

Suggested Readings

As already acknowledged at the start of this chapter, attention is a topic of great interest to psychologists, and countless articles and books have been written about the subject. For those who would like to do some serious reading in psychology, Cowan's *Attention and Memory* (1997) is a detailed look at what current psychological research and models can tell us. For readers who are willing to plunge into some highly technical writing and who know something about neuropsychology, *The Attentive Brain* (1998), an anthology edited by Parasuraman, covers research on what we currently know about how the human brain attends to stimuli and how it maintains this attention.

Much less daunting and much more directly relevant to SLA, Stevick's second edition of *Memory, Meaning, and Method* (1996) is a marvelous compendium of insights on how a language learner's attention depends on the interrelationship of the three words cited in the title. For readers who would like to learn more about memory and the rich variety of situations in which it is employed, Neisser's *Memory Observed* (1982) is a treasure trove of "natural" experiments about human memory. Despite the fact that it is a book written almost exclusively about first language use and is devoted mainly to the way people jointly negotiate meaning in conversational contexts, *Using Language* by Clark (1996) is "salt and peppered" with references to attention and contains several pages (pp. 274–282) describing ways in which people use eye contact, etc. to maintain an interlocutor's attention during a conversation. No SLA researcher has written more insightfully about the role of attention than Schmidt. Among his many articles on the topic, two are especially useful summaries. "Consciousness and foreign language learning: A tutorial on attention and awareness in learning" (1995) is breezy and reader friendly. For a more intensive examination of the issues, see "Implicit learning and the cognitive unconscious: Of artificial grammars and SLA" (1994).

5

COGNITION

We are called *Homo sapiens*, the species of animals that is "wise" or, to translate directly from the Latin root, the animal that is "tasteful," the creature that has "good taste." Given the notable evidence of lack of wisdom and good taste in our species throughout human history, either *Homo loquens*, the "talking" hominid, or Aitchison's "the articulate ape," might be a more accurate appellation. Recently, we have even been called "the symbolic species" (Deacon, 1997).

Even though we humans may not be the wisest and the most tasteful of God's creatures, there is overwhelming neurological and behavioral proof, nonetheless, that we are certainly the most cognitive. In comparative size and in sheer neurological complexity, the human brain is by far the most complicated computer in the animal kingdom, and in terms of individual precocity, social organization, and environmental impact, people dominate the globe, for better and for worse. The driving force for this evolutionary achievement, is, of course, the human brain, which is not only quantitatively much more complex than the central nervous system of any other living organism, but has also developed qualitatively into a structure unique to biological history (Corballis, 1991). Even if we look at human evolution only in terms of language, and ignore all other aspects of human development, there is overwhelming evidence for complexity and uniqueness in our species (Lenneberg, 1967; Lieberman, 1991; and Hauser, 1997).

All this is a way of saying that cognition explains everything. Attention may be at the center of the PLACE acronym, but the C for cognition accounts for all the other components that make up this model of SLA. Without a human brain and mind, People, Languages, Attention, and Emotions cannot exist, for cognition defines, refines, and confines every aspect of our social, linguistic, attentional, and emotional behavior.

We take cognition for granted so much of the time that we don't stop to think about thinking. The following story incorporates all of the five key components of this book and gives us a chance to reflect on the way cognition pervades human experience. As this anecdote unfolds, consider, first of all, the way it weaves together different people, what they say, what fixates the attention of the main character, and how passionate emotions fuel the story. Consider too the manner in which schemas are introduced, causes and effects are linked, events are sequenced in a logical manner, and how, at the end, the entire joke depends on our ability to make very subtle inferences. In sum, the whole joke hinges on cognition.

It seems that there was once a jealous husband who was always suspicious of his wife, perhaps with some justification. One morning, after he left their apartment building to drive off to work, he was overcome with a strong premonition that his wife was about to be unfaithful to him, and he immediately turned his car around and sped back to their apartment. Sprinting upstairs, he pounded on the door and demanded to be let back in. His wife, surprised and slightly disheveled, opened the door after a moment's delay, and the now enraged husband hurtled from room to room searching for the suspected interloper. His wife protested vehemently that she had been alone the whole time, but her startled look and the fires of his jealousy had by now totally consumed him. He ran to the front window and looked down just in time to catch sight of a handsome young man stepping out of the entrance of their building. The man paused a moment at the threshold to readjust his tie, and as he stopped, he seemed to be smiling with an air of smug satisfaction. Overwhelmed with rage, the husband turned to seize the nearest large object, and with the superhuman powers that come only in a fit of passion, he managed to grab their refrigerator and shove it through the window so that it hurtled down on the young stranger, killing him instantly. At the same moment, the jealous husband's heart was unable to bear the heat of the moment any longer, and he died instantly of a heart attack.

The scene suddenly shifts to the gates of heaven where Saint Peter sees a man coming toward him to request entrance into paradise. It is the young stranger who had just a moment before stepped out of the apartment building to start a fresh day. "Why are you here?" Saint Peter inquires, and the man replies that he had just begun a new job in a new town and had just stepped outside with eager anticipation when he was instantly killed by some falling object. The heavenly guardian expresses his regrets and, finding the young man an innocent victim of foul play, immediately welcomes him into heaven. A second person then steps reluctantly toward the heavenly gates. "Ah, Saint Peter, I beg your mercy," blurts out the now mortified husband. "All this time I was inflamed with misplaced jealousy of my faithful wife, and in a fit of senseless passion, I happened to spot that young man underneath my apartment window. Thinking he had just had an affair with her, I grabbed our refrigerator and threw it out the window, instantly crushing him to death. Miserable sinner that I am, I know I don't deserve to enter the pearly gates!" "My son," replies the Saint in a tone of conciliation, "although you have committed an egregious sin, still, you are full of remorse and repentance. Because of this, even you can enter heaven," and he leads the gratified husband through the gates. At this moment, Saint Peter turns to see yet a third figure approaching the heavenly gates, and so asks once again for identification. "Well, you're never going to believe this," the stranger begins, "but I was hiding in a refrigerator in this guy's apartment…".

SCHEMATA

Philosophers have long argued that our perception of the world is not a photograph, accurately reproduced by our senses, but a portrait, sketched and colored by our preconceptions (Kant, 1781). More recently, psychologists have developed several different types of models to account for the way cognition shapes our perceptions and our memories of events (Barsalou, 1992). One of the earliest such approaches was developed by Bartlett (1932), who suggested that people tend to alter their perceptions and memories of events to fit their internal **content schemata**—their expectations about situations and events based on their real-world experiences. ("Schemata" is the Greek plural form of "schema," and is frequently used in the singular form to mean "schemas.")

Going back to the story about the jealous husband, one of the major reasons the anecdote is coherent and comprehensible (though, admittedly, bizarre), is because most of the events fit our schemata, at least the schemata of contemporary American culture. Americans live in a world where jealous spouses check up on their partners, where apartments have refrigerators, and even where the entrance to heaven is manned by an inquisitive Saint Peter. Because a great deal of schemata is shaped by culture, if this joke were told to someone completely unfamiliar with the aspects of American culture just listed, there would be very little understanding of the story itself, let alone an appreciation that the whole episode was meant to be a joke.

On the other hand, a great deal of schemata is universal and shared. For example, the story would grind to an abrupt halt in the mind of any listener if the husband had seized a walrus rather than a refrigerator, to cite just one of the many ways universal schematic expectations could have been violated. As Bartlett pointed out in his research, memory of events, as well as comprehension, can be skewed by schemata, and thus not all of what we remember is an accurate perceptual observation. You will, no doubt, "remember" that the mysterious third stranger who approached the pearly gates in the story was a man—presumably, the illicit lover that the jealous husband's wife had secreted in the refrigerator, but go back and reread the two final sentences. The story never actually reveals the third person's gender!

Our years of enculturation and education also leave us with schemata about language usage. As a native speaker of English, you probably never noticed that the first paragraph of this little story was in the past tense, but the second paragraph is told in the present. An alert and grammar-conscious nonnative speaker would probably notice this, and for an advanced ESL class, one that focused on university-level writing for instance, the explanation a teacher might give would be that this use of the "historical present" makes the second half of the anecdote more immediate and also signals to the listener that this is the most relevant part of the entire discourse.

Note too that the joke begins with *It seems that there was once...* which, like other "top-down" discourse markers such as *Once upon a time...,* tells the listener that the speaker is not going to relate a true incident or begin a lecture but is about to narrate a tale, parable, or joke. Native English speakers know from the schemata they have picked up about the use of English discourse markers like these that what they are about to hear will not be something transactional, but probably something interactional. So along with content schemata, learners also have to acquire **discourse schemata**, and learn to recognize the subtle signals that each language employs to provide listeners or readers with important top-down information about the discourse they are about to decode.

In sum, since our schematic experience is constantly interacting with our attempts at linguistic communication, language use and language acquisition constantly compel us to be thinking about every aspect of what we perceive, experience, and remember. Thus, cognition controls every moment of our consciousness, and because of this, it also shapes every aspect of the way we set about learning a new language. To cite just one pedagogical application of this claim, Anderson (1999) provides an excellent illustration of how schematic knowledge can influence reading comprehension.

5.1 *How Cultures Package Schematic Knowledge Differently*

ESL instructors should know all about content and discourse schemata because they constantly confront examples of these constructs in their daily teaching. If you are currently teaching an ESL class, or are living in an environment where you can easily get in touch with a group of people from another linguaculture, try this exercise designed to uncover differences in schematic knowledge. In the process, I hope you'll also begin to unpackage your own schematic knowledge—expectations that you may have held for many years but have not been explicitly aware of. Here are some examples to get you started, but feel free to come up with your own illustrations.

(1) **Discourse Schemata: Addressing Envelopes.** Ask your class (or anyone from a different culture) if there are any differences between the tradition in their culture and the American tradition of addressing envelopes to post in the mail. As a starter, ask if they always put the return address in the upper left-hand corner of the envelope and place the stamp in the upper right-hand corner. For addresses, do they always start with name, then street address, then city, then state, and finally postal code? What are some permissible variations of the "normal, American" system. Can you stick the stamp on upside down, for instance?

(2) **Discourse Schemata: Tell a Joke.** How do people from different language backgrounds tell a joke? Do any, for example, begin by saying, "Now I am going to tell you a joke?" And what about the ending: Is there a convention for delivering the punch line? Or is there necessarily a punch line? And is a joke in one language funny in another?

(3) **Content Schemata: What Do You Eat for Breakfast?** Now let's switch to the larger and more complex world of content schemata. Since food is part of universal culture, it is always a topic of interest. "What makes a good breakfast" or "what do you eat for breakfast" all food-related questions that should trigger plenty of insights about content schemata.

(4) **Content Schemata: What Does a Color Symbolize?** Color perception is physiologically consistent, but color classification and symbolism are not. When I grew up in China, red was the color of happiness, but white was the color of death; consequently, it was not viewed as entirely auspicious for a bride to wear white on her wedding day! Take the English expression, "I'm feeling blue." Does "blue" mean "sad" in all cultures? What are the connotations of some other colors for your informants?

PROCESS, STYLE, AND STRATEGY

The technical vocabulary of SLA is no different from the professional argot of any discipline; sometimes different terms are used synonymously, but more often than not, a slight change in terminology may signal a significant change in meaning. Brown (2000), who does an excellent job of introducing many of the basic concepts and vocabulary of SLA, makes a distinction between processes, styles, and strategies, terms that many people frequently and confusingly use as synonyms for the same cognitive operation. **Process** refers to any general cognitive ability that all people employ in learning. Processes are universal and include such skills as identification, categorization, association, and memory. For example, you might suddenly encounter a pleasant smell while on a morning jog and *identify* it as coming from a flowering shrub and, an instant later, you might be able to *categorize* it as honeysuckle. But your mind usually doesn't just stop at categorization. It immediately goes on to *associate* that smell with summer evenings and that association might, in turn, trigger a long-term *memory*—perhaps of childhood vacations with a beloved grandmother on a farm. In the space of one or two seconds, your mind has raced through several different cognitive processes and has instantly evoked schemas that may have almost nothing directly to do with the initial stimulus, the aroma of a flower you just ran past. Because cognitive processes are universal and, as the illustration just cited indicates, because they are also intertwined, they play a powerful and pervasive part in every aspect of SLA.

Unlike processes, **styles** are not universal but are preferences that individuals employ in different learning situations. Styles are heavily influenced by culture, so a certain style tends to predominate in one culture, but another culture may nurture a very different style of learning. They can also be idiosyncratic, so that two learners from identical cultures may still display two very different styles of SLA. Notice how learning styles contrast in the following excerpts from two different language learners.

Learner's Account #10

While trying to read hiragana [Japanese syllabic writing], I must have been doing some sort of writing in the air or on the table with my finger, because my teacher noted afterwards that I am clearly a very kinesthetic learner. This I believe to be true, because I was much more successful on the exercise we did in class where we were given a kinesthetic stimulus—for example, for the travel scenarios where we were given maps to trace our routes.

A Student of Japanese

Learner's Account #11

During the week following my first class meeting, I practiced writing Korean letters. For this task, I made up a story or phrase to connect the sound to each letter. This imaging strategy proved successful for certain sounds. For example, the Korean letter for /m/ is shaped like a box. I wrote this letter more than a hundred times, each time saying, "Mmmmm… my mouth is shaped like a box when I say mmmm."

A Student of Korean

Both of these students were Americans and shared similar cultural styles, but they chose alternate routes when faced with the task of acquiring a very different writing system from the English orthography with which they were familiar. The first student tried to employ body movements to help her out, whereas the second relied more on auditory cues. Of course, all people from all cultures use all of the senses available to them when learning a new task; conversely, it is also true that some individuals are so exceptionally gifted in their processing abilities in a particular sensory modality that they are remembered as geniuses. Gardner (1993) writes in detail about the extraordinary creative talent of people like Martha Graham in dance or Igor Stravinsky in music, who became world famous because of their exceptional ability in one "style" of creativity (what Gardner calls "kinesthetic intelligence" and "musical intelligence" for Graham and Stravinsky, respectively).

But in looking at more ordinary examples, where these two language learners are trying to pick up a new orthographic system, we can see that some people depend more on one sensory style (kinesthetic), and some on another (auditory). To cite an analogy drawn by Brown, in the game of tennis, every player must be able to play a complete game; nevertheless, some players rely on a devastating serve, whereas others might favor a strong two-handed backhand. Any competent tennis player must be able to both serve the ball and return it backhand, but individual players tend to develop different parts of their game, and this reflects their "style." Language learners are no different, and in addition to their individual predilections, they also tend to favor learning styles that are nurtured by their mother culture.

The final term of this three-part definition is **strategy**. Strategies are the narrowest and most specific of the three terms defined here; they refer to steps students take to solve very particular language learning problems. The use of **mnemonics**, memory tricks or devices, is an excellent illustration (e.g., an ESL student pictures a "seesaw scene" to recall the three forms of the irregular verb "to see" in English—see/saw/seen). Brief jingles or rhymes are another demonstration of strategies (e.g., "*I* before *e* except after *c*"). Another strategy is to use **keywords**, where a learner invents a situation in which a word in the target language sounds similar to a word in the student's mother tongue.

Learner's Account #12

I had Emily [my 10-year-old friend] help me think of keywords today. For "sofu" (grandfather, in-group) and "ojisan" (grandfather, out-group), she suggested, "Think of your gandpa lying on the couch and your grandma comes in and says, *Oh gee*, you're on the *sofa* again!"

A Student of Japanese

Unfortunately, *strategies* may not be the best choice of terminology here, especially when we consider the military origins of the word. A more accurate term would be *tactics*, since we are looking at localized and specific solutions to immediate language learning problems. Strategies, in contrast, deal with wider and more far-ranging problems and could be more appropriate as a synonym for *styles*. But even though some SLA experts have sought to redefine *strategy* in this manner, the terminology in our field is confusing enough, so we shall remain content with the idea that strategies refer to very specific SLA tactics.

If we look back now on these three different levels of cognition, we can summarize the contrasts in the following manner.

PROCESSES
- universal—present in every human being and in all cultures
- pervasive—found in every situation in which learning occurs
- examples—categorization, association, problem-solving, memory, etc.

STYLES
- cultural and individual—people prefer to adopt certain styles over others
- limited—a certain individual in a specific learning situation almost always opts for a particular learning style
- examples—relying on visual cues, using deductive logic, paying attention to bottom-up details, etc.

STRATEGIES
- specific to the situation—a person adopts a particular strategy to solve a specific language learning problem that arises at that moment
- highly limited—learners usually cannot transfer strategies to other situations (e.g., the strategy for remembering "see/saw/seen" is useless for learning any other irregular verb forms)
- examples—keywords, rhymes, mnemonics, flashcards, etc.

PROCESSES: MEMORY

When we pause to consider all the various cognitive processes that influence our ability to acquire any new information (let alone a whole new language) there is no doubt that the one most prominent in the minds of every learner is memory. Granted, other processes are crucial to cognition, and it is inconceivable that anyone could successfully perform even a few seconds of any daily activity without being able to identify, categorize, or associate objects, to name just a few of these universal forms of cognition. But cognitive processes like these, fundamental though they may be to all human and animal behavior, deal with minute and discrete bits and pieces of language and not with the larger, higher level linguistic chunks with which students and teachers are most concerned.

SLA researchers like Flege and Hillenbrand (1987), Major (1987), and Scovel (1995) have studied or written about these cognitive processes as they pertain to the ability of native speakers to recognize quickly and accurately the foreign accent of nonnatives, but their work has been largely confined to identifying or categorizing diminutive segments of phonetic performance, such as voicing differences in initial stop consonants or very small acoustic differences between English vowels. A cognitive process that is much more relevant to language learning and teaching, and that preoccupies learners and teachers to a much greater extent than these "lower levels" of thought, is the fascinating field of memory.

How often language students lament the fact that they simply can't remember all the new material that confronts them each day of class. How frequently learners long to upgrade their memory as easily as they upgrade that of their computers, so that they can double or triple their foreign language vocabulary. And it's not just students who yearn for better memories. How regularly teachers fail to remember their students' names (as the little episode used to introduce the previous chapter attests). Alas, memory in SLA seems to go downhill as rapidly as memory for everything else. In the terse terminology of cognitive psychology, human memory is definitely "capacity limited" (Broadbent, 1952). Or as one wag has so insightfully put it, "memory is the thing we forget with!"

Actually, this witticism is extremely discerning, for memory is really nothing more than selective forgetting. Imagine for a moment that you, as a foreign language student, actually had a "photographic" memory. There are, as a matter of fact, well-documented cases of mnemonists, individuals with a super memory (Luria, 1968), but even they remember things in a highly selective fashion. Neisser (1982) chronicles accounts of mnemonists from several cultures, among them the Shass Pollak, Talmudic scholars from Poland, who were able to memorize thousands of pages of the Talmud so well that if you stuck a pin into a word on any page of this lengthy text these memory experts could tell you instantly what word was in the exact same spot on any page underneath! These scholars' awesome display of remembrance was still limited, however, for they would have the same trouble you or I would experience recalling the names of people met at a public reception or recounting verbatim a page of new material just read. But pretend, for a moment that you really were able to remember every single piece of new information you saw or heard in your German class, and that the teacher gave you the following phrase to remember: *Mein grosser Freund hat einen neuen roten Wagen.* ("My tall friend has a new red car.")

Of course you would remember this utterance upon first hearing it (although this alone would not guarantee that you would pronounce the sentence correctly whenever you were asked to reproduce it). But if such a phenomenon as "photographic" recall actually existed, you would imprint into your memory every piece of information that you were exposed to at the same moment you heard the sentence. You would remember the teacher's position and posture in the front of the classroom, you would recall in exact detail everything she wore, everything that was on the desk beside her, everything that was written on the blackboard behind the desk, every crack and chip of paint on the wall around the blackboard, every detail of the clock hanging on the wall, etc., etc.!

Naturally, as a student of German, you wouldn't want this. Like King Midas, whose wish that everything he touched would turn to gold was granted, and who instantly grew to curse the very faculty he had longed for, you would quickly protest that you didn't want to remember *everything*, but only the German you were exposed to in your language class. And upon reflection, you might not even want to remember such a useless and uncontextualized piece of German as *Mein grosser Freund hat einen neuen roten Wagen!* Once again, we see the power of cognition at work. Good language learners are not vacuum cleaners, sweeping up every detail that carpets their classroom. They must constantly sift the *emic* from the *etic* and try to remember only relevant information. To turn the emphasis on memory around, learning a language doesn't involve remembering what is important, it's simply learning to forget everything that's not. Easier said than done!

For *emic* and *etic* see p. 72.

Decades of psychological research have clearly demonstrated, first of all, that there is no such thing as memory, there are only memor*ies*. In the broadest sense of the term, the most primitive type of memory is **reflexes**, behaviors that we do not acquire but are born with as innately specified "memories" from our biological heritage. All babies "remember" how to suck or to exhibit a startle reflex. But examples that are much less rudimentary and are more representative of what we normally consider as memories are found in the tripartite distinction among declarative, procedural, and episodic memory (Koffka, 1935/1963; Tulving; 1983).

Declarative memory is the typical exemplar we think of when we talk about memory. Definitions, dates, names, phone numbers, and e-mail addresses are samples of this type of knowledge. When we complain about our memory, we are invariably talking only about this form of recall.

But in many ways, more crucial to the functioning of everyday life is **procedural memory**, the ability to remember not *who*, *what*, *why*, or *when*, but *how*. Examples of procedural knowledge abound in the simple daily tasks we take so much for granted: remembering which finger to move to type the letter *o* on a keyboard, knowing exactly when and to what extent to push in the clutch when shifting gears in a car, recalling the correct sequence of movements for the flutter kick when swimming freestyle, and even such mundanely trivial tasks as perceiving just when to stop extending your arm as you reach for a glass of water. Notice from these illustrations that procedural memories occur simultaneously and usually result in a series of concurrent and coordinated actions. Because of this, they are an excellent demonstration of what psychologists call **parallel distributed processing** (**PDP**). This means that your brain must concurrently remember to stop your arm at just the right moment as you reach for your glass and, at the same time, remember to produce the right sequence of muscular motions to allow you to continue speaking to the person seated across the table from you. PDP is an attempt to explain part of the complexity of human cognitive behavior because, on close examination, complicated phenomena such as human speech involve not one linear-sequential process but a multitude of simultaneous and complex events (Rumelhart and McClelland, 1986).

A third form of memory is **episodic**, which records a holistic impression of an entire event. Classic examples of episodic knowledge are remembrances of things past—the room, the time, where you were standing, etc. when your baby daughter took her first steps.

Evidence for this tripartite distinction comes from several sources, but probably the most convincing arises from the massive amount of research conducted by neuropsychologists over the second half of the twentieth century. One source of neuropsychological evidence is the unfortunate consequence of brain damage. Depending in large part on whether or not the injury is focal, on what caused the cerebral damage in the first place, and also upon the location of the neurological trauma itself, patients can exhibit disability in one of these types of memory but not in the others.

To cite just one of innumerable circumstances, damage to the right parietal lobe (just above and behind the right ear) usually adversely affects procedural memory but not the other two types of memory. The patient normally suffers no aphasia and no loss in declarative and episodic memory, but it is very common for him or her to "forget" how to do even common, everyday procedures such as tying a shoe or cooking an omelet. Damage to other areas of the cerebrum results in other kinds of differential memory loss and convincingly demonstrates the existence of separate and independent stores of knowledge.

Frameworks

Declarative memory vs. procedural memory

When neurological damage is not focal but diffuse and pervades the entire cerebral cortex, very often the only type of memory that is spared is episodic. Patients suffering from advanced stages of Alzheimers, for example, tend to lose a great deal of their declarative abilities (forgetting the names of their children) and their procedural knowledge (puzzling over how to warm a cup of coffee in the microwave), but sometimes maintain, in marked contrast, a remarkable recall of personal episodes (relating in detail how they learned to ride a bike, an event that may have transpired 60 years before!).

See also Stevick *What's at Stake?* (1998).

Stevick (1996) has presented the clearest and most useful exposition to date about the way memory relates to SLA. The first half of this greatly revised edition of his earlier work is a useful introduction to most of the concepts and findings of psychological research, including the three-way division of remembered knowledge just discussed. A dichotomy he discusses at great length, and one that has consumed a great deal of attention among learning psychologists (Cowan, 1997), is the distinction between **short-term memory (STM)** and **long-term memory (LTM)**. Like all categorical contrasts, this binary classification tends to oversimplify the varieties of behaviors that people demonstrate in various learning situations, but it is a long-standing metaphor that has been somewhat legitimized by decades of experimental evidence. In a nutshell, the former is the temporary store we use for brand-new information (e.g., names of strangers we have just met, telephone numbers given over the radio or TV, or a sentence about a tall friend and a red car just heard in our German class). Unless we immediately record, rehearse, or in some other way attempt to capture this fresh information in our long-term memory, the material is instantly lost and irretrievable. Notice that STM, not LTM, is most typically "the thing we forget with." Memory span for STM is much shorter than most people realize, for it lasts only a few seconds, and never more than about 20 seconds. LTM is the much larger trove of memories and contains information we may have acquired just a minute ago or the reminiscence of the first time we sallied forth on a bicycle some 60 years previous.

Many factors affect what we ignore or what we record from the flood of information initially available to us, but memory storage is most directly influenced by attention (Cowan, 1997). Based on his reading of the psychological literature in this large and complex field, Stevick has proposed a revision of the popular STM/LTM dichotomy in order to create a memory model that might be more useful to those interested in SLA and in foreign language teaching.

Figure 5.1 **Stevick's Model for Memory** (1996:65)

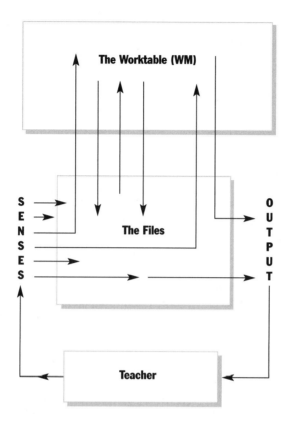

This model depicts several refinements over the simplistic STM/LTM contrast and, in addition, seems to proffer several implications for SLA. First of all, reflecting the results of much of the more current psychological research, the arrows from The Files (a term that covers all stored information a learner brings to any new learning situation) going "up" to Working Memory (WM) suggest that STM is not just a passive, time-limited filter, but is just as active and robust as LTM (i.e., it is "working" memory). Second, what gets noticed and stored into The Files from WM is the outcome of a complex process that may involve several interactions between the two memory systems and is also a consequence of continued but varied input from the Senses. Finally, as suggested by the PDP model mentioned above, this model indicates that the process of committing something to memory is facilitated by coterminous pathways that, because they provide concurrent and complementary information, greatly help to help to enhance memory storage. Among the several SLA examples Stevick cites in his book, the following about learning a new word in Turkish illustrates how this model functions in a lively and active manner.

A learner of Turkish, for example, who hears the word *heyecan*, may have to go through three round trips from working memory to the files and back: (1) Have I heard this word before? Yes. (2) When, and in what context? Last week, in a discussion of popular music. This may lead to identification: (3) What did it mean in that context? It meant something like "excitement."

(Stevick, 1996:65)

Notice how even the "simple" acquisition of a new word in a foreign language (in this case, a demonstration of declarative memory) involves a complex array of concurrent and sequential memory-related processes that entail both WM and The Files. Also observe how declarative memory can be facilitated by episodic memory (in question 2) and can also include procedural memory (if the student tried to pronounce this word out loud to help expedite memory storage).

In summary, we can conclude that what we label as a single construct, "memory," manifests itself in human learning behavior under many guises. We also see that memory is unarguably the most salient example of the way human cognition controls the nature and extent of SLA for all learners. Finally, as described and depicted by the model proposed by Stevick, we realize that memory is not a simple, calm, and orderly process of inputting one new piece of data at a time, like a person inserting coins into a vending machine, but that it often involves almost a cacophony of concurrent and sequential negotiations, not too dissimilar from the frenzied transactions that occupy the floor of a stock market.

SENSORY MEMORIES

For Mariko's experience, see p. 28.

Several years ago, one of my former students, Barbara Stoops, was teaching in Japan, after a stint as an English teacher in Malaysia, where she had become acquainted with the fruits of Southeast Asia. English was a required course for the Japanese university students Barbara was teaching, and like most of their counterparts around the world, Japanese students are not typically highly motivated to study for a required subject, especially one such as English with which they have struggled for many years. Like Mariko Okuzaki, the teacher whose voice we heard in Chapter 2, Barbara went out of her way to make her English class more interesting by doing such things as introducing unusual objects and even strange smells into her classroom. Listen to one such happening.

Barbara Stoops

We all know that effective teaching will engage learners' interest on many levels. A student of English is more likely to learn "apple" by tasting one than simply by memorizing it on a word list. So, when our textbook, *Culture Connection*, brought up the fruit called durian, I took it as a golden opportunity.

This was a content-based intermediate level class for Japanese university students, meant to sensitize them to cultural differences and improve their English as well. We were embarking upon a unit about food—a favorite topic—and the text used durian as an example of "an acquired taste." "According to a Chinese saying, 'The durian tastes like heaven, smells like hell!'", said the book (p. 66).

"How many of you have tasted durian?" I asked. Of course, none. So feeling clever, I went to Kobe's Chinatown and bought one on sale. Triple-wrapped in plastic, it still made its presence known on the subway home, and even more strongly inside the staff refrigerator at work. The scent, to me, was a strange combination of garlic, sweat, and open latrines. I felt a Proustian delight at the memories it evoked of rain-drenched Malaysian evenings, and looked forward to my students' reactions.

Sure enough, in class they were properly impressed, taking deep, disgusted breaths over the lumpy yellowish mass (a requirement) and playing a cheerful kind of "chicken" to see who would be brave enough to taste it. None proclaimed it delicious, but when I offered up leftovers some students took them home. Next week was a new topic, and I didn't think about durian again until almost a year later, living in San Francisco, when a letter came from the teacher who'd replaced me. He had the same students for their second year, and asked them to write about what they remembered from the year before.

"DURIAN!" they wrote. "It was HORRIBLE! I took it home and my mother was angry with me." 90 percent of them put *durian* as their strongest memory from a year of seminars. But, I ask myself, "What did they learn?"

Upon reading this, you might have immediately thought back on Mariko's account of her use of peanut butter on apples in her class, or you might have tried to tie this story in with types of memory just introduced above. It seems certain that most of Barbara's students had a strong episodic memory of their encounter with durian and that its smell was hard to forget!

But this particular Teacher's Voice is not really about types of memories, or the use of realia in language classrooms, or even about durian. It turns instead on that simple but provocative final phrase, "What did they learn?" *What did they learn?* This vexing question lies at the heart of reflective teaching. But it also goes directly to the very soul of cognitive psychology. *What did they learn?* And from this stream a series of similar queries, *How do they learn? Why don't they learn? Why should they learn?* And so on and so on. Cognition never stops!

STYLES OF SLA

Much more has been written about contrasts in learning styles in the SLA literature than about cognitive processes, largely because the latter are universal and do not vary among groups of learners. But because cognitive styles are shaped by cultural and/or individual differences, and because they are usually quite conspicuous to language instructors (especially those who have just begun to teach in a new cultural setting), there is the possibility that certain styles might enable students to become more effective language learners, at least for certain tasks. For example, Wesche (1981) conducted a study in which she grouped students into language classes that either matched or contradicted their learning style (e.g., highly analytic learners were placed in "analytic" classrooms

Cognitive styles

or, conversely, in classrooms that depended a great deal on good memory, not on the ability to analyze). Not surprisingly, the students who studied in situations that matched their learning preference performed better and were less disgruntled than the unfortunate students who were mismatched. Aside from very broad generalizations like this, much of the SLA research on learning styles is varied in its experimental design and somewhat unconvincing in its findings.

An initial problem with this area of inquiry is that a very wide range of constructs are subsumed under the general rubric of cognitive style. Brown (2000) lists some of the representative research and cites such diverse examples as field independence vs. field dependence, left vs. right-brain functioning, tolerance of ambiguity, reflectivity vs. impulsivity, and visual vs. auditory preferences. To these Ehrman (1996) adds sequential vs. random, concrete vs. abstract, and deductive vs. inductive.

A second limitation of this type of research is the tendency to present these styles as polarized pairs. This in itself poses several problems. For one thing, it can create a situation in which the existence of a learning style is defined by the absence of its contrasting alternate. This seems to be the case in the work done on field dependence (Jamieson, 1992), where the instrument used, the Group Embedded Figures Test (GEFT), is simultaneously a measure of both field dependence and independence, since high GEFT scores show that subjects are field independent and low scores reveal that they are field dependent.

Yet another obstacle is that by presenting cognitive styles as contradictory pairs, many insights into individual or cultural variation are lost. Most learners in most situations do not function in either X or Y style, for instance, but can probably be placed on a sliding scale between the two polar extremes. Also, it is quite likely that some learners in some situations can be good at both field dependent and independent processing, or, to take a much unhappier case, there are also some learners who might be equally weak at both, at least in some language learning situations.

But the third and most vitiating criticism of all is that whereas there's some evidence that certain cultures nurture certain styles, these differences do not seem to correlate consistently with language learning performance. Hansen (1987), for instance, gave a battery of cognitive style measures to groups of Asian ESL students and found that although certain groups differed significantly in their learning styles (e.g., the Pacific Islanders tended to be field dependent and impulsive, whereas the Japanese were much more field independent and reflective), these style differences did not correlate with success in their ESL performance as measured by test scores.

It shouldn't really be so surprising that such a complex activity as SLA cannot be neatly explained by the predominance of one cognitive style over another, especially since language acquisition varies enormously when we consider all the different ways people learn different languages around the world. Nevertheless, a couple of useful speculations can be made about the relationship between cognitive styles and SLA performance, especially if we avoid these narrower, binary categorizations and look at broader generalizations.

Skehan (1998) devotes an entire chapter of his detailed SLA text to a cogent and trenchant review of the learning styles literature and suggests that one fruitful way to summarize much of this research is to plot the individual differences that exist among learners on a graph that is circumscribed by two dimensions of style. The first dimension (the X-axis) is the degree to which the learner approaches language learning as a memory task. As just pointed out, memory is a universal process, but language learners vary in the extent that they feel it is necessary to employ memory in SLA situations. The other dimension (the Y-axis) refers to the amount of analysis learners devote to language learning tasks. Learners whom we might call the "grammarians" view language learning like math problems or crossword puzzles and try to analyze all new information by breaking it down into representative components. On the other end of this sliding scale are the "chunkers," who try to associate clusters of words or phrases with certain meanings or situations. McLaughlin's SLA model discussed in Chapter 4 comes to mind here, because an analytic style relies heavily on linear-sequential ordering, while a nonanalytic or holistic style depends much more on tuning and restructuring. In any event, based on Skehan's framework, learners are not categorized by binary features but are scattered on a graph like the following, depending on their stylistic proclivities for language learning.

See pp. 78–80 for McLaughlin's SLA model.

Figure 5.2 **Dimensions of Learning Styles** (Skehan, 1998:251)

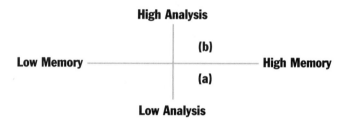

Viewed in this manner, learners aren't necessarily pigeonholed into boxes with names like field dependent or reflective but can be graphed more widely as using combinations of styles. For instance, grammarians are clearly in the top half of this depiction, but they represent a wide range from left to right on the graph. And even though "chunkers," who rely heavily on memory, will be placed somewhere in the lower right quadrant of this figure, there is still a range of possibilities open within this quadrant. For example, a "chunker" may rely heavily on memory in certain classroom situations (e.g., viewing a foreign language videotape for the first time) and be plotted in the low righthand corner (a), but the same learner may switch to a more analytic mode in a different circumstance (e.g., the teacher writes down a new rule on the blackboard) and for that situation be plotted in a higher, more analytic position on the graph (b). In sum, the approach taken by researchers like Skehan (1998) and Willing (1987) opens up the whole field of learning styles to greater individual variation and to a wider range of pedagogical situations.

STRATEGIES—SOLVING INFORMATION GAP COGNITIVE TASKS
While cognitive processes and styles are fairly general, are limited in number, and can certainly apply to all forms of learning, strategies are very specific,

almost limitless, and can be applied only to a particular language learning situation. Researchers such as Chamot and O'Malley (1987) and Oxford (1990) claim that there are not only cognitive strategies, but social and affective ones too. All of us can reflect on strategies we have used as students or ones that good teachers have modeled for us. A story is told of an anatomy professor who held almost legendary status at his medical school because of his ability to come up with spontaneous and clever strategies for helping his students remember material. Once, for example, he introduced a potentially dull lecture on the cranial nerves with the following preface. "Class," he inquired at the start of the hour, "how many eggs in a dozen? How many months in a year? How many tribes of Israel? And how many disciples of Jesus? Class, how many cranial nerves?" Not even the slowest learner in his course failed to remember that there were 12 cranial nerves, even though, quite cleverly, the instructor had never once mentioned the actual number. This is but one of innumerable strategies that could be adopted to help someone remember how many nerves there were and then go on to recall their names. Strategies obviously are incredibly diverse.

Oxford (1990) names and offers examples for over 60 language learning strategies, which she has classified into six general groups. Three of the groups typify **direct strategies**, which involve direct use of the target language to be learned; the other three exemplify **indirect strategies**, in which the language may not be directly involved, but the strategy is designed to help the learner acquire or remember a particular piece of the language. Here is her system, with a few representative examples.

Learner strategies (Oxford 1990)

Table 5.1 **Language Learning Strategy System** (Oxford, 1990:17)

DIRECT STRATEGIES	INDIRECT STRATEGIES
1. Memory Strategies • *creating mental links* • *applying images & sounds* • *employing action*	**4. Metacognitive Strategies** • *centering your learning* • *planning your learning* • *evaluating your learning*
2. Cognitive Strategies • *practicing* • *analyzing & reasoning* • *creating structure*	**5. Affective Strategies** • *lowering your anxiety* • *encouraging yourself* • *taking your emotional temperature*
3. Compensation Strategies • *guessing intelligently* • *overcoming limitations*	**6. Social Strategies** • *asking questions* • *cooperating with others*

Because this chapter focuses on the way cognition affects SLA, a cognitive language learning strategy will be chosen from the list above as an illustration —specifically, the category labeled "analyzing and reasoning." And since most language students and teachers these days are acquainted with group work and information gap exercises, a cognitive task involving information gap group interaction will be adopted based on a puzzle taken from Brown (1991:58). You may wish to try this "recipe" out on your class if you are currently teaching ESL .

A COGNITIVE REASONING RECIPE

Ingredients

- 1 ESL or Foreign Language Class (any level, but best for low intermediates)
- 1 index card for every student in the class
- 3 small prizes for the winning group (e.g., candy bars)

Directions

- Before class, prepare as many sets of three index cards as necessary.
- On the first card write, "A. There are 10 trees."
- On the second card write, "B. There are 5 rows."
- On the third card write, "C. There are 4 trees in each row."
- When you are ready for this exercise, announce to the class that they will be divided into groups of three and each group will be given the same problem to solve. The first group to come up with what they believe is the correct answer should raise their hand and whisper their answer to the teacher.
- The first group with the correct answer wins a prize.

Special Instructions

- Each student should read his or her sentence out loud to the other two—in other words, the information should be given in spoken English. However, as in a card game, they should not show their cards to the other participants.
- If some (or all) groups don't understand the task, tell them explicitly—the problem is, how can you make 5 rows of 4 trees each with only 10 trees?!
- The entire activity should take about 15 minutes. If no group figures out the correct solution within this time limit, for the sake of suspense, the teacher can withhold the correct answer until the next time the class meets.

Answer

- Although this reasoning task uses very simple language (and hence is accessible to any linguistic level), it is a difficult *cognitive* task, especially for people who do not favor a visual learning style.
- The solution is to place the trees in a star-shaped pattern so that the individual trees overlap for each of the five rows, and thus it is indeed possible to squeeze only 10 trees into 5 rows of 4!

As already indicated and as is apparent from Oxford's list, the variety of choices for language learning strategies can be expanded almost indefinitely. In this particular "recipe," a number of advantages should be evident to any classroom practitioner. In addition to the social interaction the students glean from the group work, the cognitive reasoning task is highly motivating for most students. Because the language is simple but the problem is complex, students are not frustrated about not being able to understand the task. Too often in language classes, the situation is just the reverse: Students are asked childish questions framed in second language input that is barely comprehensible. Another advantage is that cognitive tasks like these use language that is contextualized and, at least in academic situations, is authentic. Finally, since the focus and the reward are based on coming up with the solution and not with making the correct linguistic choice, communicative competence is fostered and in a fun-filled manner. Examples of pedagogical strategies like this illustrate how teachers can focus much of their creativity and energy on encouraging and demonstrating appropriate SLA strategy use, not forgetting, at the same time, that they must still take into account the students' cognitive processes and styles that will eventually shape these strategic choices.

TIME AND SLA

Up until now we have been reviewing the many ways cognition is deployed in language acquisition without considering the single most important variable affecting all human learning: time. So important is this precious commodity as a cognitive variable in experimental psychology that "reaction time" is the most commonly used measure in research. Reaction times almost always correlate directly with task difficulty, and researchers who approach SLA from the perspective of psychology have viewed time as an integral component of their theories. In her earlier model of second language learning, Bialystok (1978) divided L2 output into two types: Type I is spontaneous and immediate; Type II is more deliberate and takes place only after a noticeable delay. In beginning learners, for example, overlearned phrases, such as greetings, are typical Type I responses, since they demand little cognitive deliberation and tend to be produced quickly and spontaneously. But most SLA output is of the Type II variety, where hesitations, monitoring, and delay imply a great deal of cognitive effort. Again, we are reminded of McLaughlin's distinction between automatic (Type I) and controlled (Type II).

Two significant studies by Skehan and Foster report on the results of a factor analysis of data gleaned from the spoken English of 72 ESL learners (Foster and Skehan, 1997; Skehan and Foster, 1997). The authors measured the spoken English of these ESL students with varying linguistic tasks—telling a story, describing a personal situation, and making a decision—and then assessed the students' output according to the number of pauses they made (fluency), the complexity of the linguistic task (complexity), and the number of errors they committed (accuracy). The following table, adapted from their work as reported in Skehan (1998), reveals quite strikingly the way that time limits the capacity to perform a cognitive task. The numbers in each column refer to the degree of correlation between the tasks (listed at the left) and each factor: fluency, complexity, and accuracy. The higher the number in each cell, the stronger the correlation, with negative numbers representing inverse correlations.

Table 5.2: Correlations Between Tasks and Factors (Skehan, 1998: 168)

	Factor 1 (*fluency*)	Factor 2 (*complexity*)	Factor 3 (*accuracy*)
Narrative: pauses	.73	-.38	-.19
Personal: pauses	.88	-.08	-.15
Decision: pauses	.71	-.49	-.09
Narrative: complexity	-.50	.16	-.53
Personal: complexity	.03	.88	.12
Decision: complexity	-.26	.81	-.08
Narrative: error-free	-.18	.10	.83
Personal: error-free	-.52	-.06	.08
Decision: error-free	-.24	-.02	.72

With very few exceptions, the data from Skehan and Foster's studies demonstrate that the human mind is indeed "capacity limited" when it comes to performing demanding cognitive tasks like learning a new language. When learners focus on fluency, their output tends to be neither complex nor accurate. When they concentrate on complexity, their fluency and their accuracy suffer. Finally, if their goal is to produce error-free speech, the fluency and the complexity of their output is limited. Research like this, which delves into cognitive effects on SLA, strongly suggests that time constrains each moment of a learner's attempts to acquire a second language, especially when it comes to speaking. The implication is that learners and teachers need to concentrate on one goal at a time until that linguistic skill is automatized and the mind is free to divert attention to another linguistic goal (McLaughlin, Rossman, and McLeod, 1983). Given enough time, L2 learners can eventually acquire the fluency and accuracy of native speakers, even with cognitively complex material.

Or can they?

This simple question plunges us squarely into the middle of a second and much more controversial way of looking at how time might constrain language acquisition. There has been a longstanding belief that when it comes to language learning, kids do it best. Remarkably, the popularity and the pervasiveness of this belief are based much more on anecdotal observations than on cold, scientific fact. To take one common illustration, parents who move to a new country invariably lament the fact that they seem to be tongue-tied, even though they may have been dutifully studying the new language either on tape or in class. In stark contrast, their little children appear to absorb the new tongue like sponges. Rarely, however, do people stop and reflect on the underlying presuppositions that come packaged with these anecdotes.

Consider just one factor that should force us to reevaluate this myth that children are better language learners than adults. Supposing that you are the parent in an English-speaking family that has moved to Italy for a year, and suppose, indeed, that your three-year old is commended for her apparent fluency in

Italian while, at the same time, you are embarrassed about your "limited" proficiency. What levels of language are expected in any culture of a three-year old and a thirty-year old? Of course, we applaud a small child if she happens to be able to name a certain type of beverage, but it is entirely unremarkable when an adult can point to a cup of coffee and say the same words, "I want a cappuccino." What's cute from a kid is considered common from a grown-up! And in Italy, the adult isn't even credited with knowing an "Italian" word since the term is already used so extensively in English. So it's important to base any claims about age and acquisition on solid SLA research and not on the impressionistic and sometimes unfair generalizations that people make about the reputed linguistic precocity of children (Scovel, 2000a).

Investigations

5.2 *WHO'S THE BETTER LEARNER, ZOLTAN OR ZSUZSI?*

If we look beyond the comparatively unfair expectations we harbor for adult learners, however, we can see that in many ways, older learners are indeed better learners, both in the speed with which they pick up new linguistic information and in their ultimate level of proficiency. Consider the following hypothetical illustration of a Hungarian family that has immigrated to Canada. We'll pretend that no members of the family have ever had much exposure to English, a highly unlikely pretension given the ubiquity of English language instruction in European schooling and also the fact that many adult immigrants to English-speaking countries nowadays are fluent in English since their status as computer programmers, engineers, etc. is the very factor that permits them to immigrate. But let's suppose that this family of Hungarians has emigrated from a rural area in western Romania to settle with relatives already residing in Alberta. Zoltan, the father, is thirty-eight; Zsuzsi, their only daughter, is eight. Suppose that both parent and child are exposed to exactly equal amounts of Hungarian and English. Half the time they hear and use Hungarian at home, and the other half of the day they are exposed to English. Zoltan works as a shipping clerk; Zsuzsi is in the third grade. After exactly one month, how much English will these two learners have acquired?

Using the five different linguistic categories listed below, think of some differences between the father's English abilities and those of his daughter. You can do this investigation by yourself or collaboratively as pair work with a colleague. For each category of contrasts, write down your answers on a sheet of paper where you have drawn two columns, using the left-hand column for Zoltan and the right-hand for young Zsuzsi. In every case, try hard to think of an English expression that one learner knows but the other probably doesn't. Of course, there would probably be a great deal of overlap for both learners, but stretch your imagination and think creatively of differences between these two learners in the types of language they encounter and pick up. For example, for the first category, *Listening Skills,* you might think of phrases like the following.

Zoltan	Zsuzsi
Hey Zolt, how's it goin?	*Hi Sweetie, how are you?*
Morning Zolt, what's new?	*Good morning Suzy.*

After you've come up with a few contrasting examples for this category, think of some more for *Speaking Skills*. Record a few English phrases that you think the father and the daughter would be able to say after a month's residence in Alberta. *Reading Skills*. Now write down names, phrases, or expressions that you'd expect Zoltan and Zsuzsi to be able to read. Don't think of newspapers and books, since their English is still limited, but what about labels on cans and boxes, street signs, billboards, restaurant names, TV shows, etc.? *Writing Skills*. Now record some examples of words or phrases these two English acquirers could write on their own. Think too about the legibility of their penmanship, their ability to produce both print and cursive, and their keyboarding skills. *Vocabulary*. What English words would you expect Zoltan to know that his daughter might not recognize? How about the reverse? Can you think of vocabulary Zsuzsi would have picked up in school that her dad would be unfamiliar with?

SUMMATION

After you have recorded your samples for each of these five categories, look back over what you have written and contrast the two columns. In a way, of course, it is an unfair comparison because the child has spent most of her "English" time in a school setting, which is specifically designed to provide language instruction for Zsuzsi and her mostly native-speaking classmates, whereas Zoltan is getting paid to work, not to learn English. Still, this imbalance helps to make the case in favor of adults more striking, because disregarding age, we'd expect the immigrant with formal language instruction to be the better learner, but this is not the way it probably turned out on your list of examples.

AGE AND SLA

Now that you've had a chance to draw up some of your own examples of differences between the kinds of English a daughter and her father would pick up after receiving comparable levels of input, here are several reasons why, all things being equal, the older learner holds the advantage.

(1) Schematic Knowledge

Zoltan has three decades more experience than his daughter, and this gives him an enormous advantage as a second language learner. Let's take a very simple example. Say that both parent and child hear or see the English word *brake* and learn that it means *fek* in Hungarian. Young Zsuzsi has only a primitive conception of "braking" because of her young age and lack of experience. For her, "braking" is essentially a synonym for "stopping." The father, conversely, immediately conjures up all sorts of experiential knowledge when confronted with this word. "Braking" can instantly trigger visual schemata of different types of braking systems (bicycles use calipers, cars and trains use drums and shoes, airplanes use spoilers and reverse thrusters, etc.). The word or concept can also evoke knowledge about the process (traffic safety, reaction times, braking distance as a function of speed and vehicular weight, etc.). All of this is to say that when we compare the consequences of acquiring a single new word in English, for Zsuzsi, they are very limited, but for her father, they are quite profound. At best, the daughter is prompted to associate *brake* with the word *stop*, but for her father, *brake* in English opens up a brave new world of terminology.

(2) Metalinguistic Knowledge

Because of his relative cognitive maturity, Zoltan also has **metalinguistic** awareness. He knows a lot about the structure of language and can use language to talk about language. Although he may not know many linguistic terms, even in his native Hungarian, he intuitively realizes that English may have homonyms, just like his mother tongue, or like Romanian, another language he knows well. Consequently, after only a few exposures to what sounds like the word *brake* in the English used by his coworkers ("Careful, Zolt, don't *break* it!"), he assumes that it doesn't mean *fek* in Hungarian but is a different word and may even be spelled differently from *brake*. Because she is still so young, Zsuzsi is only dimly aware of homonymy and so could easily be confused by the fact that the two different meanings are signaled by the same sound.

(3) Literacy Knowledge

If you look back at your examples of reading and writing, surely you will have recorded some fairly significant differences between the two learners. Hungarian and Romanian are both alphabetic languages and both use the Roman alphabet, so anyone who is literate in either of these languages can apply an enormous amount of literacy knowledge to the acquisition of English, which is an orthographic cousin to these central European languages. Even without a university education, Zoltan is much more literate in his mother tongue than his daughter, and can not only transfer his phonetic decoding ability from one language to the other, but can also transfer the vocabulary he has gained via literacy. Because of their common European heritage, both Hungarian and English contain many common "learned" words borrowed from Latin and Greek. This vocabulary is available to Zoltan, but not, by and large, to his daughter. She has not spent decades of her life decoding script, either, so her attempts to read English in school are almost as labored as her endeavors to decode Hungarian. Her father enjoys the additional benefit of having learned Romanian because they lived as part of the large Hungarian minority in Transylvania, so he has developed keen metalinguistic awareness about literacy. This prepares him in all sorts of ways to anticipate different spelling rules, to be more flexible in decoding letter-to-sound correspondences, and to make more intelligent guesses about how a word should be spelled. He also has had several decades more experience writing than his daughter, so his small motor coordination and his eye-hand movements would be much faster and more accurate. Finally, he is likely to have had some experience with a keyboard and would pick up typing skills faster than his daughter.

So are kids "better" language learners? From the short investigation of differences between an older and younger learner that you just undertook, the answer appears to be "no." What about in the long run, however? What if we came back after 30 years to this town in Alberta and reassessed their English competence? In particular, what if we examined their pronunciation? Would the now 68-year-old Zoltan still outshine his daughter?

THE CRITICAL PERIOD HYPOTHESIS

Since this area of SLA has been a particular fascination for your author, it is difficult for me to discuss it in a manner that is both brief and impartial. It is also a challenge to know where to deal with this issue in this text because it is so comprehensive; it involves people, language, attention, cognition, and even emotion, to a certain extent. I have decided to place it here, at the conclusion of this chapter on cognition, because it seems to fit most comfortably into the domain of cognitive science.

The critical period hypothesis (CPH) (already introduced in Chapter 3) contends that nature has created a narrow, temporal window of opportunity for optimal language learning, and this period usually extends only to about puberty. Once you are a teenager, so the argument goes, you will never be as good a language learner as you were when you were a child. The CPH is conceivably the most contentious issue in SLA because there is disagreement over its exact age span; people disagree strenuously over which facets of language are affected; there are competing explanations for its existence; and, to top it off, many people don't believe that it exists at all (Scovel, 2000b). As our contrastive analysis between Zsuzsi and Zoltan suggested, older learners enjoy many advantages over younger ones. However, the CPH claims that after 30 years residence in Canada, Zsuzsi's English would be ultimately superior to her father's, despite the fact that she started off with the "disadvantage" of being a child. But this was her very strength, according to the CPH.

Building on the initial ideas generated by Penfield (1963) and Lenneberg (1967), I published a set of claims about the limited but profound effects of early second language acquisition when juxtaposed against the results of later instruction (Scovel, 1969). I elaborated on these claims, the evidence to support them, and speculations about their origins in a book that appeared almost two decades later (Scovel, 1988). Because so much has been published about the CPH, and because it continues to generate great interest among some SLA researchers, let me first state my position on the topic, then contrast this with the views of others who have researched this complex phenomenon. I start with my own views not because they represent the majority viewpoint (as a matter of fact, they may depict a distinctly minority opinion), but because they have often served as the initial interpretation of the CPH and especially of the "strong" version of the theory. That is, I have continued to hold that exceptions to the CPH are exceedingly rare and that virtually all learners (not just a simple majority of learners) experience critical period constraints in their second language performance.

Before listing the different viewpoints expressed by SLA scholars, it is instructive to point out that some authors have written extensively about the critical period but appear to avoid committing themselves to any definite position. Bialystok and Hakuta (1994) and Cook (1996) have written excellent surveys of SLA, but appear to take no definitive stand on the CPH. Most people who have investigated the topic do commit themselves, though, and have aligned themselves with one of three positions.

There is a Critical Period but it is confined only to foreign accents.

This is the view suggested by Lenneberg, and one that I have espoused over the decades. There are many different sources of evidence for this version of the CPH, and they are detailed in Scovel (1988), but the quickest way to capture the essence of this approach is to consider what I call "the Joseph Conrad phenomenon." Conrad remains one of the most respected novelists of the English language, but not everyone knows that he was born in Poland and did not acquire English until he was a young man. Though he matured into such a brilliant user of the language that his writing brought him fame and financial success, his pronunciation remained decidedly nonnative throughout his life. His English vocabulary, syntax, and literacy were supranormal; his accent in the very same language, however, instantly identified him as a linguistic alien. My version of the CPH explains this massive mismatch in L2 performance by claiming that, for neurological and biological reasons, given all the right conditions, anyone can acquire the phonology of any language like a native before about the age of 12. After that age, although native-like performance is ultimately attainable in all other aspects of language acquisition, despite even the best of conditions, L2 learners will be forever constrained in their acquisition and end up with some degree of foreign accent. This, of course, does not mean they cannot be eloquent or intelligible in a foreign tongue (Henry Kissinger is just one of millions of worldwide examples), but it does mean that as soon as they start to speak, they are instantly identified as foreigners. In my view, the CPH holds only for foreign accents and is probably accounted for by neurological factors that are genetically specified in our species.

There is a Critical Period not only for accents but also for syntax.

This version is relatively recent, especially when contrasted with my version of the CPH just introduced, and again, though many have written about this particular viewpoint, it is particularly well researched and promulgated by the work of Johnson and Newport (1989) and, more recently, by Slavoff and Johnson (1995). In essence, this view holds that the most interesting maturational constraints on language acquisition are seen in the acquisition of syntax, especially the more subtle and more difficult aspects of grammar such as English determiners (*the* and *a*), and the third person singular present tense marker (*My friend loves almonds*). Johnson and her colleagues have tapped this syntactic knowledge via grammaticality judgment tests. To nonnative speakers who started learning English beginning at different ages, they give sets of sentences, many of them ungrammatical (e.g., *Tom is reading book in the bathtub*). The subjects' task is to identify which sentences are acceptable in English and which aren't. In general, the researchers found that those who acquired English before their teenage years were just as good as native speakers in separating the linguistic wheat from the chaff, whereas those who learned English after the critical period often made errors in grammaticality judgments. Several prominent figures in SLA find this evidence convincing and argue for this more general claim that the critical period extends beyond phonology and into syntax (Long, 1990; Skehan, 1998). I myself am not so persuaded that syntactic aspects of language are also constrained. Among other criticisms I have about these data is the questionability of basing evidence wholly on grammaticality judgments that seem to be highly metalinguistic, unauthentic, and affected by all sorts of non-linguistic factors (Schutze, 1998). Another problem is trying to explain why there should be age limitations in the acquisition of grammar. Since neurological explanations are clearly inadequate, some contend that once learners reach puberty, for some reason, their ability to rely on universal grammar (UG) is either lost or overridden by cognitive maturation (Bley-Vroman, 1989). But the evidence supporting this contention is weak, and there is lack of unanimity among scholars over the role UG plays in SLA, if it does at all (see Cook, 1993, Chapter 9 for a summary).

There is no Critical Period, not even for pronunciation.

We should remember, to begin with, that except for sounding like a native speaker or for acquiring high-level grammatical skills, in most facets of SLA, there seem to be no constraints at all for older learners, and, as we witnessed with the comparison between Zsuzsi and Zoltan, in the acquisition of L2 literacy, pragmatics, vocabulary, etc., adults usually surpass children. Based on this, it seems illogical that there should be a critical period for any aspect of SLA for adult learners, and that the right amount of motivation and opportunity is all that is necessary for any adult to ultimately acquire native-like syntax or pronunciation. At this point, it's essential to separate experiential evidence from experimental. Because SLA research is a science, it bases most of its claims on fair and well-controlled experiments that adhere to acceptable scientific paradigms. Personal experiences are not a valid foundation for supporting or rejecting theories, at least if we play the game according to the rules of science. So no matter how accurate or how winsome they may prove, anecdotes about adults who learned a foreign language so well that they easily passed themselves off as native speakers cannot be used as valid evidence against the CPH.

There have been, however, serious, experimental attempts to train adults in an L2 so that they sound exactly like native speakers. Early studies by Neufeld (1979) have been followed by more recent and more persuasive experiments by Bongaerts and his colleagues (Bongaerts, van Summeren, Planken, and Schils, 1997). Also, a variety of arguments and evidence can be found in an anthology edited by Singleton and Lengyel (1995). Several of these studies appear to provide strong evidence that, given precise phonetic training, or having had enough formal education and exposure to a second language, adult learners can indeed acquire a foreign language so well that when they record their voices on a tape, they can actually trick native-speaking judges into believing that they themselves are natives.

I have discussed some of the problems with this evidence in my earlier book (Scovel, 1988), and I have other concerns with the more recent work in this area. I find the data mustered by Bongaerts et alia quite compromised when we discover, on scrutinizing their results, that some of the voices of native speakers used on the tape as controls are judged nonnative by the judges. It's quite baffling when a sizable percentage of the L2 learners (the nonnative subjects in the experiment aiming for the norm) are better than the norm (the native speakers themselves)! I think what's happening here is confusion about dialects and which dialect of British English (in the case of Bongaerts' work) is to be used as a norm (Scovel, 1997). Put another way, the CPH for "foreign" accents may very well extend to dialectal accents as well. This could explain why some very good English-speaking Dutch speakers sound more like "native" British English speakers than some people who were actually born and raised in the United Kingdom.

The jury is still out as to which of these three versions (or alternative hypotheses about the CPH) is most strongly supported by the SLA evidence, and this should not be too surprising given the enormous individual variation we find among the hundreds of millions of people around the world who have become bilingual. There is universal agreement, however, even among those of us who are adherents to the first version of the CPH, that all learners can improve their ability in an L2, even if they are older adults, and even if we're only talking about pronunciation ability. This should be good news for both EFL learners and teachers. Learning an L2 is a journey, not a destination, and travel guides are always welcome!

CONCLUSION

Cognition is present in every aspect of language acquisition, and that is why this chapter, more than any other, has been so wide-ranging and, at the same time, so incomplete in its coverage. Schemata, memory, analytic styles, task-based strategies, time-limited attention, and critical periods are representative, but they barely scratch the cortical surface. All kinds of diverse learning behaviors are packaged into cognition, and so it's a little bit like a refrigerator: You never know what you'll find in it next! But we are not just cognitive animals. As the opening story of the insanely jealous husband attests, we are fueled by passions as well, and they play an equally important role in SLA. Just as E completes the spelling of the PLACE framework, so too does the next chapter on Emotion introduce the concluding component of language learning.

Suggested Readings

A scholar who has long been active in SLA research has recently written an introduction to SLA that focuses largely on the central theme of this chapter. As the title suggests, Skehan's *A Cognitive Approach to Language Learning* (1998) tries to redress the imbalance of the influence of linguistics on SLA by concentrating its text on cognitive processing and how it helps shape the course of language learning. Two chapters in a book already cited, *In Other Words* (1994) by Bialystok and Hakuta, provide a briefer review of cognition and SLA (Chapter 3, "Brain," which is really about the CPH, and Chapter 4, "Mind"). For readers who would like to delve deeper into cognition, Barsalou's *Cognitive Psychology* (1992) is a serious but understandable introduction to what we know about how the human mind works. This chapter has not even mentioned the ways that social and philosophical perspectives influence our views of cognition, but for teachers who are interested in this broader approach to human thinking and learning, Williams and Burden have published a constructivist and social interactionist perspective, *Psychology for Language Teachers* (1997). An entire issue of *Studies in Second Language Learning,* edited by Tomlin and Gernsbacher (1994), was devoted to a wide-ranging and somewhat theoretical discussion of "Cognitive foundations in second language acquisition."

It is hard to think of cognition and language and not also consider the field of psycholinguistics. There are many texts published in this field, but three that come to mind are: Berko-Gleason and Ratner (eds.), *Psycholinguistics* (1993), an anthology that delves into a variety of topics in some depth; the new edition of Carroll's *Psychology of Language* (1999), which is a lengthy, single-author text; and my own introduction, *Psycholinguistics* (Scovel, 1998), which, in contrast to the other two, is short and pithy. It is also difficult to discuss the human mind without referring to the human brain. Neurolinguistics, the field that examines how the brain processes, stores, and produces language, is an equally large field and, like psycholinguistics, has its own journals, texts, and research centers. Of the many books written about this field in the past 10 years alone, I commend two, largely because they are so different. *The Lopsided Ape* (1991) by Corballis is a sweeping review of how such diverse topics as evolution, handedness, language processing, etc. relate to the human brain. Obler and Gjerlow's *Language and the Brain* (1999) is a much shorter and more recent introduction to what we know about the brain and language processing and production (including bilingualism).

The past 20 years have witnessed a growing interest in learning styles and strategies. Three books that cover this area of cognitive pedagogy in great variety and with relatively little overlap are Oxford's *Language Learning Strategies: What Every Teacher Should Know* (1990), Reid's (ed.) *Learning Styles in the ESL/EFL Classroom* (1995), and Ehrman's *Understanding Second Language Learning Difficulties* (1996). No book does a better job of discussing the relationship of human memory to SLA than Stevick's *Memory, Meaning, and Method* (2nd edition, 1996), especially the first six chapters, and Stevick's *Working with Teaching Methods: What's at Stake?* (1998) provides much insightful discussion and many practical examples of how teachers can make language more memorable.

As already acknowledged, the Critical Period Hypothesis has been a particular interest of mine over the years, so there is much I could recommend to the interested reader. I could start with my own book, *A Time to Speak* (1988), but unfortunately it's out of print! I do have a short and recent review of many of the issues; it deals with age and acquisition and gives an overview of the CPH and other topics ("The younger, the better myth and bilingual education" in Gonzalez [ed.], *Language Ideologies: Critical Perspectives on the Official English Movement*, 2000a). For a more technical discussion of the CPH, see my article in *ARAL 2000* (Scovel, 2000b). For contrasting perspectives on the CPH, Singleton and Lengyel (eds.) have compiled a useful anthology, *The Age Factor in Second Language Acquisition* (1995).

6

EMOTION

The previous chapter began by reviewing the claim that among all the members of the animal kingdom, we are the most cognitive. Given the relative size of the human brain, and, much more important, the neurophysiological complexity of our central nervous system, especially the neocortex, almost no one would dispute the contention that we, among all animals, are the most cerebral. But it might strike you as a bit curious if, in the same breath, a similar argument were launched for classifying humans as the most emotional of all creatures. An apothegm attributed to Mark Twain helps introduce this very possibility: "Man is the only animal that blushes, or needs to!" Being "naked apes" (Morris, 1967), at least from the viewpoint of comparative primatology, our blushing is readily apparent, and from traditions as ancient as Genesis, our nakedness might very well also account for our sense of shame. It takes only a moment's reflection, then, to see that, contrary to our normal perception of ourselves as a species, we are just as emotional as we are cognitive. A superego does not preclude an id.

With the growth and popularity of cognitive psychology, researchers have not tarried long in noticing the natural connection between our enormous cognitive development as a species and the possibility that human cognition can organize and even enhance emotions. In a significant review of the psychology of emotion, Strongman (1987) introduces up to 50 competing perspectives on the nature and cause of human **affect** (the more technical term for emotions) and emphasizes throughout his text that feeling is inexorably linked to thinking in all human behavior.

The centrality of cognition in explaining emotional behavior runs counter to the popular dualism that pervades so much of our culture. The purveyors of pop psychology observe, for example, that in English we often begin an utterance with I *think*… or I *feel*…, and these pseudo-psycholinguists then go on to claim that the first phrase introduces habits of the mind whereas the second is a preface to habits of the heart. This might hold true under certain rare circumstances but, by and large, these phrases function as synonyms in English, and they share a very odd grammatical characteristic that you can try to uncover for yourself.

A THOUGHT EXPERIMENT: WHAT'S SO ODD ABOUT *I DON'T THINK* AND *I DON'T FEEL?*

Here's a little linguistic puzzle that should demonstrate to you why the English verbs *think* and *feel* are actually very similar. Because this exercise introduces one of the many ways English grammar differs from most other languages, and because these phrases are extremely common in colloquial English, you might even want to use these examples in class, if you happen to be teaching intermediate or advanced ESL students. Consider these first four sentences.

(1) She <u>says</u> she will visit San Francisco.
(2) She <u>claims</u> she will visit San Francisco.
(3) She <u>thinks</u> she will visit San Francisco.
(4) She <u>feels</u> she will visit San Francisco.

There is no problem in understanding them; the grammar seems straightforward, and the four verbs appear to function in an identical manner. When we look at the negative forms of these four utterances, however, something funny seems to be happening. The first pair, (5) and (6), mean exactly the opposite of their affirmative counterparts (1) and (2), but look carefully at (7) and (8), for they do indeed negate the meaning of (3) and (4), but in a very peculiar way.

(5) She <u>doesn't say</u> she will visit San Francisco.
(6) She <u>doesn't claim</u> she will visit San Francisco.
(7) She <u>doesn't think</u> she will visit San Francisco.
(8) She <u>doesn't feel</u> she will visit San Francisco.

If you are a native speaker of English, these phrases roll so easily off your tongue that you may have trouble detecting the difference between the first negative pairs (5 and 6) and the second (7 and 8). (One of the few advantages nonnative speakers enjoy over native speakers is that the former can often recognize patterns in a second language because they can look at the language objectively. Fish don't know that they're wet; amphibians do.) If you can't get what's happening here, go on to the next set of examples, and the discrepancy between verbs like *think* and *feel* and most other English verbs should becomes plain. Notice that (7) means exactly the same thing as (9) and (8) is identical in meaning to (10), but that (5) does *not* mean (11), nor does (6) mean (12). What on earth is going on here?

(9) She <u>thinks</u> she won't visit San Francisco.
(10) She <u>feels</u> she won't visit San Francisco.
(11) She <u>says</u> she won't visit San Francisco.
(12) She <u>claims</u> she won't visit San Francisco.

This chapter is not an introduction to English grammar, so we don't want to get mired down in syntactic explanations, but it is obvious from these examples that *think* and *feel* are very similar, because they share this strange grammatical pattern that almost no other verbs in English follow. Verbs like *say* and *claim* are normal because when they are negated, the meaning is exactly the opposite, and this, of course, is the way most verbs function in most languages. Oddly, the *thinking* verb and the *feeling* verb do not follow this pattern. If you negate them (examples 7 and 8), you still mean the subject of the sentence *thinks* or *feels*! Notice too that although (9) and (10) are grammatical, they sound a little atypical, as if spoken by a fluent ESL student, and that (7) and (8) are much preferred by native speakers of English.

All of this strongly suggests that *thinking* and *feeling* as English words are not as different as many might be led to believe. Furthermore, this might be a small piece of linguistic evidence to buttress claims by psychologists like Strongman that we are extremely emotional animals because we can think so deeply about our feelings.

MOTIVATION

Of all the affective (emotional) factors discussed over the years by both teachers and SLA researchers, by far the most predominant is the complex interplay of variables subsumed under the term "motivation." So popular is motivation as an explanation for student performance (or, more often, for lack of it) that a British psychologist has called it "the dustbin of educational psychology" (McDonough, 1981). Many a language teacher has faced an audience with an approach similar to that of the politician on the stump, who tried to enthuse his lethargic listeners with a purely rhetorical question. "My friends," the orator enjoined, "which is worse, ignorance or apathy?" After a brief pause, a voice from the crowd bellowed back, "We neither know nor care!" Again we see linguistic evidence, at least in English, of the common twinning of thoughts and feelings, or, as in this case, an unfortunate lack of both!

But emotions and motivation are not just observed by teachers and public speakers, they are felt very deeply by language learners. The following diary entries written honestly and colorfully by two equally earnest students illustrate how quickly our feelings can warm or chill our desire to pick up a new tongue. The first student's enthusiasm is balanced by the second's disheartenment. As language learners ourselves, we have probably experienced similar emotions, and the students whom we currently teach are just as likely to have shared the same sentiments in our classroom.

Learner's Account #13

I was surprised at how much better I felt having a like-minded soul with like sensibilities, a funky and hip chick next to me, signing with me for the whole class hour (one-and-a-half hours). At one point early on, she turned to me and said, "I love this class!" Her comment was infectious. Soon thereafter, I realized I too loved the class.... We learned new words, and I noticed that I enjoyed this class more than any other to date, but why? I had practiced! I had memorized the alphabet and so could ask questions in finger-spelling. I felt an overall assurance—an esteem that gave me an ease and desire to take part.

A Student of American Sign Language

Learner's Account #14

A hot day with our class in a hot room. At this moment, the last thing I want to do is to hear Japanese and actually pick it up. Just got back Quiz #7—42 out of 50 points. Not bad. I need to feel good about this because I know Quiz #8 will be worse. The woman in front of me got a 33 out of 50 [happy face!]. Competition arising perhaps? New katakana characters are being presented. The teacher is just writing them on the board and not explaining stroke order! I'll need to figure this out for myself later. She just announced the midterm would be on Monday. I'm screwed! That sinking feeling. Just went over vocabulary for Chapter 9. Lots more words to memorize. The overall feeling in class today was lazy, bored, and frustrated. I believe this was a direct effect of the heat, the fact that a midterm was mentioned, and the teacher's attitude.

A Student of Japanese

One indication of the almost obsessive preoccupation educators have about motivation is the degree to which it has been defined and redefined. In their extensive review of the literature as it pertains to SLA, Crookes & Schmidt (1991) counted up 98 definitions grouped into 9 major categories. With this many variations of a single term, it is hard to get a fix on a central and common meaning, though the majority agree that motivation deals primarily with emotions, as implied by the etymology of the word. However, here are three key characteristics of motivation that most teachers would concur with: direction, persistence, and degree of activity of the target behavior.

Almost every discussion of motivation in SLA research begins with the famous dichotomy between instrumental and integrative motivation, introduced by the Canadian scholars Gardner and Lambert (1972). Motivation that is **instrumental** refers to practical, professional, or economic reasons for studying a new language. Examples would be a Korean businessman acquiring English, a British archaeologist about to spend a year in Egypt studying colloquial Arabic, or an American Buddhist scholar learning Pali in order to enjoy direct access to religious texts.

Reasons for **integrative** motivation are more personal, the archetypal situation being when a person falls in love with and "marries" into a new language. Originally, it was assumed that integrative motivation was the more effective, even if it didn't involve falling in love, but recent work by Gardner (Gardner and MacIntyre, 1991) has revised this rather oversimplified assumption and provides experimental evidence that instrumental and integrative motivation correlate with each other to some degree when measured by self-report questionnaires given to L2 learners. In addition, it demonstrates that, all in all, it is the amount of motivation that matters, not the type.

Another motivational dichotomy that superficially resembles the well-known pair originally introduced by the Canadian researchers is Brown's differentiation between intrinsic and extrinsic motivation. Based on the work of Deci (1975) and several others, Brown (2000) defines **intrinsic motivation** as pursuing an activity such as language learning for its own sake, with the learner often incurring a sense of self-actualization or self-determination. The joy is in the journey, not the destination. **Extrinsic motivation** is just the opposite: All the rewards are outside of the language learner and external to language learning as well. As already observed, it may seem that this pairing overlaps closely with Gardner and Lambert's, but it would be misleading to simply equate intrinsic motivation with integrative, and extrinsic with instrumental. Instead, it is more helpful to consider both pairs as defining separate sets of contrasts, and then go one step further and use these terms to create a two-by-two matrix from which are generated four contrasting situations, each varying in the way it draws on different types of motivation.

Figure 6.1: Matrix Based on Brown (2000) and Gardner and Lambert (1972)

	Intrinsic	Extrinsic
Integrative	(1) marrying a speaker of another language	(2) sending your children to a heritage language school
Instrumental	(3) the hero of the movie "Breaking Away"	(4) studying a language to enhance your career

Despite the fact that this matrix neatly packages two pairs of contrasts together, two points should be kept in mind about the emotions that fuel our efforts as language learners. First, the four categories exemplified above should remind us that, like all other SLA constructs, motivation does not function like a binary bit of information—it is neither X nor Y, nor is it confined to the four-way contrast depicted here. Motivations are multiple and range along a continuum, and maybe there are indeed 98 different kinds! Second, for the purposes of illustration, motivation is boxed into distinct situations in this matrix, but we shouldn't forget that because learners' emotions constantly change, perhaps more rapidly than their cognitive states, even if the situation is held constant, as it is in the table, motivations can change within that same context. In other words, an instrumental-extrinsic learner (4) may on some days—or in some moods—feel more integrative and slide over to the instrumental-intrinsic category (3). In sum, what appears to be a fairly circumscribed and neatly labeled territory to SLA researchers is, in reality, a dynamic sea of currents, especially when it comes to emotions. Having said this, however, there are real world situations which seem to ebb and flow quite distinctly in the way L2 learners are motivated.

Situation (1) in Figure 6.1 is the easiest to imagine; it has been the source of many a novel and movie. A lonely American soldier goes off to serve his tour of duty in Korea, falls in love with a young Korean woman, gets married, and they return to the States to live and raise a family. The woman is moved to acquire English because it brings her closer to her husband and her children and because it helps her adjust and acculturate to the new land that will become her permanent home. Because this is a book about language acquisition, we will not look at a new area of research that examines the very opposite process, **language loss**, but in this scenario, it is quite possible that the woman will experience some attrition in her native Korean. This phenomenon raises many sociolinguistic and psycholinguistic questions about bilingualism (Seliger and Vago, 1991).

Situation (2) is the hardest for most people to appreciate, largely because of the apparent contradiction implied by the juxtaposition of integrative with extrinsic motivation. There are nice illustrations of this setting in countries like Canada and the United States, though, especially in the heritage language schools. Many immigrant families (like the Chinese) want their children to learn and maintain their mother tongue even though they are being raised in a virtual ocean of English. At the same time, they are wholeheartedly in support of having their kids become native speakers of English and often do not endorse bilingual education programs in the public schools. In order to preserve their Chinese-speaking heritage, these parents organize and fund their own schools (usually held on Saturday mornings and/or weekday afternoons) where their children learn Chinese within a fairly traditional curriculum.

In many ways, Saturday morning Hebrew schools for Jewish children preparing for their religious rite of passage could be placed in the same box as heritage language schools. Note that from the learner's perspective, that is, from the viewpoint of the kids themselves, the motivation is mixed. It is clearly integrative, because even the most recalcitrant child realizes that the L2 experience is not for fame and fortune but to forge family links. On the other hand, the motivation is definitely extrinsic because it's the parents, not the children, who have created the program and have compelled their offspring to attend. They, of course, would much rather spend their Saturday mornings mall-crawling with their friends or slumped on a couch playing video games at home!

The third situation is also a bit unusual. In the movie "Breaking Away," a teenager growing up in a college town in Indiana has just graduated from high school and is trying to find himself. He gets caught up in bicycle racing and starts training madly, fueled by images of his heroes, the Italian road racers who dominate the sport, at least at that time. He starts learning and speaking Italian, much to the consternation of his Midwestern-values father who feels that his son should stick to "American." Here we have the somewhat unusual juxtaposition of integrative and extrinsic motivation. Italian is used as a vehicle to the subculture of road racing, not as a bridge to Italian people and culture. But no one is forcing our hero to acquire the language except the boy himself; for him, the language is tied to his success as a bike racer and is thus linked to self-actualization and self-esteem.

Situation (4), like the first one, is almost a stereotype of the "foreign language as an instrument" approach and is easier to envision than (2) and (3), for instrumental and extrinsic motivation are often lumped together, although as we have just witnessed, this certainly is often not accurate. There are literally tens of millions of people who exemplify this fourth type of learning in just one country alone! In contemporary China, a considerable minority of the populace is enthusiastically seizing the opportunity to study English, not because everyone nurtures warm feelings for English-speaking cultures (in fact, for some individuals, the sentiments are decidedly negative), but because they have utilitarian motives. English will give them a high-paying job with a joint venture firm or an ability to read widely in the technical literature of their chosen profession. For most of these people, courses in general English are required by their company, their school, or their governmental office, so the impetus for acquiring this foreign language comes from outside and above them.

Again, as mentioned in the introduction to these four situations, learners can vacillate among these emotions, so it's entirely possible that many Chinese start to develop intrinsic motives too. Chinese engineering students might get personally excited about improving their English after being introduced to the world-wide web, so if we follow any L2 learner over the years, we see a natural ebb and flow of different motivating forces. That is why a static depiction such as this matrix only hints at the range of ways in which motivation can influence the course of interlanguage development.

In all of the discussion thus far, motivation is seen as primary and deterministic; it is the egg that hatches the chicken. But is it possible to reverse this perspective and view the language learning experience as the chicken that lays the egg of motivation? In an article that summarizes several diary studies written by people while they were studying a new language, Bailey (1983) (who included excerpts from her own SLA journal) suggests that language learners may very well be self-fulfilling prophets when it comes to SLA. Those with a successful self-image enter a new language classroom with confidence and the expectation that they will succeed. Conversely, those who may have experienced difficulty in previous attempts to acquire a new tongue often begin their L2 studies with a poor self-image, at least in terms of language acquisition. It is but a short step from Bailey's contrasting self-images to motivation. One would assume that learners with former SLA experiences that were positive would have a successful self-image and would begin a new language with confidence and with motivation. Of course, to be fair, the reverse would hold for individuals at the other end of the spectrum.

Hermann's (1980) **Resultative Hypothesis**, introduced in Chapter 2, draws all these speculations together into a formal claim about language learners. In a nutshell, the hypothesis contends that success in L2 classrooms fosters increased motivation in any subsequent language learning. Several studies have corroborated this claim. To cite one, Strong (1983) discovered that the Spanish-speaking children who did well in ESL classrooms were also more positive in their attitudes toward English speakers and generated more contacts with English-speaking students. Remember Gardner's claim that it is the overall amount, not necessarily the type, of motivation that counts most in SLA. If this is true, the studies by Bailey, Strong, and others that support the Resultative Hypothesis indicate that, irrespective of what combination of motivations learners may harbor at any one time in their L2 acquisition, the impact of positive past experiences can be highly motivating. As language teachers, we cannot change our students' pasts, but at the very least, we can create opportunities for successful self-images, and this should result in more highly motivated learners in the future. To paraphrase the quip tossed back at the politician who had asked his audience about ignorance and apathy, when language learners *know* (the language), they *care* (about learning even more).

For more on Hermann's Resultative Hypothesis, see p. 32.

QIN HAIHUA

In my own Teacher's Voice at the end of Chapter 1, I briefly shared with you accounts of two different students. Carlos and Minami were their pseudonyms, but they were very real students with very different life experiences and motivations. Over the years, I have taught literally thousands of "Carloses" and "Minamis," and I have often wondered about the types and degrees of motivation they bring to my classroom. I have no SLA evidence to confirm this, but from my long career as a language teacher and my somewhat shorter experience as a learner of other languages, I sense that of the five major components of SLA discussed in this book, Emotion is the single most influential, although, of course, it is shaped and sharpened by many other factors. As a teacher, I like to think that I have some control over my students' motivation, but when reflecting back on my term-to-term experiences, and on the Carloses and Minamis I have taught, I must admit I tend to harbor the suspicion that my in-class influence is fairly minimal.

Several years ago, my son and I were competing in the same triathlon, and he was waiting patiently for me at the finish line, having completed the race as one of the fastest competitors an hour earlier than I. He greeted me with a broad smile and, half in jest but half in honest resignation, he looked at me almost with compassion and said, "Dad, you can't put in what God left out!" Maybe this is equally true for motivation. I do not wish to connote a sense of negative fatalism here, for there are many students who walk into our ESL classrooms fired with a passion to learn the language. Here is the voice of one such remarkable learner, Qin Haihua, now a teacher at Nanjing Normal University.

Teachers' Voices

Qin Haihua

To me, English means something new, something out of my reach that I would like to know about. In secondary school, English was my favorite and best subject. I was a science student at that time, and university English departments are usually only open to arts students. However, in 1990, the English Department of the University of Nanjing began to enroll science students. So I chose this department without hesitation. I majored in English language and literature. I have to say that I am not qualified to be called an English-literature major, because the literature I have read is too limited; but all the same, English has brought me a new world.

With the study of English, I have access to something foreign, something new to me that I have never known before. For example, there are so many interesting foreign customs. Valentine's is such a beautiful day, not only for lovers, but also for friends and relatives. And I will never forget the Christmas Eve of 1991 when we 10 girls, in white, stood in a row, holding candles in our hands and singing "Silent night, holy night." The lights were all out, the audience so quiet; I was lost in the calm and peaceful night and felt such a soothing feeling I have never felt before. When I read *The Gadfly*, I burst into tears when Arthur and his girlfriend bade each other farewell. In *A Passage to India*, my mind went along with Aziz's uncontrolled emotions of warmth and friendliness and coldness and hatred. There is so much flavor that I could not know if I did not know English. Nor would I have had a friendly conversation with an old Australian lady about the chrysanthemums in the warm sunshine....

Many of my former college classmates are now working in foreign trade companies, banks, insurance companies, and so on. They are making money because these are all profitable jobs. But I don't think they are using much English except for some simple business correspondence. What is the point of spending four years studying and then giving up English almost completely after graduation? My classmates have abandoned their specialization, nor are they well qualified in the fields in which they are now working because they did not study them when there were in university.

Maybe I am quite wrong to be thinking this way. If English is no more than a tool, why should I stick to it and become a tool of a tool? One should be clever enough to make use of it. Now that the chief criterion for success is how much money a person can earn, I clearly belong to the unsuccessful group. Maybe I should drop teaching English and go for a job that will make me "successful." But I always hold the idea that English is a friend I cannot easily desert, one that has opened a new and attractive world for me. Many people disagree, and it is difficult to say which of us is right, for we clearly have different standards of judgment.

There is much to reflect on in what this teacher has voiced. One of the first things to strike you about Haihua's writing is her eloquence in English—a language she learned in a foreign setting with limited opportunity to interact with native speakers. Of direct relevance to the topic just discussed is the question of what kind of motivation (or motivations) this learner has experienced. But more profound issues abound. The impact of singing in a new language—candles, choirs, and Christmas: what a marvelous illustration of episodic memory! The impact of literature—to read about characters who never lived and yet to nurse feelings for them as if they were intimate colleagues. The metaphor of English as a tool and of an English learner being a tool of a tool. The metaphor of English as a friend.

What about your classroom? What emotions do your students feel? What emotions do you yourself experience as a teacher for an hour, for a day, or even for a career?

ANXIETY

Second only to motivation, anxiety is the most talked about emotion in the field of language learning and teaching, but I feel it is the most misunderstood affective variable of all. To begin with, I think that part of this misunderstanding stems from the way in which the general public uses this term as a synonym for fear or phobia, but to be rigorous, anxiety should be distinguished from these more powerful emotions. Fears are natural and normal: Fear of falling is innate and very useful in helping to preserve our species. Phobias are unnatural and very rare: Acrophobia is a pathological fear of falling. **Anxiety** is most accurately used to describe a vague sense of unease. Unlike the other two emotions, it is usually not triggered by a specific stimulus, and both self-report and physiological measures reinforce our anecdotal observations that anxiousness is not as strong an affective response as fear or phobia.

When we look at anxiety in relation to language teaching, we tend to encounter, most unfortunately, an overly simplistic approach to this affective variable. Many of the "humanistic" methods that were especially popular in the sixties and seventies made the assumption that anxiety was a single psychological construct and invariably had a negative effect on learning. It was generally believed that the more teachers did to try to eliminate this emotion from the classroom, the better things would be for the students. There have even been a few SLA researchers who have made the same assertion. Krashen (1982) holds that all L2 input is funneled through what he calls an "affective filter" that, when raised, can constrict the flow of language input to the learner. According to this affective filter hypothesis, an emotion like "high" anxiety can impede language acquisition, but, to quote directly, "low anxiety appears to be conducive to second language acquisition, whether measured as personal or classroom anxiety" (Krashen, 1982:31). The following entry from a language learning diary seems to illustrate the point Krashen is making, although given that the student is describing the last hour of a three-hour evening foreign language class, one wonders if fatigue and not anxiety is the feeling that actually overwhelms her here!

Learner's Account #15

The third hour is when I got completely lost. Although I understood the lesson while it was being presented, absolutely none of it stuck. I had reached a saturation point and dreaded continuing with such complex material after so much expended effort. Fear and anxiety converted to anger, agitation, resistance, and clock watching. I was even forgetting material I had performed well at the beginning of class, confusing "watashi wa" with "kochira wa," and staring blankly when the instructor called on me.

A Student of Japanese

I have long argued that to view anxiety as an enemy of language acquisition is unreasonable, inaccurate, and indefensible (Scovel, 1978; 1991). Other SLA scholars have expressed similar opinions that anxiety should be viewed more broadly (Scarcella and Oxford, 1992; Ehrman, 1996). Returning to Kleinmann's 1977 study of avoidance, which was introduced in Chapter 3, part of his research dealt with the potential effects of affect on the English learned by his Arabic- and Spanish-speaking ESL students. Among the tests he administered to his students was a self-report measure designed to reveal their degree of **facilitating anxiety**. On the self-report test, this is equated with the tendency of students to agree with such statements as "Nervousness while using English helps me to do better." You may recall that Kleinmann's study revealed that, for the most part, his ESL students displayed a strong inclination to avoid using syntactic structures in English that differed demonstrably from the grammar of their mother tongue. There were exceptions, however. Some Arabic learners tried to employ expressions in English that were markedly different from Arabic, and some of the Spanish-speaking students behaved in a similar way. When Kleinmann correlated the avoidance behavior of all his students with the results of the self-report anxiety test, he discovered a revealing pattern.

For Kleinmann's study, see pp. 58–63.

Table 6.1: Correlations Between Measures of Anxiety and Avoidance Behavior
(Adapted from Kleinmann, 1977 and Scovel, 1978)

Language	Anxiety Type	Use of English structures normally avoided by the Spanish speakers	Use of English structures normally avoided by the Arabic speakers
Spanish speakers	Facilitating	p<.01 correlation	no correlation
	Debilitating	no correlation	no correlation
Arabic speakers	Facilitating	no correlation	p<.05 correlation
	Debilitating	no correlation	no correlation

A quick glance at this table shows that, in general, anxiety shows few correlations with avoidance behavior among the two different groups of ESL students, and none of the students who scored high on debilitating anxiety revealed significant correlation coefficients. But look at the two groups of students who self-reported themselves as high facilitating anxiety types. For the Spanish speakers, these students were the exceptions who tried *not* to avoid English structures usually avoided by the Spanish speakers. In other words, these students were the rare ones who tried to use English patterns that differed demonstrably from their native Spanish. Likewise, the Arabic students who scored high on facilitating anxiety also were exceptional; they were the few Arabic speakers who tried to tackle the more difficult patterns of English. Do these data then tell us that anxiety is the enemy of the language learner or the classroom? No. Most teachers want their ESL students to attempt difficult structures in English, especially high intermediate level students like the ones Kleinmann was teaching. Students normally avoid such structures because, for one thing, it allows them to be more accurate. But avoidance is clearly a flight response and a strategy that ultimately delays acquisition. All in all, the table validates the positive role anxiety can play in the language classroom, and this finding is reinforced by other anxiety studies of ESL and foreign language learners (Scovel, 1978).

Were anxiety as simple as many would like to believe, a description of this pervasive emotion would end right here, but like so many psychological constructs, the more we examine it, the more complicated it gets. Despite the efforts of some SLA scholars to make sense of the anxiety research (Horwitz and Young, 1991), our understanding of its relationship to language learning is mostly piecemeal and pales in perceptiveness when compared with the work done by applied psychologists in other fields, most notably, sports psychology. The following study is revealing in that it identifies yet another pair of contrasts, and it nicely illustrates the way that anxiety is neither good nor bad when it comes to human behavior; it remains a natural emotion that plays varying roles on the emotional stage of our life.

Sonstroem and Bernado (1982) wanted to study the effects of anxiety on sports performance, and like all good researchers, they began by narrowing down their domain of inquiry. Specifically, they settled on a longitudinal study that focused on the effects of two different anxiety types on basketball performance over time. Before the season began, they gave self-report anxiety questionnaires to a group of college-level women basketball players and used the results to categorize all of the athletes into one of three categories. **High trait anxiety** players were those whose natural personality trait was to be "Nervous Nellies," the fidgety nail-biters who seem always worried about something. Another third were the "what, me worry?" **low trait anxiety** types who seemed to be always composed. The final third, as you may imagine, were **moderate trait anxiety** types whose responses placed them in the golden mean.

The investigators then waited until the end of the basketball season to collect their next data, which were based entirely on information the coaches provided. This information came in two forms. First, they asked the coaches to divide all of the playing time each athlete had into three situations depending on the **state anxiety**—the amount of anxiety induced by the situation itself, irrespective of individual differences in personality. The conditions were: low state anxiety, where there was very little pressure on any of the players (e.g., the beginning of games or the end of games where the outcome was clearly in one team's favor), moderate state anxiety, where there was increasing pressure (e.g., at the end of a game where it might have been possible for the losing team to catch up), and finally high state anxiety, where the pressure and excitement were almost overwhelming (e.g., the score was tied with only a minute left in overtime). The second kind of data they garnered from the coaches was an objective measure of each player's performance in each of the three "state anxiety" conditions, based on a complex formula that took into account the number of points scored, rebounds made, and so forth, per minute of playing time. Thus, at the end of the season, Sonstroem and Bernardo came up with the following graph that caught all the variables they had quantified for the players during the season.

Figure 6.2: Basketball Ability and Anxiety (Sonstroem and Bernado, 1982)

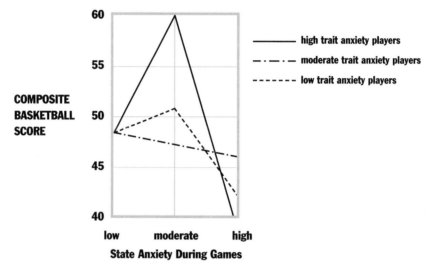

The lack of simple linearity and the disparity among the slopes of the performance lines in this graph immediately demonstrate that no simple correlations between anxiety and athletic performance obtain here. Further, at least in the realm of sports psychology, anxiety does not necessarily inhibit performance. The up-then-down slopes depicted in this graph are a common phenomenon in psychology and are referred to as the inverted U curve (or, sometimes, the inverted J curve). Because the data in this study are limited to only three points on the graph and are linear, not geometric, the results only very crudely represent an inverted U curve. Nonetheless, all of this confirms the **Yerkes-Dodson law of arousal**, which is used to name phenomena of this sort. It holds that psychological arousal initially increases behavioral performance up to a certain point, after which there is a rapid decline (Ehrman, 1996). Psychologists like to capture this concept with the folksy aphorism, "The same heat that hardens the egg melts the butter." Although additional factors can vitiate the generalizability of this "law," the data presented in this graph seem to fit, assuming that arousal and anxiety can be considered emotional equivalents in this context. In sports psychology, there have been many attempts to use the Yerkes-Dodson theory (usually under the rubric of "Peak Performance") to enhance athletic performance, and it has even been extended to self-help programs. The potential exists for adopting peak performance even into language classrooms.

Returning to the graph, what kind of trait anxiety typifies the best basketball players, at least among female athletes? Notice that there is no clear-cut answer. Put another way, the question is inappropriate. A better tack to adopt in addressing these data is to ask, in which situation does each type of trait anxiety excel? From the graph, we see that the high trait anxiety players are by far the superior performers under moderate and even low state anxiety conditions. The moderate trait anxiety athletes outperform all their peers under high state conditions. Even the low trait anxiety types, who lack so little internal arousal that they appear to be motivational tortoises, eventually win the race against the high trait rabbits under high state anxiety conditions. The high trait players have such an enormous fall-off under stressful conditions that the lowly low trait athletes can outperform them in this particular setting.

Granted, it is a giant leap from studying basketball performance to trying to replicate this experiment with language learners, even if we substituted TOEFL scores for the composite basketball numbers. But it would be extremely surprising if trait and state anxiety didn't play similar roles in terms of language acquisition performance, and in the future, SLA researchers might profit from trying to adapt research designs from other areas of applied psychology so that learners and teachers can gain a deeper appreciation of the complex role that anxiety plays in human learning and skilled performance. In sum, anxiety can be a significant player in the game of language acquisition, but its effects are neither simple nor solely negative.

6.1 *EXAMPLES OF MOTIVATION AND ANXIETY IN YOUR CLASSROOM*

By now you can see that the research in SLA and related disciplines introduced in this chapter goes against the popular beliefs of many language teachers. Typically, we think of motivation and anxiety as single concepts. Typically, we also think of motivation and anxiety as either present or absent in any given learning situation. And, again typically, we like to believe that motivation is "good" and anxiety is "bad."

> Your task in this investigation is to sit down with a partner and discuss your responses to the two numbered topics below. What examples, experiences, and perspectives dealing with emotions in the classroom do the two of you have in common? What are some ways in which the two of you differ, and why? If you are teaching and have the time and interest to involve your students in a formal survey about the role of emotions, Brown (1989;1991) has developed and adapted several questionnaires that you can give to your students (or teaching colleagues) to help measure the effect of affect and personality on the learning of a new language.

(1) Motivation is usually thought of as a good thing. In other words, only when it is absent is it viewed as potentially debilitating. But have you ever had students who seemed to be fueled by *negative* motivation?

What exactly was going on? Consider the way motivation relates back to some of the social variables we discussed earlier in this book (e.g., culture shock and acculturation). What can you as a teacher do to motivate students more positively in the language classroom?

(2) First, share with your discussion partner some memories or experiences you have had with the *positive* effects of anxiety on performance in sports, music, or a similar area in your life. Performers of all kinds experience anxiety, although they tend to describe their feelings with lots of different words—"excitement," "nervousness," "butterflies in the stomach," etc. During the performance, this affective arousal is very often described with positive and facilitating imagery—"in the zone," "runner's high," "second wind," etc. Athletes, musicians, and other performers frequently view "anxiety" as something that enables them to reach peak performances. Now, with your partner, try to think of ways "anxiety" can enhance the "performance" of your students. Can ESL students ever feel that they can be "in the zone"? Can there be a "learner's high"? Even a "teacher's high"?

EMPATHY

At first blush it may seem that empathy, the ability to "walk in someone else's shoes," is a warm and fuzzy sentiment unrelated to the task of picking up a new language, especially within the confines of an academic classroom. However, like so many affective factors, it deserves our consideration. For one thing, one of the benefits language teachers in training can gain from studying a foreign language is that they can reawaken their previous experiences as language students and can develop a greater empathy for the social, linguistic, attentional, cognitive, and emotional challenges all learners of a new tongue experience. The following journal excerpt well attests to such a benefit.

Learner's Account #16

I bonded with another classmate during the break about our humiliating experience last week. She too had believed herself quickly adept at language and was shown her place. We both agreed that our empathy toward our own students had risen dramatically. Often, teaching class, I wonder how it is my students just don't get it; now I have a much better idea.

A Student of Japanese

Another way of considering the role of empathy in SLA is to view it as a stage in the process of acculturation. Scarcella and Oxford (1992) discuss four levels of increasing cultural awareness that are related to the overall development of foreign language students, and they name their highest and fullest level of cultural sensitivity "empathy." Like all the other terms used in this book, though, it helps to begin the discussion by narrowing down the range of meanings that appear in general usage and by adopting a definition that has been carefully framed by people who have expended considerable effort in studying the construct. In the somewhat cold terminology of psychiatry, **empathy** has been pedantically and ponderously defined as "a process of comprehending in which a temporary fusion of self-object boundaries, as in the earliest pattern of object relations, permits an immediate emotional apprehension of the affective experience of another, this sensing being used by the cognitive functions to gain understanding of the other" (Guiora, 1965).

Whew! More tersely, and perhaps more precisely, empathy refers to "the permeability of ego boundaries." As is true of all emotional behavior, there are extremes. Normal empathy ranges in the middle, but an almost complete lack of empathy can be found in sociopaths, who are trapped by an inability to share feelings outside of themselves. But you can also have too much of a good thing, for if ego boundaries are completely permeable, it is hard to tell where you as an individual end and another personality begins. What does the SLA research tell us about how the normal range of empathy between these two extremes might affect language learning performance?

The most well-known study on the relationship between empathy and SLA performance was undertaken by a team of researchers at the University of Michigan in the early seventies. Guiora, Beit-Hallahmi, Brannon, Dull, and Scovel (1972) attempted to quantify empathy and correlate it with pronunciation accuracy in an elaborate and well-funded experiment. A key challenge to investigating any emotional variable is being able to measure it with numbers. For the anxiety studies, we could see that most investigators tapped this emotion by asking subjects to self-report their own perceptions, to "take your emotional temperature" (Oxford, 1990:167), but this is a highly subjective way of quantifying affect. Although there are several tests of a subject's empathy awareness used by psychologists, they too are fairly subjective or difficult to use with language students who have not had extensive training in counseling.

For this reason, Guiora, who headed the team, decided to develop a "transpositional" research design. In essence, **transpositional research** is an attempt to bridge the gap between the abstract world of beliefs and the observable world of behavior by using an intermediary measure that is both quantifiable and presumed to be linked directly to the abstract construct. This kind of experimentation attempts to wed the two historical poles of psychology, introspection and behaviorism. Based on his own research experience and that brought to his team by other members, Guiora chose alcohol as the transpositional measure for an elaborate experiment designed to correlate empathy and success in language learning. Because of its neurochemical effects on the nervous system, one of the consequences of alcohol ingestion is a release of inhibitions that normally suppress empathy to some degree. (At least this is one popular psychological explanation for the popularity of this drug.) If this is true, where alcohol is given in moderation, empathy should be increased in concert with the amount of alcohol administered, and careful and well-measured administration of alcohol could serve as the transpositional instrument for determining the degree of empathy a language learner possessed. But how can you quantify SLA, or more precisely, which aspect of language acquisition would be most affected by empathy?

Again, the scientific tradition dictates that researchers delimit the domain as much as possible. Based partly on his own experience as a fluent polyglot, Guiora felt that empathy would most tightly correlate with accuracy in pronunciation. Intuitively, it seems logical that of all the various skills one needs to master in acquiring a foreign language, learners who are especially empathetic would be the ones most likely to *sound* authentic in a new tongue. Skills such as vocabulary acquisition and grammatical competence seem to correlate more closely with linguistic and cognitive precocity, but it is reasonable to assume that someone who can "feel with" a speaker of another language would also be able to model the voice characteristics of that speaker more accurately.

Since I was fortunate enough to be a member of Guiora's team, serving as the linguist and language learning consultant, it was largely my responsibility to come up with a satisfactory foreign language pronunciation measure. We wanted to ensure that our subjects had not had previous exposure to the language we had chosen for them to learn. After all, if we were to measure pronunciation accuracy in French, there would be a good chance that some had already studied this language; consequently, their fluency would reflect their educational experience, not their emotional talents. Fortunately, I had lots of experience with Thai and would be returning to Thailand shortly after the experiment, so it would be easy for me to recruit native speakers to judge the pronunciation performance of the subjects. Additionally, Thai is tonal and has other phonetic features that make it relatively challenging for English speakers to acquire, and because the majority of students at the University of Michigan had never heard of it, let alone studied it, Thai was chosen as our dependent variable to determine if empathy did indeed increase pronunciation accuracy.

I developed a detailed linguistic measure that used tape-recorded attempts by the subjects to replicate Thai phrases of various lengths which they heard via headsets. Native speakers of Thai then graded each syllable of the subjects' attempts on the basis of several phonetic categories, and the combined scores for each subject served to rank them according to their pronunciation accuracy. This ranking was then correlated with a separate ranking of the subjects determined by their amount of empathy, or to be more accurate, the amount of alcohol they had ingested.

One of the intriguing aspects of conducting SLA research is that problems arise from the most unpredictable and surprising sources. The decision about the amounts of alcohol we were to use is an apt example. The actual measurements to be used were not in dispute; abundant research and ethical protocols helped to determine the actual amounts to be given to different groups of subjects (one, one and a half, two, and three ounces in a mixed drink). The challenge lay in coming up with a placebo drink to avoid the so-called "cocktail party" effect. Empathy might be heightened simply by having subjects mingle in a social situation that replicated a party. In other words, how could we tell whether it was the alcohol (our controlled independent variable) or the conviviality (an uncontrolled and intervening variable) that accounted for the presumed increase in empathy in our participants? To counter this possibility, we decided that everyone would get a drink, but only some would get a placebo, and during an unanticipated number of Friday afternoons, our team gathered to sip various foul-tasting concoctions, until one of the members created an alcohol-free mixture that was indistinguishable from the more potent drinks to be apportioned.

Two other alcohol-related factors had to be controlled for in our experimental design. Obviously, this chemical affects the mind and the body in many ways other than its reputed effect on empathy, and since pronunciation does involve neuromuscular control, we knew there was going to be a trade-off between the facilitating empathetic effects and the debilitating loss of synaptic functioning. Since we couldn't prevent this loss of neuromuscular programming, we decided at least to measure it, using the digit-symbol test, a simple measure of both mental acuity and writing speed. We assumed that the digit-symbol data would provide a base line against which we could separate out the gradual decline of mental and physical skills from the hopefully beneficial effects of empathy on L2 pronunciation.

One more addition to our experimental design, which at the time appeared to be almost trivial, turned out to be the factor that completely confounded this entire, meticulously prepared enterprise. Subjects were screened for gender (this study involved only males) and other factors such as weight. A one-ounce drink would clearly have less of an effect on a 220-pound person than someone half this size. We also selected out the few candidates who had had some experience with the Thai language. We also gave each person who was selected a set of instructions about when to come to the experiment. We arranged to have the subjects arrive in cohorts so that we could effectively dispense the drinks, keep surreptitious records of who got what, and then run them through the digit-symbol test and record their attempts to pronounce Thai. Knowing that the effects of alcohol are also mitigated by food in the stomach, we asked each subject in the instructions not to have anything to eat for several hours before arriving at the site of the experiment. As part of the check-in process, however, among other things, we noted whether or not the subjects had adhered to our enjoinder to avoid eating. Not too surprisingly, we discovered that about half the subjects had eaten something (mostly light snacks), but quite surprisingly, this insignificant fact turned out to have major repercussions in the way the experiment was written up and the way the results have been perceived for decades after!

Several months after the experiment was completed, I was able to mail back the scores from the pronunciation evaluations that I had supervised after my return to Thailand, and the data were collated, a statistical analysis was run, and the study was eventually published a year later. The data that garnered all of the attention are depicted in the following figure. Even the lay public learned about the study because it was written up in the first issue of *Psychology Today* with a headline that shamelessly testified to the American public's fascination with style over substance. The story about the empathy experiment was titled "Thai-ing one on!" And to this day, this study is known in SLA lore as the experiment that "proved" that a little nip can help you improve your accent in a foreign language. Many otherwise objective and reputable reviews of SLA research (e.g. Bialystok and Hakuta, 1994) have perpetuated the myth that Guiora and his colleagues demonstrated that empathy via alcohol improves pronunciation, and based on the following graph, the claim at first appears to be justified.

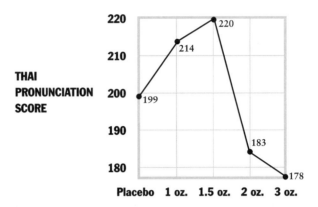

Figure 6.3: Thai Pronunciation and Alcohol Consumption After Ingestion of Sugar
(adapted from Guiora et alia, 1972:425)

The dramatic rise and fall of the Thai scores in this figure evoke memories of inverted U curves and the Yerkes-Dodson law. The rise in scores with increasing amounts of alcohol ingestion strongly suggests that an increase in empathy does correlate with improved pronunciation ability in a new language, especially if contrasted with the results of the digit-symbol test (which are not depicted here). In all cases, not surprisingly, the subjects in the experiment experienced a decline in their digit-symbol scores, with the "placebos" scoring highest on this measure and the "three-ouncers" scoring most poorly. The gradual and inevitable demise of psychomotor abilities with ingestion of increasing amounts of alcohol, as documented by the digit-symbol scores, eventually overcomes the apparent beneficial effects of empathy in the pronunciation scores, and that is why, about half-way across the graph, the Thai scores start to plummet. Psychomotor loss overcomes empathy's gain. This graph has created the myth surrounding this famous alcohol and empathy experiment, but it is just part of the story.

The other half of the story begins with the title of this graph. Notice that it refers to the effects of alcohol on L2 pronunciation *after ingestion of sugar* (n.b., "sugar" refers to the food that some of the subjects had eaten as a snack some time before the experiment). This graph reports on only a little over half of the subjects (47, to be exact). What happened to the other subjects, and why did the eating of snacks suddenly appear as a major variable in this study? It turns out that after the original statistical analysis was run, the increasing amounts of alcohol ingested had no statistically significant effect on the Thai pronunciation scores, at least not when all of the subjects were lumped together. Because this had been a well-funded study, and because the research team felt that their intuitions about the potential relationship empathy and SLA performance were justified, they performed an ex post facto analysis of the data looking for clues they had possibly missed in the first round of analysis. (Because I was now living in Thailand, I was no longer an active participant in the study.) It was here that the team discovered that the subjects could be divided into two fairly equal subgroups: the 40 who obeyed our instructions and did not have any snacks before the experiment, and those who did not and had something to eat (the 47 people whose performance is recorded in Figure 6.3). The 40 who had followed instructions were reported on in this second graph (Figure 6.4).

Figure 6.4: Thai Pronunciation and Alcohol Ingestion on Totally Empty Stomachs
(adapted from Guiora et alia, 1972:425)

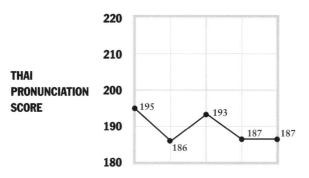

The results depicted here suggest a very different picture about the way empathy via alcohol might affect the course of SLA pronunciation. Clearly, there is nothing resembling the Yerkes-Dodson law, and the results of the Thai test mirror almost exactly the results of the symbol-digit tests for all the subjects; there is a general decrement in performance with increasing amounts of alcohol ingestion. If we combine the results of both figures into one pool of data (which was the original design of the study), it is evident that the performance of the subjects depicted in Figure 6.4 washed out the desired results that were achieved by the subjects in Figure 6.3. In other words, if we look at all 87 subjects together, there is no statistically significant effect of alcohol (empathy) on SLA performance. The 1972 article offered an attempt to justify the sudden imposition of the snack vs. no snack condition as a major variable in this otherwise elaborately planned experiment, but the justification is vitiated by the fact that the subjects who disobeyed the instructions they were given are the very ones who are promoted as the exemplars of the research hypothesis. There's a saying among statisticians that if you torture the data enough, they will admit to anything!

So what conclusions can be drawn from this comparatively lengthy analysis of a single and rather dated exploration into one emotional variable? First, even among academicians, interesting results often garner much more attention than authentic results. The idea that a margarita can help your Spanish or sake can improve your Japanese is much more marketable than the notion that empathy is a difficult construct to measure. Second, even well-funded studies conducted by experienced and well-intentioned scholars and published in well-respected journals are open to question. Ultimately, we are all our own experts when it comes to applied science, and SLA research is no exception. Third, as acknowledged in both the design and the interpretation of this experimental study, surprises can happen, and sometimes they turn out to be more consequential than all of the pedestrian and unsurprising planning that goes into an experiment in the first place. Finally, it is my personal opinion that Guiora's basic premise is correct—that empathy, abstract and difficult to verify though it may be, is closely related to pronunciation accuracy. I base this completely on the intuitions I have gleaned from my experiences as a language learner and teacher.

In my view, this particular study failed not because the fundamental hypothesis was wrong, but because alcohol has too many confounding effects to be used as an appropriate instrument for transpositional research. One exciting possibility for future SLA inquiries is the development of an experiment that might ultimately bridge the link between empathy and language learning which Guiora and his colleagues had tried so desperately to forge.

OTHER AFFECTIVE VARIABLES

Motivation, anxiety, and empathy are the emotions that have dominated this chapter because they have tended to preoccupy language teachers the most or have attracted the most publicity. But just as cognitive processes, styles, and strategies vary, emotions differ enormously too. A variety of affective factors have been discussed by SLA researchers: self-esteem (Brown, 2000), tolerance of ambiguity (Ehrman, 1996), risk-taking (Larsen-Freeman and Long, 1991), extroversion and introversion (Torkelson, 1995), and even the Myers-Briggs personality test (Carrell and Monroe, 1995). Investigations into the possible relationship between these emotions and success in SLA have been even more speculative, more conflicting, and less clear-cut than the research already reviewed or cited concerning "the big three" affective variables that were discussed earlier in this chapter.

Skehan (1989) does a thorough job of covering many of these studies and, in general, finds them wanting. For instance, it is often assumed that people with more outgoing and extroverted personalities will be more successful language learners, in part because their sociability will place them in situations where they will naturally be exposed to more L2 input than introverted learners (Seliger, 1983). Skehan found that, like the myth that anxiety is invariably debilitating, the belief that extroversion is a facilitating trait lacks consistent support. Compared to the majority of studies done on social, linguistic, or cognitive factors affecting interlanguage development, research on affective variables is less credible. This does not mean that emotions are not as important in influencing SLA as other topics introduced in this book, but it does suggest that they are harder to define and more difficult to investigate, at least within the confines of applied linguistics and psychology. The study conducted by Guiora et alia is an excellent case in point. Their work failed to prove that empathy correlates with success in acquiring a new phonology; nevertheless, since this failure could very well be the result of flaws in the experimental design, it is possible that empathy *is* linked to L2 pronunciation success, even though this was not demonstrated scientifically.

Stefanie Brown has been teaching mostly Mexican-American students in a central California middle school for several years, and during this time has experienced "a variety of challenges and joys, both expected and unexpected" (to use her own words). Despite the fact that this book focuses on the learner and learning and, in this particular chapter, on how the emotions of the learner affect what the student learns, teachers also have emotions, believe it or not, and these emotions naturally influence and are influenced by the feelings of their students. This interaction is usually much more intense with teachers like Stefanie because those who instruct younger children spend many more hours a day with their pupils than those who teach adults. And feelings like motivation, anxiety, and empathy are more apparent in classrooms like Stefanie's where there is an unusually large number of socioeconomically disadvantaged children. Listen to this account about one of her students, and consider the interchange of emotions that both "Gloria" and her sensitive and sensible teacher brought to the classroom.

Stefanie Brown

Gloria (name changed to protect her identity) arrived in my seventh grade science class nine weeks after the school year began. She had only been in this country for three years and was struggling to acquire her English language skills. As a sixth grader, she spent her entire year in a bilingual class, where the majority of instruction was in Spanish with a couple of classes spent on developing English (known in my school district as ELD—English Language Development). During seventh grade, having passed the test for basic English language skills, Gloria was transferred to a class of students with higher English proficiency. This meant that nine weeks into the school year, she entered new classes with students who were acquiring English skills in classes conducted only in English. She was clearly behind on two accounts: She had missed nearly nine weeks in her new classes, and she did not seem to possess the same level of language skills as the other students in the class.

She was a shy girl with large dark eyes and a pleasant personality, but time and time again, she turned in assignments that were barely comprehensible. She grew steadily more depressed and introverted. With 34 needy students, I didn't have the time during class to assist her every minute. Unfortunately, she didn't ask for my assistance either. After a couple of weeks, I asked her stay after class to talk about her work. Eyes cast downward, Gloria immediately began to cry stating hesitantly, "I try hard, but no understand, not'ing." Since she was obviously distraught, I decided to place her next to a "buddy," another girl who comprehended more English than she, but who also was fluent in Spanish. While the quality of her work did not improve noticeably at the onset, her attitude did. Since many of my assignments include partner or group work, she began to contribute and participate more. As her attitude and participation improved, so did her class work. She sat in the very front of the room, so I was able to monitor her slightly more than the other students. I would often hear Gloria's buddy instruct her on the correct way to spell something or explain concepts crucial to the assignment. Sometimes these explanations would be in mixed Spanish and English, sometimes only in Spanish.

After several months, Gloria's assignments became more comprehensible and her English language skills increased. I spent extra time with Gloria after class, providing her with additional reading and writing practice to help in her second language acquisition. She also participated in our after-school tutorial program, "Ayude" ("help" in Spanish). I taught Gloria in my science class for eighth grade as well, where I certainly witnessed a remarkable increase in her English! I felt fortunate to have seen such a dramatic change in this once shy and depressed girl. Gloria's grades, which were D's and F's, rose to C's and B's. Why not A's, you ask? While I knew that she was quite capable of earning A's at this time, she began the familiar adolescent activity of flirting with the boys—the joys of puberty! With time and effort, I am sure that Gloria will succeed in school as her English proficiency continues to grow.

CONCLUSION

It is somewhat sobering to reach the end of this chapter with the realization that of all the SLA variables discussed in this book, emotions are the ones we are still struggling to come to grips with. The great irony is that they could very well end up being the most influential force in language acquisition, but SLA researchers have not even come close to demonstrating such a claim. A large part of the problem is the wide variety of constructs that are subsumed under the term "emotions." To further complicate matters, we have seen in this chapter that even "one" emotion (e.g., anxiety) is actually multifaceted. More than any other topic covered in this book, affective variables are the area that SLA researchers understand the least. For language teachers, however, they may be the factor that matters the most. So, unfortunately, the contributions to our understanding of SLA reviewed in this chapter are minimal, but they are not completely insignificant. First of all, we have learned that the most important single affective variable, motivation, is defined and shaped by differences in SLA environments. Second, we have seen direct evidence that the effects of anxiety on language learning often differ from the myths about this emotion that have been popularized by various language teaching methodologies. Finally, through the careful reading of the unusual experiment by Guiora et alia, we have come to realize that it is exceedingly difficult to measure and manipulate such a complex emotion as empathy. But this, of course, does not mean that this construct, or any of the other emotions brought up in this chapter, is not important in the learning of a new language. Like language learners, SLA researchers still have a great deal to learn.

Suggested Readings

Although neither the title of the book nor the topics of the individual chapters refer directly to emotions, Stevick's *Working with Teaching Methods* (1998), published in this TeacherSource series, is filled with direct and indirect references to the ways affective variables interact with our teaching and our students' learning. His unique perspective on affect and learning is aptly characterized by his claim that success or failure in language learning largely depends on "what goes on inside and between the people in the classroom" (Stevick, 1998:xii).

Probably no one has written more about motivation and SLA than Gardner, and for a summary of much of the work he and his Canadian colleagues have done on the topic, see his *Social Psychology and Second Language Learning* (1985). Gardner and MacIntyre (1995) provide an update on the Gardner-Lambert model of motivation in an article entitled "An instrumental motivation in language study: Who says it isn't effective?" My 1978 article on "The effect of affect on foreign language learning: A review of the anxiety research" is reprinted in Horwitz and Young (eds.), *Language Anxiety: From Theory and Research to Classroom Implications* (1991), which is itself a thorough summary of diverse research on anxiety and SLA.

Brown is one of the few scholars in the field who has written consistently and insightfully on affective factors. Chapter 6 of the most recent edition of his *Principles of Language Learning and Teaching* (2000) offers a nice review of the major emotional variables, including some not mentioned in this chapter. Brown has also published two shorter books dealing with language learning, both written for the lay public and both containing useful exercises and questionnaires designed to make the language learner more aware of affective and personality variables. They are *A Practical Guide to Language Learning* (Brown, 1989) and *Breaking the Language Barrier* (Brown, 1991). Two chapters in Skehan's *Individual Differences in Second Language Learning* (1989) also address emotions and SLA: Chapter 4, "Motivation" and Chapter 6, "Additional cognitive and affective influences on language learning." Finally, Chapter 7, "The affective dimension: motivation, self-efficacy, and anxiety" in Ehrman's *Understanding Second Language Learning Difficulties* (1996), discusses various ways in which emotions can affect the course of language learning.

7

EPILOGUE

By now it must be manifest that Second Language Acquisition is sweeping in scope and complex in content, and teachers must begin to wonder if there is anything in the field that is relevant or applicable to the work they are called to do each day. SLA researchers themselves grapple with this same issue, and many of them believe that SLA theory makes bad pedagogical practice. As I admitted to you at the very beginning of this text, I have almost always been both an ESL teacher and an SLA researcher, and not being a dualist myself, I have felt uncomfortable with the notion that language learning could be neatly divided into either "theory" or "practice." This "divide and conquer" mentality oversimplifies the nature of language acquisition, and it also creates a separate and unequal perception about who does what. SLA researchers, mostly men and mostly university types, are the ones who are privileged to study theory and handle data, and ESL instructors, mostly women and mostly K–12 teachers, are left with the difficult task of dealing with students. Even the metaphors we sometimes use to describe these two different activities betray the gross inequality that pervades this dichotomy. Researchers work in the "ivory tower" while teachers "labor in the trenches." I cannot pretend to redress any of the inequities our cultural histories have forged, but I do believe that work in SLA and work in the classroom share much in common, and it is the purpose of this epilogue to demonstrate that social interaction is just as vital for teachers and researchers as it is for interlocutors acquiring a new tongue.

We see again and again that SLA researchers owe an enormous debt to what they have learned from observing students and teachers in the language classroom. Many prominent SLA researchers, investigators like Ellis, Lado, Larsen-Freeman, Long, Skehan, and Stevick, based much of their research on their direct experience as language teachers and classroom observers. And in this book, we have seen very specific insights that have come directly from the work of SLA researchers who were simultaneously teaching ESL classes as they investigated theoretical issues (e.g., Acton's work on perceived social distance and Kleinmann's study of avoidance). Language teaching and SLA research have historically been mutually dependent, and the two have been twinned sometimes within the same person or sometimes paired between different people. It would therefore be a misrepresentation to assume that contributions to our understanding of language learning have come largely from the theorists.

For perceived social distance, see pp. 26–28. For Kleinmann's study of avoidance, see pp. 58–63.

I began the book by baldly admitting that there are no cheap and easy answers to the many questions we have about how people learn languages or how we can teach them better. Consequently, I will not be giving you any answers in this brief conclusion. Rather, I can only choose to share a few observations. And in keeping with my personal experience as a teacher/researcher and with my professional view that SLA and teaching are best regarded as sharing much in common, these final observations are based on both experiments and experience—a little of each, but a lot of both.

(1) Individual students differ from each other far more than any single group of learners differs from another.

Especially in Chapter 2, where we focused on groups of people, we've examined the way SLA could be sliced and diced sociolinguistically. Nonetheless, we don't teach "Spanish speakers," or "children", or "Buddhists;" we teach Carlos, or Gloria, or Minami. We teach persons, not people. By and large, SLA research is engrossed with groups of learners, and its conclusions, in turn, are generalizations about large numbers of subjects (e.g., people who have ingested one and a half ounces of alcohol; speakers of Arabic learning English; all native speakers who have acquired a second language after puberty). Even longitudinal studies of a single subject are still framed as if they were relevant to huge numbers of learners. It is ironic, for example, that one of the best known theories for explaining the People factor in SLA (Schumann's Acculturation Model) originated from the study of a single subject, a young Spanish immigrant to the United States.

For more about Schumann's Acculturation Model, see p. 25.

SLA researchers are not the only ones who make generalizations about groups of people, of course. All of us do this all the time, and from this facile form of stereotyping we develop schemata for making useful everyday generalizations at best, and biases against other races, genders, and cultural groups at worst. But as I tried to emphasize in my Teacher's Voice in Chapter 1, our work as teachers tends to focus on individuals. Because we see them every day, because we teach language—a subject that invariably relates to deep interpersonal needs—because we know their names and recognize their faces, even after they have graduated from our classrooms, our students are always persons to us, not anonymous faces in a monolithic group. Therefore, we need to realize that whatever our students learn in our language classes always, *always*, depends first and foremost on all the individual variables that make up that single person. Only in an indirect and secondary way do group forces play a role in shaping a student's interlanguage.

Despite the fact that most of the SLA research summarized in this book deals with groups and not with individual learners, what experimental evidence is there to support this strong contention that individual variation predominates and that ESL teachers should view their students individually? Well, as a matter of fact, every chapter of this book is replete with explanations why one language learner differs from another. In terms of People, there are the influences of socioeconomic class, opportunities for social interaction, the amounts of exposure to English depending on what country an ESL student comes from or what the language planning policies of that nation may be. In terms of Language, there are the contrastive differences between a student's mother tongue and English and these diverge into a variety of combinations. A language like Spanish shares a similar orthography and lexicon with English but can differ markedly in grammar (for instance, Spanish is a "+pro-drop" language, and adjectives tend to follow nouns). On the other hand, a language like Japanese uses a completely different writing system from English and, except for English loanwords, has no overlap in vocabulary, and yet these two languages share some common grammatical features (adjectives precede nouns, and there is a past tense). Even ESL students who speak the "same" mother tongue can demonstrate the effects different dialects have on their attempts to acquire English. Speakers of southern Chinese "dialects" (representing the great majority of immigrants to inner circle countries) speak English with a different accent from ESL learners whose native language is Mandarin. And we have only scratched the surface in enumerating the variables that have been identified by SLA research and that can account for contrasts in the way individual learners may deviate in their attempts to master a second language. Each learner brings to the classroom varying clusters of attention types, cognitive styles, learning strategies, degrees and kinds of motivation, forms of anxiety, amounts of empathy, and so on. Maybe the motto of the ESL teacher should be *ex uno plures* "from one (classroom) many (individuals)!"

(2) Social interaction both fuels and lubricates all language acquisition.

You don't have to be a card-carrying Vygotskian to recognize the importance of social interaction in both first and second language acquisition, especially if your goal is authentic communicative competence. Naturally, if the target of your teaching is to have students remember petty paradigms like *sing-sang-sung*, then your students needn't interact with each other—or with you, for that matter, because computers and programmed learning can take care of this kind of "teaching" very nicely. However, I trust that most language teachers foster a more enlightened awareness of the linguistic needs of their students, and realize that unless their students learn to communicate in the classroom, they will never be able to communicate in the workplace, let alone the kitchen. Social interaction must involve the teacher in many ways because, just as the parent plays the unwitting role of a catalyst in nurturing young children through their linguistic zones of proximal development, so too does the teacher intentionally intervene in encouraging ESL students to acquire more complex ways of communicating.

But social interaction should take place not just between teacher and student; interaction needs to occur between student and fellow student, a point that traditional teacher-fronted instruction fails to apprehend. Pair work, group work, project work, information-gap activities, and task-based syllabi are some of the classroom procedures that come to mind when we consider some of the ways we can translate social interaction into pedagogical practice. And referring back to computer-assisted language learning, software programs that incorporate procedures such as the ones just listed are very useful in integrating social interaction into the contemporary technology of language instruction.

(3) Learners are constantly influenced by their mother tongue and by the language they are trying to acquire.

Learning a new language is very much like immigration—not in a literal sense, although those of us who teach ESL in inner circle countries are aware that most of our students are newcomers to the land as well as immigrants to the language. But here, I am referring to the metaphorical similarities between the experience a person undergoes when trying to learn a second language and the process of emigrating from one's mother culture to a brave new world—and a very strange one at that. Just as immigrants are torn, sometimes for life, by competing loyalties between the old and familiar and the new and exotic, so language learners are caught between the habits of their mother tongue and the challenging new rules and patterns of the second language.

In Chapter 3, we reviewed many of the linguistic factors that account for a learner's interlanguage, and we ended up acknowledging that to account accurately for a learner's performance in the target language, we must consider several factors: the differences between the mother tongue and the language to be learned, irregularities in the second language itself, the possibility of UG effects, and so forth. All of this suggests, to those of us who are language teachers, that our students are up against a lot more than we generally think.

Typically, many ESL instructors are quick to attribute any errors students make to their mother tongue, but we have already learned that interlanguage performance is much more complicated than this. Just as a friend or a social worker cannot do much to change the cultural forces that tug and pull at an immigrant, especially during the early stages of acculturation, neither can a language teacher ameliorate the effects of competing linguistic paradigms on the student of a second language. But language teachers can be sympathetic!

Given all the swirling symbols competing for the attention of a foreign language learner, especially during the first year or two of study, it is quite remarkable that most students are able to communicate in the target language. And it is wise to remember Cook's concept of multi-competence. Beginning ESL students are rapidly adding to the native speaker competence they already have in their mother tongue (or, in some cases, in two primary languages), so however much they may struggle in English, their SLA performance is a sign of added, not diminished, linguistic prowess. For me, the study of interlanguage should be a crucial component of any teacher training program, because such an inquiry teaches us to be understanding, tolerant, and sensitive to the plight of any learner attempting to become bilingual.

(4) Errors are invariably the sign of a motivated and intelligent student!

Let's make a couple of points clear at the outset. I've never met a teacher or a student who, given the choice between flawed or error-free performance, would opt for the former; so, granted, the ultimate goal of any language learner is to produce and to comprehend the target language with close to the accuracy and fluency of a native speaker. Even this goal isn't completely precise because SLA research has taught us that, with rare exceptions, all second language learners will speak with a foreign accent, so we must first acknowledge the fact that speech that is fluent and intelligible but accented is "error-free." In addition, going back to the view that in this new millennium, the international language is World English*es*, as long as ESL learners acquire one of these accepted varieties of English, again we can conclude that they are fully competent bilinguals. And a final caveat—remember that we are talking about SLA "errors" and not performance mistakes.

The traditional view of errors (i.e., the perspective language teachers held before the advent of SLA research) is that errors are evidence of failure—they tell the teacher where the student went wrong. It may be a bit bold to suggest that SLA studies have turned this view completely on its head and go on to claim that now we believe that all errors are a sign of success and tell us where the student has gone right, but this extreme is much closer to reality than the other. To begin with, errors show that the student is motivated to learn the new language, and this is evidenced in several ways. In a typical "drill and kill" classroom, students can languidly parrot the teacher whenever she or he commands, "Repeat after me...." Because the students are replicating the teacher's L2 output as faithfully as a duplicating machine or a tape recorder, the chances are very small that any of them will make a mistake. However, anyone who has observed such an activity in a language classroom, or who remembers such exercises from their own foreign language training, can vouch for the fact that the students do not find this type of activity particularly motivating. But when a student attempts to create a response to a fellow student's (or teacher's) question and makes an error in the attempt, the chances are very slim that the student wasn't trying. How unfair, in cases like this, to criticize students for not being motivated whenever they make an error!

Second, recall the research on avoidance behavior discussed in Chapter 3. When See pp. 58–63. students reach the intermediate or advanced level of linguistic competence in a second language, they have learned alternative ways of saying or writing things, and so now they are capable of committing sins of omission: They can avoid difficult structures in the target language, not make any errors at all, and sometimes sound as if they are really competent. A native speaker of Spanish who is fairly good in English can artfully avoid the problematic infinitive clause (reviewed in Chapter 3) and can come up with the impressive "You suggested that he should close the window" as a paraphrase of "You asked him to close the window." The whole point is that by *not* making an error, the learner ultimately demonstrates a lack of motivation to acquire this more difficult English structure.

Finally, errors are, for the most part, a demonstration of originality, creativity, and intelligence. Any parrot can mimic the teacher and any duplicating machine can copy from a printed text, so surely there is no originality or creativity in producing something in English that doesn't break any rules. But you know for sure your students aren't copying when they come up with a gem like, "in the highlands we raise wheats, and in the lowlands we raise corns." And the very fact that an otherwise unintelligible student claims to work in a factory that makes "boring balls" proves he is far from boring in his attempts to learn English. I once wrote an article entitled "I am interesting in English," which was a direct quote from one of my Thai students, who, by the very fact she said this, proved she was indeed interesting in (my) English (class)! But students who commit errors are not only creative, they demonstrate that they are also intelligent learners. Their errors come from positive and negative transfer from their mother tongue; they come from false analogy and overgeneralization of rules and patterns in English; they come from attempts to simplify the input or the output to reduce the strain on working memory. In sum, errors are the outward manifestation of an inwardly active mind.

(5) Students are always paying attention; the real question is, to what?

After more than three dozen years of teaching, I have as much experience as the next teacher with wandering eyes, nodding heads, and (my personal favorite) the sudden lurch of a body about to doze off, sending books and papers flying off the desk of the embarrassed but sleepy-eyed offender! Why don't they pay attention? Just as common are the many times when I get feedback from students by their questions in class or their answers on a test that they didn't seem to hear what I said. "Weren't they paying attention?" I ask myself. The natural tendency is to blame the students for not attending, but we saw in Chapter 4 that, like everything else in SLA, attention is not as simple as all that.

For examples like these, and in similar experiences you have had as a teacher, it's not that the students have switched off their attentional searchlights, they are simply focused on a different terrain from the one on which your attention is fixed. Or to put it more accurately, their peripheral attention is always on what is happening in class (unless, of course, they are completely asleep). But the problem is that we teachers are a greedy lot—we demand their focal attention too! Varying the ways in which material is introduced, coupling the language taught to specific communicative tasks, changing the activities and the tempo of the lesson, and trying to employ differing learning styles and strategies over the course of the curriculum all help, but none of this guarantees the capture of focal attention.

SLA research provides some encouragement in the face of this pedagogical problem, however, especially when we consider McLaughlin's distinction between two very different but concurrent forms of learning. When we think of attention, we inevitably think about incremental learning (the left-hand side of the tree depicted in Figure 4.2 on page 80) but we should remember that a lot of learning takes place as a holistic gestalt—one day we don't have it, but the next day we do. This is especially true of skills like learning to ride a bike, or to whistle, or to pick up a new sound, or phrase, or structure in a second language. Remember too that it's next to impossible to determine how attention is allocated in holistic learning, because there is no specific task or stage to attend to. All of this goes to say that we teachers can never assume that our students aren't learning when they don't appear to be paying attention. Perhaps they are, even when heads are turned or eyelids are drooping!

(6) Content and discourse schemata play a powerful role in shaping language learning behavior.

Behaviorists will feel uncomfortable with the mentalistic implications of the first half of this observation, for they believe that we should avoid speculating about what is inside people's heads when they do something. Cognitivists, in turn, will rebel at the behavioristic terminology in the second half of the phrase, especially at the term "shaping." But we teachers need all the help we can get to describe and explain what our students learn or why they don't, so the choice of words is intentional here. The key point is that from the moment our ESL students step into the classroom on the very first day of school, they have already learned a great deal about people, about language, about emotions, and so forth, *and* they have already learned a lot about learning. It helps enormously if we can then try to become more aware of the schemata that our students bring into our classrooms and begin to work with these expectations, rather than against them. Let me share an illustration or two.

All students have certain expectations about what a classroom looks like and what kinds of activities will take place there (contemporary psychologists often refer to these as "frames" and "scripts"). For most students who have had their early schooling in another country, an English classroom should be filled with many chairs and desks neatly laid out in a grid pattern, and the teacher should do almost all the talking, often writing on the board and occasionally stopping to ask a student to stand and answer a question. Further, the teacher (and the textbook) is seen as the font of all wisdom about English and the final adjudicator of all questions about usage. Imagine the confusion these students must experience when they begin an ESL class in the United States or in some other inner circle nation where the teacher asks the students to move the chairs into groups or pairs and tells the students to exchange their homework with each other and correct each other's errors. Suddenly, schemata clash like cymbals!

A sensitive teacher can help by orienting the students at the start of a new class: "Here are my goals for the course, here are my expectations for you, here are the activities we will be undertaking in this class throughout the term, and here are the reasons why I have chosen these activities." An empathetic teacher can go even further by occasionally giving the students an opportunity to choose which activities they would like to pursue. Students can tune and restructure their schematic knowledge more easily and less painfully if they can anticipate what they will be asked to do and are given reasons for this.

Along with the content schemata they bring to the new ESL class, students also carry with them a great deal of discourse knowledge. Like their first language knowledge, some of these discourse schemata can transfer positively into oral and written English, and some of them can interfere because of negative transfer. Once again, language teachers can help ease students through the difficult process of learning to learn all over again if they can see where their students are coming from and empathize with their plight. One way to do this has already been alluded to in this book and is a procedure adopted by many ESL teachers and textbooks: Create opportunities in class for students to reflect on the differences between the discourse structures they have learned and the ones they are about to learn in their English class. How do you address an envelope? How do you begin a joke? How do you let someone know that it is his or her turn in a conversation? What's a good way to end an essay? How do you know someone is being sarcastic? Reflections on topics like these are helpful in any ESL class, but they are particularly effective in heterogeneous classrooms because the more diverse the examples, the more aware the students (and the teacher!) become that SLA is more than just acquiring new sounds, words, and syntax; it creates a whole new set of expectations about learning and about the ways we speak and write.

(7) Emotions are neither good nor bad; they are simply a natural part of language acquisition.

When I read what some people have written about second language learning, or when I hear certain people promoting a "unique" approach to language teaching, I sometimes get the impression that these methodologists want to turn the ESL classroom into a sterile hospital ward. No anxiety allowed here! Wash your hands of all feelings and place affective filters over your mouths before entering! In Chapter 6, we reviewed the SLA studies of affective variables such as motivation, anxiety, and empathy, and found that they are much more complex and complicated than we normally surmise in our day-to-day use of those terms. Some of them, like empathy, elude even the most sophisticated experimental attempts to quantify and correlate. And we definitely saw evidence that these sentiments cannot be lumped into categories like the good, the bad, and the ugly. Even anxiety, often considered the ugly duckling of the lot, can be beneficial for certain people at certain times in certain tasks. So second language classrooms are more like kitchens than they are like hospital wards—feelings can be messy and unclean, but they can also be funny, heartening, and spirited. Above all, they are a natural part of our class, just as they are a natural part of us and of our students.

We cannot and should not ignore our students' emotions or the feelings that we ourselves bring to the classroom. We continually need to recognize that each student brings differing emotions each day, and these sometimes fuel and lubricate learning so that it is smooth and effortless, and sometimes the whole process may grind to a halt or explode unexpectedly. We are immediately aware when the latter happens, but we frequently ignore the role of affective variables when students are placid—and often this represents the silent majority. Many times I have mistaken a student's lack of involvement in my class for shyness or boredom—only to find out later that a car was stolen, a family member had died, or a relationship had abruptly ended. How silly of me not to have first thought of natural explanations like these! Why did I fall back on the tried-and-true excuses of a traditional teacher? SLA research does not provide us with any startling new revelations about the role of emotions and how they affect language learning, but it does encourage us to look for multiple causes rather than singular explanations.

CONCLUSION

It may be somewhat disheartening for you to finish this book with the news that Second Language Acquisition is even more complex than nutrition, and that there are no fast and facile ways to become a successful language learner. But perhaps you have suspected this all along. What is encouraging to me is that, despite the enormous complexity of the enterprise, most people around the world do learn a second language, and hundreds of millions of them do this very well. As their teachers, we hope that we have played an active part in their success, and by continual study and continuous reflection, we trust that we can become even more effective participants in the miracle of language learning, which is a gift and birthright of all peoples. Finally, I hope that this book has encouraged you to ensure that your classroom will always be a place for learning.

References

Acton, W. 1979. Second language learning and perception of difference in attitude. Unpublished doctoral dissertation. University of Michigan.

Aitchison, J. 1989. *The articulate mammal: An introduction to psycholinguistics.* (2nd ed.) London: Routledge.

Anderson, N. 1999. *Exploring second language reading: Issues and strategies.* Boston, MA: Heinle & Heinle.

August, D., and K. Hakuta. 1998. *Educating language minority children.* Washington: National Academy Press.

Bailey, K. 1983. Competitiveness and anxiety in adult second language learning: Looking at and through the diary studies. In H. Seliger and M. Long (eds.), *Classroom-oriented research in second language acquisition.* Boston, MA: Heinle & Heinle/Newbury House, 67–102.

Bailey, K. 1998. *Learning about language assessment.* Boston, MA: Heinle & Heinle.

Barsalou, L. 1992. *Cognitive psychology.* Hillsdale, NJ: Lawrence Erlbaum.

Bartlett, F. 1932. *Remembering: A study in experimental and social psychology.* Cambridge: Cambridge University Press.

Beebe, L. 1988. Sociolinguistic perspective. In L. Beebe (ed.), *Issues in second language acquisition.* Boston, MA: Heinle & Heinle/Newbury House, 43–77.

Berko-Gleason, J., and N. Ratner. 1993. Language development in children. In Berko-Gleason, J., and N. Ratner (eds.), *Psycholinguistics.* Fort Worth, TX: Harcourt Brace Jovanovich, 301–350.

Bialystok, E. 1978. A theoretical model of language learning. *Language Learning* 28:69–83.

Bialystok, E., and K. Hakuta. 1994. *In other words: The science and psychology of second-language acquisition.* New York: Basic Books.

Bley-Vroman, R. 1989. What is the logical problem in second language acquisition? In S. Gass and J. Schachter (eds.), *Linguistic perspectives on second language acquisition.* Cambridge: Cambridge University Press, 41–68.

Bley-Vroman, R., S. Felix, and G. Ioup. 1988. The accessibility of universal grammar in adult language learning. *Second Language Research* 4:1–32.

Bongaerts, T., B. Planken, and E. Schils. 1995. Can late learners attain a native accent in a foreign language? A test of the critical period hypothesis. In D. Singleton and Z. Lengyel (eds.), *The age factor in second language acquisition: A critical look at the critical period hypothesis.* Clevedon, England: Multilingual Matters, 30–50.

Bongaerts, T., C. van Summeren, B. Planken, and E. Schils. 1997. Age and ultimate attainment in the prounciation of a foreign language. *Studies in Second Language Acquisition* 19:447–465.

Boysson-Bardies, B. 1999. *How language comes to children: From birth to two years.* Cambridge, MA: MIT Press.

Braidi, S. 1999. *The acquisition of second language syntax.* London: Arnold.

Broadbent, D. 1952. Failures of attention in selective listening. *Journal of Experimental Psychology* 44:428–433.

Brown, G., and G. Yule. 1983. *Discourse analysis.* Cambridge: Cambridge University Press.

Brown, H.D. 1989. *A practical guide to language learning.* New York: McGraw-Hill.

Brown, H.D. 1991. *Breaking the language barrier.* Yarmouth, ME: Intercultural Press.

Brown, H.D. 2000. *Principles of language learning and teaching* (4th ed.). White Plains, NY: Pearson Education.

Brown, J.D. 1991. Statistics as a foreign language—Part I: What to look for in reading statistical language studies. *TESOL Quarterly* 25:569–586.

Brown, J.D. 1992. Statistics as a foreign language—Part II: More things to consider in reading statistical language studies. *TESOL Quarterly* 26:629–664.

Brown, J.M., and A. Palmer. 1988. *The listening approach: Methods and materials for applying Krashen's input hypothesis.* London: Longman.

Brown, R. 1973. *A first language: The early stages.* Cambridge, MA: Harvard University Press.

Brumfit, C. 1994. The linguist and the language teaching profession: Ghost in a machine? In R. Barasch and C. James (eds.), *Beyond the monitor model: Comments on current theory and practice in second language acquisition.* Boston, MA: Heinle & Heinle, 263–272.

Canale, M., and M. Swain, 1980. Theoretical bases of communicative approaches to second language teaching and testing. *Applied Linguistics* 1:1–47.

Carrell, P., and L. Monroe. 1995. ESL composition and learning styles. In J. Reid (ed.). *Learning styles in the ESL/EFL classroom.* Boston, MA: Heinle & Heinle, 148–157.

Carroll, D. 1999. *Psychology of language* (3rd ed.). Pacific Grove, CA: Brooks/Cole.

Casey, B., C. Gordon, G. Mannheim, and J. Rumsey. 1993. Dysfunctional attention in autistic savants. *Journal of Clinical and Experimental Neuropsychology* 15:933–946.

Chamot, A., and J. O'Malley. 1987. The cognitive academic language learning approach: A bridge to the mainstream. *TESOL Quarterly* 12:227–249.

Chomsky, N. 1957. *Syntactic structures.* The Hague: Mouton.

Chomsky, N. 1965. *Aspects of the theory of syntax.* Cambridge, MA: MIT Press.

Clark, H. 1996. *Using language.* Cambridge: Cambridge University Press.

Cook, V. 1993. *Linguistics and second language acquisition.* New York: St. Martin's Press.

Cook, V. 1996. *Second language learning and language teaching* (2nd ed.). London: Arnold.

Cooke, J. 1968. *Pronominal reference in Thai, Burmese, and Vietnamese.* Berkeley, CA: University of California Press.

Corballis, M. 1991. *The lopsided ape.* Oxford: Oxford University Press.

Corder, S.P. 1967. The significance of learners' errors. *International Review of Applied Linguistics* 5:161–170.

Cowan, N. 1997. *Attention and memory.* Oxford: Oxford University Press.

Crookes, D., and R. Schmidt. 1991. Motivation and second language learning: Reopening the research agenda. *Language Learning* 41:469–512.

Crystal, D. 1988. *The English language.* London: Penguin Books.

Crystal, D. 1998. *English as a global language*. Cambridge: Cambridge University Press.

Cummins, J. 1981. *Bilingualism and minority children*. Ontario: Ontario Institute for Studies in Education.

Cummins, J. 1994. Primary language instruction and the education of language minority students. In C. Leyba (ed.), *Schooling and language minority students: A theoretical framework*. Sacramento, CA: California State Department of Education, 3–46.

Deacon, T. 1997. *The symbolic species*. New York: W. W. Norton.

Deci, E. 1975. *Intrinsic motivation*. New York: Plenum Press.

Dulay, H., N. Burt, and S. Krashen. 1982. *Language two*. Oxford: Oxford University Press.

Ehrman, M. 1996. *Understanding second language learning difficulties*. Thousand Oaks, CA: Sage Publications.

Ellis, R. 1994. *The study of second language acquisition*. Oxford: Oxford University Press.

Ellis, R. 1997. *Second language acquisition*. Oxford: Oxford University Press.

Fantini, A. 1997. Language: Its cultural and intercultural dimensions. In A. Fantini (ed.), *New ways in teaching culture*. Alexandria, VA: TESOL, 3–15.

Ferguson, C. 1971. Absence of copula and the notion of simplicity: A study of normal speech, baby talk, foreigner talk, and pidgins. In D. Hymes (ed.), *Pidginization and creolization of languages*. Cambridge: Cambridge University Press.

Ferguson, C. 1996. *Sociolinguistic perpective: Papers on language and society, 1959–1994*. Oxford: Oxford University Press.

Flege, J., and J. Hillenbrand. 1987. Limits on pronunciation accuracy in adult foreign language speech production. In G. Ioup and S. Weinberger (eds.), *Interlanguage phonology: The acquisition of a second language sound system*. Boston, MA: Heinle & Heinle/Newbury House.

Foster, P., and P. Skehan. 1997. Modifying the task: The effects of surprise, time and planning type on task based foreign language instruction. *Thames Valley Working Papers in English Language Teaching*, Volume 4.

Fries, C. 1945. *Teaching and learning English as a foreign language*. Ann Arbor, MI: University of Michigan Press.

Freud, S. 1904/1958. *Psychopathology of everyday life*. New York: Mentor Book (English translation).

Fromkin, V. 1973. *Speech errors as linguistic evidence*. The Hague: Mouton.

Furnham, A., and S. Bochner. 1986. *Culture shock: Psychological reactions to unfamiliar environments*. London: Methuen.

Gardner, H. 1975. *The shattered mind: The person after brain damage*. London: Routledge and Kegan Paul.

Gardner, H. 1983. *Frames of mind: The theory of multiple intelligences*. New York: HarperCollins.

Gardner, H. 1993. *Creating minds: An anatomy of creativity seen through the lives of Freud, Einstein, Picasso, Stravinsky, Eliot, Graham, and Gandhi*. New York: Basic Books.

Gardner, R. 1985. *Social psychology and second language learning: The role of attitudes and motivation*. London: Edward Arnold.

Gardner, R., and W. Lambert. 1972. *Attitudes and motivation in second language learning*. Boston, MA: Heinle & Heinle/Newbury House.

Gardner, R., and P. MacIntyre. 1991. An instrumental motivation in language study: Who says it isn't effective? *Studies in Second Language Acquisition* 13:57–72.

Gass, S. 1988. Integrating research areas. *Applied Linguistics* 9:198–217.

Gass, S., and E. Varonis. 1985. Variation in native speaker speech modification to non-native speakers. *Studies in Second Language Acquisition* 7:37–57.

Genesee, F. 1987. *Learning through two languages: Studies of immersion and bilingual education.* Boston, MA: Heinle & Heinle/Newbury House.

Genesee, F. (ed.). 1998. *Educating second language children: The whole child, the whole curriculum, the whole community* (6th ed.). New York: Cambridge University Press.

Genesee, F., P. Rogers, and N. Holobow. 1983. The social psychology of language learning: Another point of view. *Language Learning* 33:209–224.

Giles, H. 1980. Accommodation theory: Some new directions. In S. de Silva (Ed.), *Aspects of linguistic behavior.* York, U.K.: York University Press, 105–136.

Gonzalez, R., and I. Melis (eds.). 2000. *Language ideologies: Critical perspectives on the official English movement.* Urbana, IL: National Council of Teachers of English.

Gregg, K. 1984. Krashen's monitor and Occam's razor. *Applied Linguistics* 5:79–100.

Guiora, A. 1965. On clinical diagnosis and prediction. *Psychological Reprints* 17:779.

Guiora, A., B. Beit-Hallahmi, R. Brannon, C. Dull, and T. Scovel. 1972. The effects of experimentally induced changes in ego states on pronunciation ability in a second language: An exploratory study. *Comprehensive Psychiatry* 13:421–428.

Hakuta, K. 1986. *Mirror of language: The debate on bilingualism.* New York: Basic Books.

Hansen, L. 1987. Cognitive style and first language background in second language test performance. *TESOL Quarterly* 21:565–569.

Hauser, M. 1997. *The evolution of communication.* Cambridge, MA: MIT Press.

Hermann, G. 1980. Attitudes and success in children's learning of English as a second language: The motivational vs. the resultative hypothesis. *English Language Teaching Journal* 34:247–254.

Horwitz, E., and D. Young (eds.). 1991. *Language anxiety: From theory and research to classroom implications.* Englewood Cliffs, NJ: Prentice-Hall.

Irujo, S. 1998. *Teaching bilingual children.* Boston, MA: Heinle & Heinle.

Jamieson, J. 1992. The cognitive styles of reflectivity/impulsivity and field independence/dependence and ESL success. *Modern Language Journal* 76:491–501.

Johnson, J., and E. Newport. 1989. Critical period effects in second language learning: The influence of maturational state on the acquisition of English as a second language. *Cognitive Psychology* 21:60–99.

Kachru, B. 1985. Standards, codification, and sociolinguistic realism: The English language in the outer circle. In R. Quirk and H. Widdowson (eds.), *English in the world: Teaching and learning the language and literatures.* Cambridge: Cambridge University Press, 11–30.

Kant, E. 1781. *Critique of pure reason.* J. Meikeljohn (1934), translator. London: J.M. Dent and Sons.

Kapur, N. (ed.). 1997. *Injured brains of medical minds: Views from within.* Oxford: Oxford University Press.

Kleinmann, H. 1977. Avoidance behavior in adult second language acquisition. *Language Learning* 27:93–107.

Koffka, K. 1935/1963. *Principles of gestalt psychology.* New York: Harcourt, Brace, and World.

Krakauer, J. 1997. *Into thin air.* New York: Villard Books.

Krashen, S. 1982. *Principles and practice in second language acquisition.* Oxford: Pergamon Press.

Krashen, S. 1985. *The input hypothesis: Issues and implications.* London: Longman.

Krashen, S., and T. Terrell. 1983. *The natural approach.* Oxford: Pergamon Press.

Lado, R. 1957. *Linguistics across cultures.* Ann Arbor, MI: University of Michigan Press.

Lafayette, R., and M. Buscaglia. 1985. Students learn language via a civilization course—A comparison of second language classroom environments. *Studies in Second Language Acquisition* 7:323–342.

Larsen-Freeman, D. 1991. Second language acquisition research: Staking out the territory. *TESOL Quarterly* 25:315–350.

Larsen-Freeman, D., and M. Long. 1991. *An introduction to second language acquisition research.* London: Longman.

Lenneberg, E. 1967. *Biological foundations of language.* New York: John Wiley and Sons.

Lessow-Hurley, J. 1990. *The foundations of dual language instruction.* London: Longman.

Lieberman, P. 1991. *Uniquely human.* Cambridge, MA: Harvard University Press.

Lightbown, P., and N. Spada. 1993. *How languages are learned.* Oxford: Oxford University Press.

Long, M. 1990. Maturational constraints on language learning. *Studies in Second Language Acquisition* 12:251–286.

Luria, A. 1968. *The mind of a mnemonist.* New York: Basic Books.

Major, R. 1987. Phonological similarity, markedness, and rate of L2 acquisition. *Studies in Second Language Acquisition* 9:63–82.

McDonough, S. 1981. *Psychology in foreign language teaching.* London: George Allen and Unwin.

McLaughlin, B. 1987. *Theories of second-language learning.* London: Edward Arnold.

McLaughlin, B., T. Rossman, and B. McLeod. 1983. Second-language learning: An information-processing perspective. *Language Learning* 33:135–158.

McLeod, B., and B. McLaughlin. 1986. Restructuring or automaticity? Reading in a second language. *Language Learning* 36:109–123.

Meisel, J. 1980. Linguistic simplification. In S. Felix (ed.), *Second language development: Trends and issues.* Tubingen: Gunter Narr, 9–40.

Mendelsohn, D. (ed.). 1999. *Expanding our vision: Insights for language teachers.* Don Mills, Ontario: Oxford University Press.

Mitchell, R., and F. Myles. 1998. *Second language learning theories.* London: Arnold.

Morris, D. 1967. *The naked ape.* New York: Dell Publishing.

Nation, R., and B. McLaughlin. 1986. Experts and novices: An information-processing approach to the 'good language learner' problem. *Applied Psycholinguistics* 7:41–56.

Neisser, U. 1982. *Memory observed: Remembering in natural contexts.* New York: W.H. Freeman and Company.

Neufeld, G. 1979. Towards a theory of language learning aptitude. *Language Learning* 29:227–241.

Obler, L., and K. Gjerlow. 1999. *Language and the brain.* Cambridge: Cambridge University Press.

Oxford, R. 1990. *Language learning strategies: What every teacher should know.* Boston, MA: Heinle & Heinle/Newbury House.

Parasuraman, R. (ed.). *The attentive brain.* Cambridge, MA: The MIT Press.

Parry, K. (ed.). 1998. *Culture, literacy and learning English.* Portsmouth, NH: Boynton/Cook.

Patterson, P., and E. Linden. 1981. *The education of Koko.* New York: Holt, Rinehart and Winston.

Penfield, W. 1963. *The second career.* Boston, MA: Little, Brown.

Phillipson, R. 1992. *Linguistic imperialism.* Oxford: Oxford University Press.

Pike, K. 1954. *Language in relation to a unified theory of the structure of human behavior.* The Hague: Mouton.

Pinker, S. 1994. *The language instinct: How the mind creates language.* New York: HarperPerennial.

Porter, R. 1990. *Forked tongue: The politics of bilingual education.* New York: Basic Books.

Reich, P. 1986. *Language development.* Englewood Cliffs, NJ: Prentice-Hall.

Reid, J. 1995. *Language styles in the ESL/EFL classroom.* Boston, MA: Heinle & Heinle.

Richards, J. (ed.). 1974. *Error analysis.* London: Longman.

Richards, J. 1990. *The language teaching matrix.* Cambridge: Cambridge University Press.

Rumelhart, D., J. McClelland, and the PDP Research Group. 1986. *Parallel distributed processing: Explorations in the microstructure of cognition, Volume 1: Foundations.* Cambridge, MA: MIT Press.

Samway, K., and D. Mc Keon. 1999. *Myths and realities: Best practices for language minority students.* Portsmouth, NH: Heinemann.

Savage-Rumbaugh, S., S. Shanker, and T. Taylor. 1998. *Apes, language, and the human mind.* Oxford: Oxford University Press.

Scarcella, R., and R. Oxford. 1992. *The tapestry of language learning: The individual in the communicative classroom.* Boston, MA: Heinle & Heinle.

Schmidt, R. 1990. The role of consciousness in language learning. *Applied Linguistics* 11:129–158.

Schmidt, R. 1993. Awareness and second language acquisition. *Annual Review of Applied Linguistics* 13:206–226.

Schmidt, R. 1994. Implicit learning and the cognitive unconscious: Of artical grammars and second language acquisition. In N. Ellis (ed.), *Implicit and explicit learning of languages.* London: Academic Press, 165–209.

Schmidt, R. 1995. Consciousness and foreign language learning: A tutorial on attention and awareness in learning. In R. Schmidt (ed.), *Attention and awareness in foreign language learning.* Honolulu, HI: University of Hawaii Second Language Teaching and Curriculum Center, 1–64.

Schneider, W., and R. Shiffrin. 1977. Controlled and automatic processing I: Detection, search, and attention. *Psychological Review* 84:1–64.

Schumann, J. 1978. *The pidginization process: A model for second language acquisition.* Boston, MA: Heinle & Heinle/Newbury House.

Schumann, J., and N. Stenson (eds.). 1974. *New frontiers in second language learning.* Boston, MA: Heinle & Heinle/Newbury House.

Schutze, C. 1998. *The empirical basis of linguistics: Grammaticality judgments.* Chicago: University of Chicago Press.

Scovel, J. 1982. Curriculum stability and change: English foreign language programs in modern China. Unpublished Doctoral Dissertation. University of Pittsburgh.

Scovel, T. 1969. Foreign accents, language acquisition, and cerebral dominance. *Language Learning* 28:129–142.

Scovel, T. 1978. The effect of affect: A review of the anxiety literature. *Language Learning* 28:129–142. (Also reprinted in Horwitz and Young, eds., 1991.)

Scovel, T. 1988. *A time to speak: A psycholinguistic inquiry into the critical period for human speech.* Boston, MA: Heinle & Heinle/Newbury House.

Scovel, T. 1995. Differentiation, recognition, and identification in the discrimination of foreign accents. In J. Archibald (ed.), *Phonological acquisition and phonological theory.* Hillsdale, NJ: Lawrence Erlbaum, 169–181.

Scovel, T. 1997. Review of Singleton, D., and Z. Lengyel (eds.), *The age factor in second language acquisition. Modern Language Journal* 81:118–119.

Scovel, T. 1998. *Psycholinguistics.* Oxford: Oxford University Press.

Scovel, T. 2000a. The younger, the better myth and bilingual education. In Gonzalez, R., and I. Melis (eds.), *Language ideologies: Critical perspectives on the English Only movement. Volume One: Education and the Social Implications of Official Language.* Urbana, IL: National Council of Teachers of English.

Scovel, T. 2000b. A critical review of the critical period research. *ARAL* 20:213–223.

Seliger, H. 1983. Learner ineraction in the classroom and its effects on language acquisition. In Seliger, H., and M. Long (eds.), *Classroom oriented research in second language acquisition.* Boston, MA: Heinle & Heinle/Newbury House, 246–267.

Seliger, H., and R. Vago (eds.). 1991. *First language attrition.* Cambridge: Cambridge University Press.

Selinker, L. 1972. Interlanguage. *International Review of Applied Linguistics* 10:209–231.

Selinker, L. 1992. *Rediscovering interlanguage.* London: Longman.

Singleton, D., and Z. Lengyel (eds.). 1995. *The age factor in second language acquisition.* Clevedon, England: Multilingual Matters.

Skehan, P. 1989. *Individual differences in second-language learning.* London: Edward Arnold.

Skehan, P. 1998. *A cognitive approach to language learning.* Oxford: Oxford University Press.

Skehan, P., and P. Foster. 1997. The influence of planning and post-task activities on accuracy and complexity in task-based learning. *Language Teaching Research* 1/3.

Skinner, B.F. 1957. *Verbal behavior.* New York: Appleton-Century-Crofts.

Skutnabb-Kangas, T. 2000. *Linguistic genocide in education—or worldwide diversity and human rights?* Hillsdale, NJ: Lawrence Erlbaum Associates.

Slavoff, G., and J. Johnson. 1995. The effects of age on the rate of learning a second language. *Studies in Second Language Acquisition* 17:1–16.

Sonstroem, P., and J. Bernado. 1982. Intraindividual pregame state anxiety and basketball performance: A re-examination of the inverted U curve. *Journal of Sports Psychology* 4:235–245.

Spolsky, B. 1989. *Conditions for second language learning.* Oxford: Oxford University Press.

Spolsky, B. 1998. *Sociolinguistics.* Oxford: Oxford University Press.

Spreen, O., A. Risser, and D. Edgell. 1995. *Developmental neuropsychology.* Oxford: Oxford University Press.

Stevick, E. 1996. *Memory, meaning, and method* (2nd ed.). Boston, MA: Heinle & Heinle/Newbury House.

Stevick, E. 1998. *Working with teaching methods: What's at stake?* Boston, MA: Heinle & Heinle.

Strong, M. 1983. Social styles and second language acquisition of Spanish-speaking kindergarteners. *TESOL Quarterly* 17:241–258.

Strongman, K. 1987. *The psychology of emotion.* New York: John Wiley and Sons.

Tannen, D. 1996. *Gender and discourse.* New York: Oxford University Press.

Tomlin, R., and M. Gernsbacher (eds.). 1994. Cognitive foundations of second language acquistion. *Studies in Second Language Acquisition.* Volume 16, 129–132.

Tomlin, R., and V. Villa. 1994. Attention in cognitive science and second language acquisition. *Studies in Second Language Acquisition* 16:183–203.

Torkelson, K. 1995. Learning styles and ITA training. In J. Reid (ed.), *Learning styles in the ESL/EFL classroom.* Boston, MA: Heinle & Heinle, 134–147.

Tulving, E. 1983. *Elements of episodic memory.* Oxford: Oxford University Press.

Van Lier, L. 1995. *Introducing language awareness.* London: Penguin.

Vygotsky, L. 1962. *Thought and language.* Cambridge, MA: MIT Press.

Wesche, M. 1981. Language aptitude measures in streaming, matching students with methods, and diagnosis of learning problems. In K. Diller (ed.), *Individual differences and universals in foreign language aptitude.* Boston, MA: Heinle & Heinle/Newbury House, 119–154.

White, L. 1989. *Universal grammar and second language acquisition.* Amsterdam: Johns Benjamins.

Widdowson, H. 1996. *Linguistics.* Oxford: Oxford University Press.

Williams, M., and R. Burden. 1997. *Psychology for language teachers: A social constructivist approach.* Cambridge: Cambridge University Press.

Willing, K. 1987. *Learning styles in adult migrant education.* Adelaide: Adult Migrant Education Programme.

Yule, G. 1996. *Pragmatics.* Oxford: Oxford University Press.